# FUNDING
## DEMOCRATIZATION

**Perspectives on Democratization**
Shirin M. Rai and Wyn Grant, series editors

*Democracy as Public Deliberation*
Maurizio Passerin d'Entrèves, editor

*Democratization through the Looking-glass*
Peter Burnell, editor

*Funding Democratization*
Peter Burnell and Alan Ware, editors

*Trade Unions and Democracy*
Mark Harcourt and Geoffrey Wood, editors

# FUNDING
## DEMOCRATIZATION

Edited by
# Peter Burnell
## and Alan Ware

**Transaction Publishers**
New Brunswick (U.S.A.) and London (U.K.)

Published in 2007 by Transaction Publishers, New Brunswick, New Jersey.
Copyright © 1998 Manchester University Press.

This book is printed on acid-free paper that meets the American National Standard for Permanence of Paper for Printed Library Materials.

Library of Congress Catalog Number: 2006052957
ISBN: 978-1-4128-0600-8
Printed in the United States of America

Library of Congress Cataloging-in-Publication Data

Funding democratization / Peter Burnell and Alan Ware, editors.
    p.  cm.
Originally published in 1998 by Manchester University Press.
Includes bibliographical references and index.
ISBN-13: 978-1-4128-0600-8 (alk. paper)
ISBN-10: 1-4128-0600-3
  1. Campaign funds—Cross-cultural studies.  2. Democratization—Cross-cultural studies.  I. Burnell, Peter J.  II. Ware, Alan.

JF2112.C28F85   2007
324.7'8—dc22                                006051476

# Contents

# Tables

# Contributors

Peter Burnell, Senior Lecturer in politics, Warwick University, co-edits the journal *Democratization* and has a particular interest in Zambia. His extensive writings on foreign aid include *Foreign Aid in a Changing World* (Open University Press, 1997).

Peter Ferdinand, Director of the Centre for Studies in Democratization and Reader in Politics, Warwick University, is formerly head of Asia-Pacific Programme, Royal Institute of International Affairs. Recent edited books are *The New Central Asia and its Neighbours* (1993) and *Take-Off for Taiwan?* (1996).

Vladimir Gel'man is Lecturer in Russian politics, European University at St Petersburg. He is editor of *Ocherki Rossiiskoi Politiki* (*Essays in Russian Politics*, Moscow, 1994) and has written several articles, published mostly in Russian.

Richard Gillespie is Professor of Iberian and Latin American Studies at the University of Portsmouth. He is the author of *The Spanish Socialist Party* (Oxford University Press, 1989) and co-editor of the journal *Mediterranean Politics*.

Carlos Huneeus is Professor of Political Science at the Pontificia Universidad Católica de Chile, Santiago. He specialises in comparative politics, including, most recently, German party politics. His books include La Unión de Centro Democrático y la Transición a la Democracia en España (1985) and Los Chilenos y la Política (1987).

Maria D'Alva Gil Kinzo is Professor of Political Science at the University of São Paulo and Senior Lecturer (part time) at the Institute of Latin American Studies, London. Her many publications on parties and elections in Brazil include *Brazil: Challenges of the 1990s* (British Academic Press, 1993) and *Growth and Development in Brazil: Cardoso's 'Real' Challenge* (with Victor Bulmer-Thomas, for ILAS, 1995).

Paul G. Lewis is Senior Lecturer in Government at the Open University and has recently conducted research on party development in eastern Europe. He is the author of *Central Europe since 1945* (Longman, 1994) and *Party Structure and Organization in East-Central Europe* (Elgar, 1996)

Rosa Mulé is Lecturer in politics, University of Warwick. Her main research interests are political parties, political economy and income redistribution. She has published articles on Italian electoral behaviour, parties and public policies.

Roger Southall is Professor of Political Studies at Rhodes University, South Africa. He has published widely on Africa, including the recent book *Imperialism or Solidarity? International Labour and South African Trade Unions* (University of Cape Town Press, 1995).

Alan Ware is a Professor of Politics at the University of Oxford and a Fellow of Worcester College. His recent publications include *Political Parties and Party Systems* (Oxford University Press, 1996).

Geoffrey Wood, Senior Lecturer (in charge) at the Department of Sociology, Rhodes University (East London) has research interests in democratization and economic reconstruction in Lusophone Africa, flexibility trends in Eastern Cape manufacturing, security issues in southern Africa and political opinion surveys.

# Acknowledgements

The chapters in early form were presented at a workshop held under the auspices of the Centre for Studies in Democratisation, University of Warwick, with support from the university, in January 1997. All participants and particularly Professor Desmond King (St John's College, Oxford) are thanked for their helpful comments.

1

# Introduction: money and politics in emerging democracies

PETER BURNELL

*Funding democratization* investigates the funding of political
competition among parties and politicians in countries that can
be loosely characterized as new or emerging democracies. The
contemporary experience of countries that have recently embarked on democratic transition in central and eastern Europe,
east Asia, southern Africa and elsewhere is compared with the
formative years of democratization in some of today's longer
established democracies of North America and western Europe.
Chile, an example of re-democratization, and Spain, a recently
consolidated democracy, are considered alongside.

The meaning of democracy here conforms to certain fundamental and well-known procedural criteria that include competitive elections to high public office on a regular basis and which
are more or less free and fair, universal adult suffrage and certain
freedoms including most notably the freedoms of expression,
assembly and association.[1] This is a fairly formal and minimalist
use of the term democracy. The book's purpose is not to engage
with debates that compare procedural with more substantive
accounts of democracy, for example contrasting representative
with highly participatory forms. Nor does it aim to mark out
electoral democracy from liberal democracy, or to argue that certain countries are better described as democracies than pseudo-
democracies, semi- or quasi-democracies or similar terms that
are current in the democratization literature.[2] No presumption
is made that countries which feature below will not one day
experience a 'hollowing out' of democracy, democratic decay or
even democratic reversal. Another possibility would be stasis –
no further progress of democratization or democratic deepening.
However, key characteristics of a country's regime for funding
political competition could be a significant influence on its

probable fate. And for 'mature' democracies too, democratization is unfinished business. There one finds politicians keenly looking out for new techniques to raise resources, governments deliberating reforms or regulatory frameworks for political finance (funding and expenditure), and academics comparing the merits and disadvantages of private and largely public-based approaches to political finance. The definitive formula for optimizing the funding of political competition eludes even the longest lived and most prestigious of democracies.

## Democracy, democratization and political competition

There is of course far more to democratization than the activities of political parties and their leaders.

During political liberalization, the main motor of change can be social movements, civic associations and forms of non-governmental organization, perhaps bringing about the collapse of an authoritarian regime almost unaided. Since 1989 civil society has come to the forefront of attention. Its true significance and its relationships to the state and market, even the very meaning of the term, are prompting considerable debate. But also, so-called pacted transition to democracy can be negotiated among relatively unaccountable elites in an *ancien régime* – the military, the bureaucracy, personal rulers or leading political families – without much reference to political parties. Indeed, parties, or parties other than the ruling party, might be legally proscribed prior to democratic breakthrough. Even then, parties could struggle to emerge from the shadows of civil society. At such times of flux, deciding on whether an actor is a civic action group (politically partisan or otherwise) or instead looks like a proto-party, a *de facto* party or some other kind of political group can be difficult, and its status may oscillate over the period of political transition.

When the opportunity arises to begin 'crafting' the new democratic order, a much higher premium tends to be placed on such things as leadership skills and the techniques of constitutional drafting than on issues to do with political finance. This has always been the case; for example Germany's Basic Law is silent on the issue of political financing and when it was drawn up in 1948–49, the idea of public political financing 'did not even occur to anyone'.[3] In regard to the longer term prospects for democratic consolidation,[4] democratic sustainability and persistence in the face of 'shocks', a considerable literature dwells on the importance of environmental and intrinsic factors separate from the state of the parties and candidates, the party system and political finance. *Inter alia* the following needs have been identified: to inculcate the elements of a democratic political culture (what Almond and Verba call a civic culture)[5] which secures a consensus on the new rules of the political game, to develop a vibrant civil society (that term again), and to establish a market economy and achieve a fairly even spread of favourable socio-economic attainments such as literacy and material prosperity. A belief that the last is important to the democratic outlook goes back at least as far as Lipset's seminal article (1959);[6] more recently, Przeworski *et al.* argue that the chances of a democracy surviving will hinge on its enjoying economic development, not on the length of time it has endured since first introduced. They claim this makes democratic consolidation an empty term; in principle, no democracy's future is guaranteed.[7]

Yet for all the uncertainties surrounding the meaning of democracy and its conditions and prerequisites, and despite a prevailing ignorance about the processes involved in democratization, a safe assumption is that a central role is played by political competition between parties and individual politicians. Thus for example Shin (writing on east Asia) says parties 'play a pivotal role in consolidating democratic gains'; Sandbrook (an Africanist) judges that the 'consolidation of democracy entails, above all, the institutionalisation of parties and a party system'; and the Stockholm-based International Institute for Democracy and Electoral Assistance states simply that parties are 'the nerve centre of democracy'.[8] Establishing parties' contribution to democracy is all the more important where a significant section of the populace is suspicious of political parties because of their past performance.

The party system that evolves in a country will ultimately be structured by a number of forces ranging from ideological and social cleavages to the choice of electoral system. But in order for there to be political competition, resources – particularly money – are essential.

### Costing democracy

In their broadest sense the costs of democracy extend much further than just the financing of recurrent political competition. Such things as public expenditure on maintaining an autonomous judiciary and running local government – public goods (like competitive politics) that help ensure the rule of law and a measure of political decentralization – could be reckoned among the expenses. Also, there are the economic costs involved in the sort of lengthy consultative procedures for decision-making on issues of public importance that democracy can often entail, even in circumstances that require urgent action. On the one side, the legislature's ability to scrutinize effectively the executive requires that it be given adequate research and information resources. On the other side, in recent years 'gridlock' has appeared to be part of the price that Americans must pay for upholding their approach to democracy, setting branches of government against one another in an intricate arrangement of checks and balances. Democracy understood as popular rule allows public policy on complex and weighty issues to be decided by a majority of the people – possibly ill-informed, reluctant to participate and easily misled – rather than by a technically qualified or passionately interested elite. This too might be considered one of democracy's potential costs. Where the democratic way leads to compromises that seem politically rational the results, for instance decisions on resource allocations, can sometimes look economically irrational and unnecessarily burdensome to the exchequer.

Moreover, even in respect of underwriting political competition, there is more to the matter of money than how the contestants finance their political organization and election campaigns. For example, in some of the poorest countries a notable task of international assistance in recent attempts to establish democratically elected government, particularly in countries emerging from civil war like Cambodia (1993) and Mozambique (1994), has been to facilitate the election arrangements – identifying a suitable electoral system for the country, creating the machinery for staging elections, organizing voter education exercises in citizen rights and civic duties, supplying the ballot boxes, and paying for teams of international and domestic observers to monitor the election campaign and guard against electoral fraud on polling day. Between 1992 and mid-1994 the United Nations was faced by requests from no less than fifty-two member states for technical assistance with the holding of elections. In these circumstances international verification of the freeness and fairness of the election can be far more significant than the financial assistance, in securing acceptance of the outcome by all the contestants.

In many wealthier democracies especially, political finance also involves extra-party actors making substantial commitments of resources to the conduct of public debate, even though they have no intention of contesting public office themselves and might not fund parties or politicians directly.[9] But they do have political objectives, including helping shape public policy agendas, gaining access to people in power and influencing electoral outcomes. By this of course one refers to pressure groups, interest groups and similar organizations. So prominent are they in the United States that the impression is easily gained that civil society far outranks political society *qua* parties as an engine of political activity. Of course, in the United States many civic groups and 'political action committees' collectively contribute large sums to the election campaigns of individuals running for Congress. In much poorer countries, however, political society and non-partisan civic groups can be in serious competition with one another for the limited pool of available resources; there is a possibility that many of the latter will be crowded out of the domestic market for private funds. Parties and politicians in office (or those who can credibly pose as future office-holders and make promises on that basis) are better placed to attract support from donors motivated by desires for some favour in return. There are also special considerations in respect of an independent media – an elemental constituent of civil society, according to some analysts. The links between politicians and the mass media such as through ownership or control of newspapers and broadcasting systems and the media's behaviour must be taken into account when gauging the scale and distribution of political resources in the wider sense. Whether they advance or retard democratization, their impact cannot be ignored in this, the 'information age'; they may overwhelm more narrowly defined issues of political finance.

Thus, the costs of democracy and the resourcing of democratic politics both go far beyond just the financing of political competition; similarly, economic power and finance can be politically potent in ways other than the funding of parties, candidates and election campaigns. But equally the power of money to influence the results of political competition should not be overestimated.[10] The evidence shows there is no necessary correlation between the magnitude of finance available and political success, whether measured in terms of an individual's standing within a party, a politician's or party's vote-catching performance, their ability to dictate the terms of political debate or capacity to govern effectively. To become a successful competitor other ingredients may be essential, ranging from charisma to a shrewd political brain, party discipline and organizational competence, a good 'nose' for policy positions that will look credible to voters and, perhaps, a degree of luck. Even the legal permission to register as a party or to stand as a candidate for public office cannot be take for granted.

By the same token financial weakness need be no absolute bar to exercising political influence, for instance by being a small but crucial partner in a coalition government, or by launching policy initiatives that are subsequently appropriated by wealthier and more powerful parties. The Free Democrats and the Green Party in Germany respectively illustrate these two points. An abundance of political finance is self-evidently neither a sufficient nor, perhaps, a necessary condition for a country to have a positive experience of democratization. Where money exerts excessive influence on the behaviour of politicians or the voters, such as through the bribery of one or both of these groups, then democracy will be undermined.

Something else that is worth remembering is that the amounts and distribution of political finance are themselves not independent variables. They will be influenced by the fund-raising strategies pursued by politicians, the codes of conduct they observe and their expenditure habits, by statutory requirements and controls (for example trade union funding of parties is prohibited in South Korea and Brazil) and by the legislation of public support, pecuniary and non-pecuniary, for parties and for candidates and their expenses. The point is particularly apposite here. For while the two categories, established democracies and emerging democracies, both contain great cultural, social, economic and political diversity, the latter category differs from the former in at least two respects. First, new democracies obviously have less relevant experience of their own to draw on when devising arrangements for political finance. Indeed, some look outside for guidance or advice. Re-democratizing countries are differently placed again.

Second, however, emerging democracies are more free to make choices. Once made, these choices, like decisions on, say, whether to adopt a parliamentary or a presidential model of democracy, or like the overall shape that a party system takes after it begins to bed down, can be difficult to erase.[11] The reference to party system is especially pertinent. For, as with the choice of electoral system, the rules and formulae governing the allocation of public funds to political competition can be so devised as to encourage certain systemic tendencies, such as an early 'petrification' of the party map by favouring the already established and the larger parties, and by concentrating resources inflows in the hands of the party bureaucracies.[12] A different set of rules, or private funding with a very personalized or clientelistic orientation (and/or a different election system), would facilitate the proliferation of parties, cliques and tendencies and might encourage hyperfactionalism. The prospect of public funding could persuade a range of civic associations to attempt to transform themselves into parties. These effects might preclude political stabilization in the short run. But they could also help advance the longer term democratic prospects by allowing society leeway to establish a political alignment that offers the most appropriate balance and spread of political representation. A partisan or politically contentious approach to determining legal frameworks for political finance and their administration, for example rules determining state funding, can itself bring a fragile new democracy into disrepute, threatening to undermine smooth progress if not its very survival.

## Money for democratization, and the issue of corruption

Notwithstanding the caveats made so far, money is an asset valued both for its symbolic and its practical worth in political competition between parties, among candidates and between rivals or factions within party-like formations. Its value is heightened in societies where politicians are expected to attend to the welfare requirements of constituents and where vote-buying is customary.[13] Of course, several kinds of potential resource may be regarded as substitutable to a certain degree.

The list includes volunteer labour, free access to training programmes and advice on how to become an effective political organization, grants of office equipment and entitlement to use public buildings for meetings, free air time and space for political advertising in the mass media, tax concessions on income and tax incentives for donors, and reimbursement by the state of allowable expenditures. But each will be fitted to a specific purpose and will have its own consequences. Money is unusual in that it can be transformed into other kinds of instrumental goods and services far from the point of origin, constrained only by legal and practical limits on procurement. However, it should be noted that money cannot always buy some of these other, more specialized resources.[14]

But where will the money come from? Will there be enough, and what happens when parties go into debt? In poor countries, where basic human needs are unmet, can (or should) the state afford to finance political competition? And in some former one-party states the very idea of state funding suffers from its reputation in the past, and is liable to perpetuate an identification of the state and the party in power with all the connotations of patronage and abuse of public resources that formerly prevailed.[15] There, a danger could exist that parties will be remote from the people, uninterested in cultivating broad-based involvement, and not accepted as part of society. State funding may be a Trojan horse for state intervention and control. What effect will the patterns of available funding have on the type of party system and the number of parties? How do they impinge on the internal life and structure of parties:[16] for example on relations between the national and sub-national levels of party organization? Particularly important is whether the financial arrangements give prominence to individual political entrepreneurs, or instead favour party organizations and control by the party bureaucracy. This is especially pertinent to 'delegative democracies' (commonly found in Latin America), where presidentialism can reach such a pitch as to erode the executive accountability of government. The consequences for democratization may be considerable, for in the long run parties offer a wider range and greater continuity of the functions essential to democracy than even the most capable of personal leaders can. The ways in which political finance impact on how parties and politicians involve the party membership, connect with affiliated bodies and relate to voters and the general public are also matters of profound importance to the quality of democracy. Do the financial arrangements have any specific consequences for the style and content of political debate? What does the condition of political finance reveal about society's attitudes and affections towards their system of political representation? Should it be a concern that the funding of political society might crowd out civic associations from the private market for funds?

Of course a number of these questions have been addressed by scholars in respect of more established democracies in western Europe and in the United States.[17] There, different approaches to political finance have been studied quite intensively, particularly the effectiveness of modalities of state assistance as devices to counter the political inequalites that can flow from substantial private economic discrepancies.[18] Also, at the time of writing the connections between private money, politicians and political competition have come to the fore in public debate and journalistic coverage in both the United States and Britain, in circumstances surrounding respectively the 1996 presidential election and the 1997 general election.

Yet political finance has barely figured in the bourgeoning literature on democratization and in accounts of newly emerging democracies.[19] One reason could be that almost insuperable obstacles inhibit the assembling of an accurate and comprehensive database of political finance; there are significant variations between countries, but even in the older democracies one cannot be sure how meaningful the data in the public domain are. Indeed, recent discourse on political funding seems to have been hijacked by a fascination with the phenomenon of corruption in its various guises, 'sleaze' and political scandals generally, some involving pecadillos unrelated to money. The reason is obvious: a constant stream of *causes célèbre*, all around the world. Our levels of awareness have been fuelled by the enthusiasm of rival politicians to discredit their opponents (by unvarnished rumour-mongering, among other means), investigative journalism, judicial inquiries and, in a number of developing countries, external scrutiny from foreign aid donors and particularly the World Bank (which now places a crusade against corruption at the leading edge of its campaign for better 'governance').

At times the accusations of corruption do not distinguish between illegality and impropriety, or are aimed at practices

that may attract disapprobation but are by no means univers-
ally condemned. Nevertheless, in regard to some countries, for
instance Italy and Colombia, a customary assumption is that
the amount of 'black money' circulating in politics has far
outweighed those political expenditures and party incomes that
are formally declared. This is what Gel'man has called, in the
Russian context, the tip of the iceberg.[20] It is true that drawing
conclusions on the basis of studying only the tip of the 'iceberg'
would be somewhat misplaced. Also, the appearance of corruption, and attitudes taken towards it, clearly have an important
bearing on the condition of democracy and democratic prospects. Meny goes so far as to claim that corruption is at present
fuelling a growth of anti-politics and cynicism.[21] Moreover, in
the new democracies whose governance capabilites are limited
and attachment to the rule of law is weak, the difficulties in
enforcing legal controls on political finance could be magnified,
especially in the early stages of political transition. For there
may still be widespread uncertainty over the the rules of the
game of political competition and their application. In some
such countries even the state is a new and incomplete entity,
the ethos of public service not fully developed. In these circumstances foreign corporations might consider offering bribes
to be less risky business practice than in a number of the older
democracies.

Nevertheless, the greatest threats to political order and to
democratization may not lie in corrupt political finance. Parties
and the effectiveness of political competition can weaken for
many reasons unconnected with there being too much (or too
little) money in politics, or the wrong kind of political money.
Moreover, just as there are notable determinants of inter- and
intra-party relations that are not reducible to the question of
who raises and who spends the funds, so there are serious financial issues apart from 'funny money' that concern the broader
agenda of what kind of plural politics can, or is likely to, emerge.
Hence, this volume is not primarily about corruption, although
inevitably certain manifestations will be noted in the examination of some countries more than others.[22]

## Funding regimes

Funding regimes for political finance and related resources
can be classified under a number of bimodal headings, each of

which could have specific implications for the development of parties and party systems and so for the democratic outlook. Examples with respect to funding source and practice are: governmental versus private, domestic versus foreign, legal versus illegal, institutional versus non-institutional, overt versus covert, and a few large sources versus many small sources. Competitive political systems can be classified in accordance with such dimensions. Thus for instance a polity where all the main parties and candidates draw on similar sources or types of source (such as state subsidies) could be distinguished from one where the contestants collectively or separately draw on several sources or types of source. A further variant would be where the competitors who are most successful in winning elections and filling public office differ systematically from their unsuccessful opponents, in terms of the sums at their disposal and where their funds come from. The type of funding regime, interacting with the electoral system, can have quite distinctive implications for parties internally and for party systems. Thus for example in some countries where there are multi-member constituencies, candidates have tended to develop their own individual funding lines, and political competition has been structured around personal allegiances and the distribution of favours, rather than around principles and issues, as has been typical in Japan.

In theory, political contributions can be obtained in a variety of ways. The particular mix will reflect the circumstances and character of a society, its culture and wealth profile, and local traditions. In principle, there could be particular models of political funding that are only suited to certain societies, or to specific historical phases. A comprehensive typology of sources would include the following:

1 statutory public support, including on a basis of matching private funds;
2 legitimately acquired personal fortunes of politicians;
3 levies on salaries of party officers, especially those who are on the government payroll, or entry fees which candidates for public office must pay in order to have their party's endorsement;
4 party members' subscriptions and the sale of party cards;
5 income from assets previously acquired by a party or its leaders as a result of their belonging to the former ruling

elite (for example as members of a *de jure* one-party state or military government);[23]

6 trading income from enterprises set up and owned by the political organization or its subsidiaries and not spun out of the power structure of the pre-democratic state;

7 legitimate sponsorship by local business, wealthy patrons and nationals resident abroad, and returning émigrés;

8 other affiliated or sympathetic non-affiliated groups in civil society, such as trade unions, religious groups, ethnic associations and pressure or interest groups;

9 the general public, for instance through direct mail fundraising drives;

10 foreign owned corporations and/or their locally incorporated subsidiaries;

11 other friends overseas;[24]

12 foreign governments and their agents acting bilaterally;

13 inter-governmental organizations such as the United Nations;

14 political parties or party foundations (like Germany's Stiftung) in other democracies;

15 private international foundations;

16 corrupt use of the public purse and of discretionary powers of the state;

17 organized crime outside government.[25]

Usually funds are solicited by political actors, but monies may also be pressed upon them without special request. Resources may be offered on a partisan or a non-partisan basis, to organizations or to individuals personally. The immediate purposes to which finance is directed and the ultimate objectives of those who provide it can vary (as can the reasons for an established relationship of financial support, or outstanding promises, being cut off or withheld). Again there are many possibilities, including: the building of party machines and party research institutes; boosting election campaigning, with a view to influencing the composition of the next government; promoting personal political advancement; gaining access for the purpose of influencing public policy and/or attaining discretionary administrative favours from government. In new democracies the ambition could be to shape the entire future landscape of political competition, by trying to fix the ideological boundaries and the balance of effective political representation, for example by discriminating against communist or extreme right wing sentiments. A 'party within a party' may be funded by outsiders in an attempt to subvert the larger group and provoke internal dissent.

The actual beneficiaries of an inflow of funds will not always coincide with the providers' intended destination or stated purposes.

## Funding democratization then and now

The established democracies have taken a close interest in the democratization processes going on elsewhere in the world.[26] In some poor countries with weak democratic credentials, where large inflows of international economic assistance are made conditional on compliance with certain democratic norms and 'democracy assistance' is being received, one might judge that a form of dependent democratic development is being attempted. However, neither the past nor the present experience of the established democracies – not even the most Messianic – can be assumed to offer ready templates for emerging democracies, in respect of political funding. There are several reasons for this. And just as economic historians mull over the advantages and disadvantages of being a late latecomer to industrial development, so there is a mixture of positive and less favourable arguments for countries commencing democratization now.

Especially notable is the fact that, although government's role tends to be bigger in the late twentieth century in most places than it was in, say, the United States in the 1870s,[27] democratization today proceeds in parallel with economic liberalization and deregulation, almost everywhere. The dominant neo-liberal agenda recommends initiatives to 'downsize' or at least restrain the size of the public sector, and to reduce social welfare provision. These changes undercut the usual advantages of being the party in power and able to shape public policy and public spending in ways intended to mobilize electoral support. The pool of state patrimony and discretionary powers from which ruling parties may be continually fed is squeezed.[28] But at the same time opportunities are created for enterprising actors and others to make substantial gains from the processes by which countries' economies are being reformed, as well as from the greater market orientation that results. Examples are the contracting out of economic activities formerly in the state sector and the privatization of public assets and associated income streams, especially in countries that have only weakly developed capital markets.[29] A reasonable presumption is that a portion of these windfall financial gains will then be channelled to those political forces – 'bourgeois' or pro-capitalism – which offer to provide a secure policy environment and will guarantee the arrangements that made the gains possible, if given power.

Also, in a number of former socialist countries and developing countries like Zambia, economic restructuring has meant a measure of de-industrialization, sharp falls in real wages and increased unemployment – trends that reduce the potential of trade unions to make a significant financial contribution to party politics. This situation differs from the important role played in some of the advanced industrial countries in helping build (especially though not only) left wing parties. In the United States organized labour offered $35 million to Democrat election compaigns in 1996; in Britain affiliated unions supported the Labour Party to the tune of over £100 million (at 1995 prices) between 1979 when it lost power and 1996.[30] There seems to be nothing remotely comparable in the democratizing countries profiled in this book, not even the more urbanized and industrially developed of these countries. In places like the former German Democratic Republic for example, unions now concentrate on collective bargaining issues as they search for an identity and function distinct from the politicization associated with their communist past.

The international political climate, expansion of global communications and information networking, and the supply of internationally-sourced resources for competitive politics all differ now from conditions in the past. The collapse of the Soviet Union virtually sealed the end of cold war funding by the KGB and CIA, which benefited communist and anti-communist parties in countries in western Europe and the developing world and helped keep many non-democratic governments in power. This has not meant the end of all funding by foreign governments bent on pursuing their strategic foreign policy objectives.[31]

The globalization of financial markets, increasing penetration of national economies by multinational corporations and the exponential rise in their direct foreign investment in some 'emerging markets', and the growing porousness of state borders all mean that money can move around the world in larger quantities, faster and more easily than ever before. This includes money from organized crime and trafficking in illicit drugs, which have a combined estimated annual value of $1,000 billion.

Looking to the future, beyond the east Asian 'tiger economies' and the more dynamic economies in Latin America and former Soviet bloc, any completely new 'waves' of democratization, with very few exceptions, will have to rely on more backward parts of the developing world – countries lacking a sizeable middle class or the significant economic transformation achieved in Chile for example.[32] The 1990s has already witnessed a rise in 'democracy assistance' or 'political development aid' from bodies like the US government's Agency for International Development (annual budget for this purpose of around $400 million) and the semi-autonomous National Endowment for Democracy (founded in 1983), and Germany's Stiftung.[33] Britain joined in by establishing the Westminster Foundation for Democracy in 1992. The great bulk of such support comprises 'technical' assistance of various sorts rather than financial transfers, though at least some of it has been earmarked specifically for political parties and associated political groups.[34] Parts of central and eastern Europe as well as 'third world' countries are the targets. There is a strong presumption that parties willing to espouse liberal policies towards international trade and inwards investment receive favourable treatment.

There are some risks as well as possible benefits for both sides. The signals may be misinterpreted, and there can be unforseen consequences as a result of being drawn into a country's domestic political arena. The backers incur political embarrassment if they become identified with succesful political contenders who then stray from democratic practice; those seeking particular gains could suffer as a result of unwittingly backing losers and alienating the winners. The mechanisms by which some funds from foreigners are received and disbursed are not transparent and may be incompatible with democratically accountable arrangements inside parties. They could be thought capable of undermining a country's political independence and its national security. In the United States a political storm arose over the involvement of foreign financial support most notably from US subsidiaries of foreign firms and Asian American businesspeople (dubbed 'reverse foreign aid' by Republican Party critics), and also allegedly from official Chinese sources (which would be contrary to US election law), for Democrats in the 1996 election campaigns. Sensitivities can be just as great in smaller and poorer countries that have been subjected to external colonial or imperialistic domination in the past, or whose international stature has waned recently. Needless to say, expensive models of electioneering and campaign techniques are being exported from wealthy western countries to economically less developed countries, sometimes as part of packages of political aid.

Almost everywhere the funding of political parties and election campaigns from outside the country looks problematic. And as the South African case shows, it is problematic in different ways for the different actors who are involved.[35] So, once the process of staging elections has been installed in a country, the growing trend is for 'democracy assistance' (other than for institutions of governance) to concentrate on civic associations and non-governmental organizations. It remains to be seen whether this trend will reinforce the relative underdevelopment of political pluralism, in those emerging democracies where one party gains a clear dominance *vis-à-vis* the other parties. On the one side, the flourishing of civil society might be good for the further development of stable mature democracies (although in the United States, the cacophony of competing and conflicting group demands is being held partly responsible for the rise of political immobilism, or 'demosclerosis'). On the other side, however, history suggests that the party form of organization is more likely to offer the bundle of functions necessary to constructing democratic polities in the first place. Also, a concern in government for some overarching conception of the public good seems more likely to be advanced. Strong party government may be essential to check the threats to democracy which anti-democratic elements in (un)civil society can pose. At the same time the claims of civic associations to domestic legitimacy can be undermined by international contacts, especially those that inhibit widespread local roots. One view, espoused in relation to some African countries, is that only where multi-party democracy has been secured first will there be a chance for healthy civil society to develop freely.[36]

Meanwhile, older democracies are reappraising critically their own *modus operandi* in political finance (and even criminalizing certain informal but previously extra-legal links between money and politics).[37] They are looking for higher standards of public morality among the emerging democracies than obtained (or the law required) in their own early days. Rarely discussed is whether practices that western liberal democrats now freely censure were a valuable instrument for consolidating viable party systems in countries that have since turned into stable democracies.[38] The question is begged completely whether the presence of similar practices in emerging democracies today might also be functional, and on *balance* justifiable, at this stage in their political evolution, especially when compared with the practicable alternatives – the obvious risks notwithstanding. But perhaps this is a speculation too far. What we do know is that the presence of internationally-sanctioned norms and expectations can be particularly intrusive for the emerging democracies in fiscal crisis, desperate for foreign debt relief and beholden to the International Monetary Fund, World Bank and bilateral donors. In contrast, when Britain and the United States started building party politics, the outside world was in no position to make well-informed judgements, and its views did not carry political clout.

Something else that is different now is the way in which the political fortunes of governments, their leaders, ruling parties and their opponents can be affected by the general economic support made available to countries by the Bretton Woods institutions. Equally important are the accompanying policy conditionalities and close external monitoring which reduce the discretionary powers of government to manipulate public policy and expenditure for partisan advantage. It seems probable that these external factors could be far more significant than the international community's direct attempts to help build party politics in such countries.

## Conclusion

Taking all considerations together, then, it is not obvious that candidates to join the club of democracies in the latter stages of the twentieth century and beyond can (or even should) replicate exactly their predecessors' experience of funding democratization. However, although the context of political finance in the newly democratizing countries differs in some important respects from earlier experience of democratization, there are also some similarities between the old and newer democracies. All democracies face funding challenges, even though their precise nature takes its particular colour from the local circumstances, as will become clear from reading the chapters below. There is certainly no simple fit between excessive expenditure and its inverse – the under-provision of resources – on the one hand, and on the other hand a distinction between established democracies in the North and emerging democracies in the South. That distinction is itself a spurious dichotomy. It does not reflect accurately contemporary political developments, the regional patterns of economic progress or even the national variations in financial sums mobilized for election campaigns.[39] Moreover, both the established and the emerging democracies encompass some very different experiences of democratization, and their pre-democratic origins are similarly diverse. This raises many kinds of difficulties for comparative analysis that will be familiar to most readers. That problems of political finance are certainly not confined to emerging democracies is evident from the scholarly research into the settled democracies, for instance the ease with which legal controls seem to be avoided or evaded. Demands for reform of the way parties and election expenditures are now funded are high on the political agenda in several of these countries. But there are useful lessons to be learned from the earlier stages of democratization, too. These will be visited first, before investigating more closely political funding's contribution to democratization in some of today's newest democracies.

## Notes

Elements of this chapter draw on Peter Burnell's 'Funding political parties: a challenge for old and new democracies', to be found in the published proceedings of the symposium *Democratization in the 1990s* organized by the University of Nagoya School of Law, and Asia-Pacific Regional Studies Project (1997), pp. 199–214.

1 The issue of whether democracy entails a fundamental right of individuals to make private donations to political causes including parties without limit and free of any requirement of public disclosure is not discussed here.
2 See for example L. Diamond, 'Is the third wave over?', *Journal of Democracy*, 7:3 (1996), 20–37.

3  H. von Arnim, 'Campaign and party finance in Germany', (trans. by A. Gunlicks)
   in A. B. Gunlicks (ed.), *Campaign and Party Finance in North America and
   Western Europe* (Boulder, CO, Westview, 1993), p. 203.

4  The meaning of democratic consolidation and how one distinguishes it from
   democratic transition have yet to be settled in the literature. See J. Linz and
   A. Stepan, 'Toward consolidated democracies', *Journal of Democracy*, 7:2 (1996),
   14–33; G. O'Donnell, 'Illusions about consolidation', *Journal of Democracy*, 7:2
   (1996), 34–51 and 'Debate: democratic consolidation', *Journal of Democracy*, 7:4
   (1996), 151–68.

5  S. Almond and G. Verba, *The Civic Culture, Political Attitudes and Democracy
   in Five Nations* (Princeton, NJ, Princeton University Press, 1963).

6  S. M. Lipset, 'Some social requisites of democracy: economic development and
   political legitimacy', *American Political Science Review*, 53:1 (1959), 69–105;
   also S. M. Lipset, 'The social requisites of democracy revisited', *American Soci-
   ological Review*, 59:1 (1994), 1–22.

7  A. Przeworski, M. Alvarez, J. Chiebub and F. Limongi, 'What makes democracies
   endure?', *Journal of Democracy*, 7:1 (1996), 39–55.

8  D. C. Shin, 'Political parties and democratization in South Korea: the mass public
   and the democratic consolidation of political parties', *Democratization*, 2:2 (1995),
   20–55; R. Sandbrook, 'Transitions without consolidation: democratization in six
   African cases', *Third World Quarterly*, 17:1 (1996), 76; *The Newsletter of International Institute for Democracy and Electoral Assistance*, 6 (December 1996),
   p. 5.

9  In the US 1996 elections, $263 million of 'soft money' for issues advocacy
   (and party building), three times the sum in 1992, was raised by the Republican
   and Democratic Parties. Statutory limits on spending on individual candidate
   promotion were circumvented in this way.

10 In the United States J. Snyder has drolly observed 'despite years of research by
   political scientists and economists, the extent to which money actually buys
   political influence on a regular basis remains a mystery'. 'Long-term investing in
   politicians: or give early, give often'. *Journal of Law and Economics*, 35 (1992), 15.

11 On democratic models see Przeworski *et al.*, 'What makes democracies endure?',
   pp. 48–9; on party systems see A. Ware, *Political Parties and Party Systems*
   (Oxford, Oxford University Press, 1996), p. 303.

12 P. Lewis and R. Gillespie examine the experience of central/eastern Europe and
   Spain respectively, in this volume. On the significance of factionalism for party
   building and thereby for democratization see R. Gillespie, M. Waller and L. López
   Nieto (eds.), *Factional Politics and Democratization* (London, Frank Cass, 1995).

13 See P. Ferdinand in this volume.

14 S. Darnolf has argued (in a communication to the author) that in some African
   countries not even money can purchase the paraphernalia of modern, commercial-
   ized, techniques for electioneering such as voter mailing lists, which are made
   impracticable by limitations of the infrastructure. There may be no substitute for
   mass members to canvass support in rural areas especially. See Darnolf's *Democratic Electioneering in Southern Africa. The Contrasting Cases of Botswana and
   Zimbabwe* (Göteborg, Göteborg University Studies in Politics, 1997).

15 This point was made to the writer by Zambia's President Chiluba.

16 This is a particular concern of R. Mulé in this volume.

17 See H. Alexander (ed.), *Comparative Political Finance in the 1980s* (Cambridge,
   Cambridge University Press, 1988); Gunlicks, *Campaign and Party Finance*;
   H. Alexander and R. Shiratori (eds.), *Comparative Political Finance Among the
   Democracies* (Boulder, CO, Westview, 1994). Political finance in the United States
   has been extensively studied in the American politics periodicals; in Japan, scandals
   involving politicians and business generate much press coverage.

18 We live in an age of marketization, but the funding of political parties is one
   activity that seems unlikely to be completely handed over to the determination

of market forces. Indeed, over time the state has actually become more involved in funding election expenses, parties or parliamentary groups, party institutes and foundations, reaching two-thirds of the established democracies in the late 1980s. This represents one of the most significant changes to the environment in which parties act, according to R. Katz and P. Mair, 'Changing models of party organization and party democracy', *Party Politics*, 1:1 (1995), especially 15–16.

19 Papers on selected Latin American as well as western European countries were presented at an excellent conference, 'Financing party politics in Europe and Latin America', hosted by the University of London Institute of Latin American Studies in conjunction with Instituto Universitario Ortega Y Gasset Madrid, 25–26 March 1996.

20 V. Gel'man in this volume.

21 Y. Meny, 'Politics, corruption and democracy. The 1995 Stein Rokkan lecture', *European Journal of Political Research*, 30:2 (1996), 111–23.

22 The literature on corruption is faster growing than that on political finance more generally. Examples are W. Little and E. Posada-Carbó (eds.), *Political Corruption in Europe and Latin America* (Basingstoke, Macmillan, 1996) and a dedicated issue 'Corruption in Western Democracies' of *International Social Science Journal*, 149 (September 1996).

23 On the significance of property that formerly belonged to communist party states see P. Lewis in this volume. Just as the assets acquired from having belonged to the 'authoritarian' government that pre-dates democratization might be carried forward, the same can be true of former 'freedom fighters', insurgents and 'terrorist' organizations.

24 For example in 1995 the Friends of Sinn Féin in the United States provided over $1.2 million to Northern Ireland's republican movement.

25 The alleged infiltration of $6 million of drugs mafia money in President Samper's successful campaign in the second round of Colombia's 1994 presidential election has not simply attracted international attention but has noticeably dented diplomatic relations with the US government.

26 See L. Whitehead (ed.), *The International Dimensions of Democratization* (Oxford, Oxford University Press, 1996) and 'Concerning international support for democracy in the South', in R. Luckham and G. White (eds.), *Democratization in the South: The Jagged Wave* (Manchester, Manchester University Press, 1996), especially pp. 246–50.

27 See A. Ware in this volume.

28 See P. Ferdinand, 'The party's over – market liberalization and the challenges for one-party and one-party dominant regimes: the cases of Taiwan and Mexico, Italy and Japan', *Democratization*, 1:1 (1994), 133–50.

29 Suspicions of 'kickbacks' have arisen in some instances where the sale of public sector companies has been effected not through public share offerings or transparent competitive tender but by direct negotiation instead, often to the benefit of leading political 'insiders' or their associates. Such sales have been a reward for helping to finance an election campaign like President Yeltsin's in Russia in 1996. In India, partial decontrol of the economy is said to have introduced a far greater number of businesses to the extortionate fund-raising methods used by the parties, unlike formerly when the pressure was mainly on just a few large industrialists. See *India Today*, 31 March 1996, p. 19.

30 The unions have traditionally spent as much again on other political purposes. The contribution made by affiliated unions to Labour Party income fell from 80 per cent to 47 per cent at the time of the 1997 general election.

31 In some parts of the world assistance from outside the country to minority political groupings with whom there are shared ethno-nationalist, religious or tribal identities can be intended to encourage separatist movements, possibly in pursuit of irredentist goals. In Algeria, the Islamic Front for Salvation (FIS) which looked destined to take power through the ballot box in January 1992, before the

military intervened and interrupted the electoral process, reputedly had support from the Iranian government. Doubts have been expressed about the (now banned) FIS's commitment to democracy and to furthering democratization, at least as they are understood in the West.

32 See the chapter by C. Huneeus in this volume. The immediate outlook for genuine multi-party democracy in Middle Eastern Arab countries, poor or rich, is very uncertain given their political traditions.

33 These were given a thorough examination by M. Pinto-Duschinsky in 'Foreign political aid: German political foundations and their US counterparts', *International Affairs*, 67:1 (1991), 33–63. See also the same author's detailed study of 'International political finance: the Konrad Adenauer Foundation and Latin America', in Whitehead, *International Dimensions of Democratization* (chapter 9).

34 A critical account of the practice of 'democracy assistance' is T. Carothers, 'Democracy assistance: the question of strategy', *Democratization* 4:3 (1997), 109–32. Carothers in *Assessing Democracy Assistance: The Case of Romania* (Washington, DC, Carnegie Endowment for International Peace), p. 42 shows how US partisan assistance to Romania's political opposition, given under the guise of levelling the playing field, encouraged the ruling communist party to compensate through using its control of the state apparatus.

35 See R. Southall and G. Wood in this volume.

36 Baroness Chalker, UK Overseas Development Minister, personal interview, 10 June 1996. This view acknowledges civil society's role in bringing about the political revolutions in central and eastern Europe.

37 Thus among the first announcements of Britain's newly elected Labour government in May 1997 was a proposal that the Nolan committee of inquiry into standards in public life should look at political funding, that large private donations to Britain's parties would have to be publicly declared, and that foreign donations would be outlawed.

38 See the chapter by A. Ware in this volume.

39 There has been no shortage of campaign finance in such countries as Thailand (where the parties disbursed an estimated $800 million in the 1996 general election), Brazil (see chapter by M. Kinzo in this volume), and Mexico, where legislation drawn up in 1996 proposes to limit the amounts of expenditure and private political finance. In Britain, a Conservative Party deficit of £19 million in 1993 became a war chest of well in excess of £20 million for the 1997 general election campaign. However, in Italy, where the possibility that a Soviet-backed Communist Party could be elected to power has now disappeared, industrialists are more resistant to the calls of centre-right parties for cash support – a development that has contributed to the *de facto* restructuring of the country's party system.

# 2

# The funding of political parties in North America: the early years

ALAN WARE

This chapter examines the funding of political parties in the United States and, by way of comparison, Canada. In the case of the United States the period covered is from the 1830s to the mid-1890s while with Canada the focus is on the period from Confederation (1867) until about the First World War. Neither country at that time met all the criteria that today would be regarded as necessary for a regime to be considered a democracy. In particular, large sections of the electorate were disenfranchised. Women could not vote, nor in the United States before the end of the Civil War could the vast majority of black people. Not only were slaves deprived of the vote but so too were many so-called 'free' black men. Moreover, the Reconstruction era (1865–77) provided only a brief interlude of black enfranchisement; coercion of black voters commenced in the South after that, and from the mid-1890s onwards Jim Crow laws effectively removed civil rights for black people, including the right to vote.

Nevertheless, the political systems that developed in the United States from the early to mid-1830s onwards, and in Canada from 1867, had many of the features of representative democracies. Relatively large electorates were being mobilized by political parties that were competing for their votes. The systems of political institutions in which parties were operating were very similar to the systems in which contemporary American and Canadian parties operate, and the transition from an 'emerging democracy' to 'democracy' involved continuity rather than radical change. For this reason it is instructive to look at how parties were funded in nineteenth-century Anglo North America, because it may throw light on crucial differences in problems of party funding between those confronting regimes which are democratizing in the late twentieth century and those confronting regimes which democratized earlier. The United States will be examined first, partly because it was the longer established 'quasi-democracy' and partly because the system of party funding there was far more extensive and complex than that in Canada. However, before turning to either country the idea of corruption will be briefly considered, because charges of corruption are often levelled against both North American democracies in the nineteenth century. The argument here is that it is not helpful for purposes of political analysis to label practices as corrupt, simply because they would not be acceptable today.

## The idea of corruption in relation to party funding

When examining claims about alleged corruption it is necessary to be clear as to whether it is the behaviour of particular individuals that is at issue or the social process in which individuals operate. A process is corrupt if it tends to undermine the entire system of which it is part. Thus, if one form of party funding tended to undermine the system of free elections then it would be corrupt; in other words, corruption in this sense is connected to the idea of dysfunctionality. But, of course, a process that undermines a system in one context might not do so in another. This point is important because part of the thrust of the argument in the following sections is that many of the practices that were characteristic of party funding in nineteenth-century North America might well be corrupting of late-twentieth-century democracy, but, generally, they were not corrupting in the context in which they worked in the nineteenth century. Thus, the spoils system did not tend to weaken electoral competition, partly because of the different scale of economic enterprises in the nineteenth century and partly because of the rather different relations between government and economy evident then.

Within a given process the behaviour of individuals is corrupt if what they do violates contemporary norms about how individuals should behave in a given context. In relation to politics, allegations of individual corruption usually bear on the use made of government in promoting individual or group interests. However, since what is regarded as acceptable self-interested behaviour (in relation to the state) changes over time, behaviour that falls within the norms of one era may well fall outside it at another. Accusations of corruption made against a nineteenth-century politico must be judged by the prevailing norms of that era, and not by late-twentieth-century norms. Some nineteenth-century politicians, such as New York's William Marcy Tweed in the early 1870s, were undeniably corrupt – by the standards of political life at that time, as well as by those of the late 20th century. However, there were many others of whom corruption was alleged, and whose behaviour would not be exonerated today, but whose contemporary critics were employing different norms from those that were then dominant. Often the latter wanted to change standards of behaviour in public life, because their interests lay in doing so, and 'corruption' became a weapon in the contest with their opponents. That one would regard particular behaviour as corrupt if it were evident in a polity today is no reason for accepting the verdict of the nineteenth-century critics about their opponents.

## United States: introduction and background

It is impossible to know how much money American parties raised or spent in the nineteenth century. There are several interconnected reasons for this. First, the system of funding was highly decentralized because the political system itself was decentralized. Parties operated at the levels of local, state and federal government. Different bodies would be involved in garnering funds depending on the type of election being contested at a particular time. Of course, there were connections between the individuals and groups that raised money at the different levels, but these connections were informal even if they relied heavily on convention. This leads to a second reason.

The funding system was largely 'informal' (or extra-legal) in that it either depended on wholly personal connections – an individual or group simply being approached for money, or giving an unsolicited donation – or on systems of contribution that were neither open to public scrutiny, nor for which complete records were usually kept. Unlike membership dues in some European parties, the records of which are often available to future historians, the records that survive for American parties are fragmentary and incomplete. Furthermore, the figures that were quoted by contemporaries can be misleading – hardly any participants had a full picture of their party's funding and many of them had 'an axe to grind'. Reformers often exaggerated the amounts raised and spent by parties, in order to justify their own stance, while party regulars could do so for self-aggrandizement or as part of an intra-party conflict. One of the most famous instances of the latter was the claim by the Secretary of the Republican National Committee, Stephen W. Dorsey, that $400,000 had been spent by the party in 1880 to win the marginal state of Indiana. In fact, nothing like this amount was either needed or spent in the state that year.[1]

One of the reasons that the parties in the nineteenth century kept no record of their income or expenditure was that they were not required to do so by law. It was not until after the 1904 presidential election, when there had been allegations of huge sums of money being used to support Theodore Roosevelt's re-election bid, that the first, and largely ineffectual, federal regulation of campaign finance was introduced. Consequently, estimating how much money the parties raised and spent in the nineteenth century is difficult, and it is impossible to estimate for elections at the state and local level because there was so much variation from one place to another, and also considerable variation from one year to another. Archival evidence relating to, say, Boston tells us nothing about likely levels of party income in St. Louis or Chicago, and it was the local level of politics that really mattered in the nineteenth century. Nevertheless, there are at least estimates for presidential elections after 1860 which, if somewhat inaccurate, do make it possible to make a start in understanding the scale of party funding in the nineteenth century.

Herbert Alexander, using estimates supplied by the *Congressional Record* in 1910, indicates that in 1860 the two major parties between them spent about $150,000.[2] That was an election in which two other candidates also polled a substantial vote, so that almost certainly this figure understates the actual amount spent during the campaign. On the other hand, it is quite possible that the intensity of feeling over the issues that year meant that overall expenditure may have been rather high in 1860 by comparison with the immediately preceding years. So, if we accept the estimate of $150,000 for 1860, it indicates that about 3 cents was spent per voter. After the Civil War the amounts spent in presidential campaigns rose dramatically, though unevenly, to $1.85 million in 1876, $2.7 million in 1884, and $4 million in 1896. Although the voting population was increasing rapidly in this period, the increase in campaign expenditures outpaced it; spending was 22 cents per voter in 1876, 27 cents in 1884, and 29 cents in 1896.

It is instructive to compare this with the British experience at about the same time. The British data is much 'firmer' because the Corrupt Practices Act of 1883 required all parliamentary candidates to report their expenditures, and these expenditures were restricted to a certain amount per eligible voter. (Campaigns by the parties nationally were of very limited importance then.) That Act had a dramatic effect on campaign expenditures, which decreased by 41 per cent between the general election of 1880 and the one in 1885; this occurred in spite of an increase of 80 per cent in the size of the electorate, following electoral reform in 1884.[3] But how do total expenditures compare with those in the US? In the 1900 British general election £0.78 million was spent with 3.5 million men voting; this represents 22 (new) pence per voter.[4] At first glance, and allowing four dollars to the pound sterling, this might seem to suggest that British parties were relatively better funded than their American counterparts. But this is highly misleading. A British parliament could last for up to seven years, and, in fact, the average life of a parliament between 1868 and 1900 was over 4.5 years. Apart from parliamentary elections nineteenth-century party politics was relatively inexpensive; it was not until the later years that elective local governments were introduced, and in these contests party expenditures were low. In the United States, however, there were important, and expensive, elections every year – local government elections, state elections, mid-term congressional elections and so on – for which high levels of expenditure were necessary. Focusing on presidential elections means that only a small proportion of expenditures is disclosed, whereas when looking at parliamentary election expenditures in Britain it is virtually all party expenses that are visible.

Despite the paucity of the data, it is clear that the trend in nineteenth-century America was for the cost of election campaigning to increase, and with it increased the needs of the parties for money. Certainly party politics could not be described as cheap before the Civil War, but by comparison with the 1880s and 1890s it was. As Silbey has noted of the 1840s and 1850s:

> The amounts raised were minute by later standards. In 1852, the Democrats sought to collect $100 from each congressional district for a national party fund; about $20,000 was raised all told. In 1840, New York City's Fifth Ward Whig Committee spent $590 to rent meeting halls, print documents and hire cabs to bring people to the polls. And when Chauncey Depew ran for the state legislature in 1861, he spent less than $100.[5]

The American trend over a sixty-year period marks a notable contrast with, say, Britain where democratization was marked by an astonishing drop in the cost-per-voter of elections. The extensions of the franchise in 1867, 1885 and 1918 were accompanied by a significant change in spending on electoral politics. In the sixty years after 1867 electoral politics went from being an expensive sport for a small number of aristocratic party grandees to a low-cost operation. In the 1924 election, for example, expenditures per voter did not reach even 6 (new) pence, less than a third the amount spent per voter in 1900. The early regulation of election expenses (in the legislation of 1883 and also that of 1918) made party politics relatively inexpensive in Britain – at least until the rise of television campaigning, and the consequent much greater role played by the parties nationally in advertising themselves. However, in America the sixty years after the Jacksonian revolution saw the cost of party politics rise, although financial support for the parties continued to be fairly widely based.

### The 'myth' of nineteenth-century party funding in the United States

Both the amount of money involved in the funding of America's political parties and the informal nature of that funding contributed to the growth of a persistent myth about party finance in the nineteenth century. The myth may be outlined as follows:

> At the heart of party finance was corruption. The Jacksonians created a spoils system in which all public appointments were made on partisan grounds. The job holders themselves were expected to contribute to party coffers. So too were businesses that received contracts from governments, or expected to receive them. Corruption was

worst in the major cities where party bosses ran government as a kind of business, and where they were sustained
in power by politically malleable immigrants. Consequently,
the abuses in the system became worse over time, to the
point at which a major public revolt occurred against such
practices.

This view of the parties was propagated by Progressive reformers
and it continues to have a hold over the popular imagination.

It is a myth, not in the sense that it is fictitious for much of
what it states is true, but in the sense that the overall picture
it presents of party funding is distorted and demonized; it picks
out particular elements of financing and combines them in a
way that conceals key aspects of the process.

One point to observe is that according to the myth the public were at the mercy of politicos who had hijacked the democratic process. In fact, the spoils system on which the whole
edifice was constructed had widespread support. As Stemp notes
of the federal government, in which there were about 20,000
positions to be filled by an incoming president:

> By 1857 the spoils system was not only universally practiced but,
> according to its theoretical defenders, it had become an essential
> ingredient of effective governance in a democracy ... Hardly an
> appointment, high or low, was made on merit alone. Federal clerk-
> ships, post offices, customhouses, navy yards, land offices, and
> Indian agencies were filled with persons of varying degrees of abil-
> ity and integrity but of unswerving party loyalty. So were federal
> judgeships and district attorneys' offices ... Some applicants for
> federal appointments resorted to professional office-brokers to work
> in their behalf ... *The spoils system was not without its critics,
> but they were always most plentiful among the members of a
> defeated party* (emphasis added).[6]

At the state and, especially, the local levels of government the
same system of appointment was practised – but it was a system
that rested on a broad base; most white males were partisans
and many had a stake in a system that distributed the benefits
of office so widely.

Now it is certainly true that mass immigration to the United
States from the mid-1840s onwards, and particularly after the
Civil War, did make possible the emergence of party bosses in
the major cities. Their control over the vote could make them
an independent and unaccountable source of power, thereby
changing the balance between party and society. But there are

three considerations that the 'myth' ignores. First, with the possible exception of New York City, most of the so-called 'party machines' were much less centralized in the nineteenth century than critics maintained. Centralized machines did not develop until the very end of the century (Philadelphia being one example) or until the early twentieth century (as was the case with Chicago).[7] The second point is that the worst manifestations of nineteenth-century machines – especially the Tweed 'ring' in New York in the 1870s – were actually broken up by party politicians themselves; they were too damaging to the system of party politics to be allowed to continue. (Samuel Tilden who led the effort to overthrow Tweed was not a party outsider – he became the Democratic Party's presidential nominee in 1876.) The final point is that in any context informal, or extra-legal, systems of funding are often interpreted by critics as being far more pervaded by corruption than they really are. There is a similar myth about eighteenth-century Ch'ing China which westerners interpreted as being rooted in corruption. In fact, the informal system of funding introduced by local magistrates there was a response to a funding base that was wholly inadequate for the tasks they were required to carry out. They resorted to unofficial, that is informal or extra-legal, means of raising the necessary funds and, while in some cases this did permit the syphoning off of funds for personal benefit, many officials did not do so.[8] It is all too easy, because they are not rule-governed, to see informal systems of funding as being no more than a facade for corrupt relationships. While there were practices that would have been recognized as corrupt even at the time, much of the informal system of party funding in nineteenth-century America was not corrupt.

In the heyday of nineteenth-century party politics business people did not give to the Democratic or Republican Party in order to secure a contract with the government or to have a relative placed in public office. They gave to the Democrats (or Republicans) because they were Democrats (or Republicans), and they then hoped to be given consideration after the party won the election. To the extent that they were not in competition with others for the same contract or post, this was not an unreasonable expectation. But the more attractive spoils of office were sought by many would-be beneficiaries, and, naturally, individuals often had inflated estimates of their own value to the party. Disappointment abounded, and those who were disappointed might well rail against the spoils system, but few then threw over their partisan identities and most were to be found at future elections engaged in the same process as before. This was a deeply partisan social world; the vast majority of white, male Americans were strongly attached to one or the other political party, and, in contrast to twentieth-century America, involvement in parties included people from across the social spectrum.[9] To be a business person who made donations to his political party was to occupy a reputable role in a community, and to have 'expectations' was only natural.

## Contrasts with political funding in the late twentieth century

It should be apparent from the discussion so far that party funding in the nineteenth century differed from the practices found in the United States in the late twentieth century in a number of significant ways. (Others will become evident later.) The party-centred nature of funding was crucial. The party looked to its known supporters to contribute; until the later nineteenth century there was little casting around for funds among the affluent simply on the basis that they would be attracted to a particular issue or candidate, although that was changing by the 1880s. It was the parties that received the money, not the individual candidates, and they used it to promote the party's campaign. Candidates themselves gave money to the party – usually on the basis of an assessment that was made of them by the party – rather than being recipients of funds from the party. The wealthy whose partisan connections were weak could not expect to obtain a nomination unless there was some evidence of prior commitment to the party. Even in those states where US Senate seats could be obtained only by those with large sums at their disposal, prior association with the party was important. For example, in 1887 the *New York Times* estimated that George Hearst (William Randolph Hearst's father) had just spent half a million dollars in securing the nomination of the California state legislature.[10] But Hearst, who had set his heart on becoming a Senator, had begun his manoeuvring in the party more than six years before he got the nomination. He bailed out a San Francisco Democratic newspaper in 1880, bought it subsequently, and then obtained the support of the city's Democratic Party organization for his political ambitions.[11] The super-rich could get into politics if they wanted to, just as a Steve Forbes or a Ross Perot can today, but unlike their counterparts in the late twentieth century, a kind of 'apprenticeship' had to be served with the party before they could expect to be nominated for major public office.

This can be linked to the related point that, while money became increasingly important for parties in the nineteenth century, raising money never became the core activity of the party. In the late twentieth century there are relatively few campaigns for major offices that do not require some funds to have been raised as a *sine qua non* for the candidate actually proceeding to run for office. Only the most secure of incumbents, such as Senator William Proxmire in the 1970s, or insurgents relying on a large activist base, such as presidential hopeful Pat Buchanan in 1996, do not conform to this pattern. In the nineteenth century the central role provided by the party enabled campaign activity to get under way even if fund raising had not yet brought in the sums desired.

Furthermore, giving to the party was not confined to a relatively small 'political class'. Politics was not a minority hobby, but an activity that touched on most people's lives, and in many different ways. By no means all those involved in a party could afford to donate money, but those that could not gave their time to party work, including, for example, marching in organized party parades. Giving money was not just about trying to buy influence, or at least a hearing from the influential, it was also about being a member of a community. As McGerr has observed of the party political spectacles and pageantry, such as the torch light parades which were financed by the wealthy – they sprang in part from a powerful sense of local community.[12]

The form that party funding took in the nineteenth century can be seen as the interaction of what might be termed 'demand factors' – most especially the nature of party competition – and 'supply factors' – the various sources from which funds might be obtained from outside the party. Both of these will be examined in turn before turning to a description of the *system* of funding that resulted from what otherwise would have been a shortfall in supply if the parties had not been able to 'self-generate' funds.

### The demand for funds – the nature of party competition

Between 1836 and 1896 the United States had a highly competitive party system. For example, of the sixteen presidential
elections, there were only five when the winning party received
6 per cent or more of the popular vote than its main rival, and
in only three of these instances (1860, 1864 and 1872) was the
winning margin more than 10 per cent. In many of the states,
in quite a few congressional districts, and in most cities too
there was genuine two-party competition – first between Democrats and Whigs, then, as the Whigs collapsed in the mid-1850s,
between Democrats and Republicans. The closeness of elections meant that neither party could settle for less than all-out
effort if it was to stand a chance of victory. Moreover, such
effort was required every year. The Jacksonians in their push
for democracy in the late 1820s and 1830s had not only created
a universal white male suffrage but they had also plumped for
frequent election for most offices. Typically state governors
served for no more than two years, state legislatures were often
elected annually, and there were many local offices for which
the terms were short. (Even in 1900 fewer than half the state
governors served for terms longer than two years.) Together
with the Constitutional requirement that members of the House
of Representatives serve for no more than two years, this meant
that the party 'armies' were never really 'stood down': 'Nothing
quite matched the excitement of a presidential campaign, but
important state or city elections always seemed to be pending
somewhere.'[13]

This consideration alone would have ensured a strong demand for money, but the particular form the competition took
accentuated it. Elections were usually lost by one party rather
than won by the other – in the sense that failing to get your own
supporters out would likely cost you an election. The accepted
strategy for an election campaign was to keep the 'army' intact,
rather than proselytise for converts. There were few uncommitted voters to be won over simply because party identity
reflected patterns of membership in socio-economic and ethno-
religious groups within American society. So there could be
no question of a party taking its own supporters for granted
and directing resources at winning over the 'uncommitted'. The
whole campaign effort was geared towards maintaining passion
for the forthcoming contest among supporters, but that was

costly because it meant providing entertainments, distributing speeches, and devising many other stimuli for large numbers of people. The scale of this activity was astonishing. For example, in 1852 faced by an eligible electorate of less than 4.6 million, the Whigs printed nearly one million copies of a biography of their presidential candidate, Winfield Scott.[14] (Consequently, there were nearly as many copies of the biography as Whig voters that year: the number of voters was 1.3 million.)

An unusual feature of nineteenth-century presidential elections was that the electoral advantage normally lay with the party that had lost the previous contest, and there is some evidence of a tendency for this to be reflected in the ability to raise funds for a campaign. If the three elections affected directly by the Civil War are excluded – the wartime 1864 election and the two immediately following (1868 and 1872) during the active era of Reconstruction – there were twelve presidential elections between 1840 and 1896. Of these only three (1856, 1876 and 1880) were won by the party that held the presidency. (Moreover, one of these three is the so-called 'stolen' election of 1876 which, arguably, was actually won by the Democrats.) By comparison, in the twelve succeeding presidential elections (1900–44) nine were won by the party occupying the White House, and in the thirteen elections since the end of the Second World War seven have been won by the incumbent party. Incumbency was a liability in the nineteenth century in that once in the White House a president had the impossible task of trying to satisfy all the demands for office from the various elements in each of the state parties. All politicians believed they were owed something for their role in the electoral victory, and when they got less than they expected, discontent and internal dissent followed. A party's financing was often affected directly by this tendency of the winning party coalition to fragment. Thus, although the data may be somewhat unreliable, it appears that at every election from 1884 to 1896 the party in the White House was outspent by its opponent – and on every occasion it lost.[15]

If the major element in nineteenth-century party strategy was to keep one's own party together, opportunities could present themselves, nevertheless, for reducing the other party's vote. The third and minor parties that arose from time to time were likely to draw their support disproportionately from one of the two major parties. Having a minor party slice away as much of your opponent's support as possible could mean the difference between victory and defeat in a particular state. For this reason, it was well worth while for a major party to provide financial backing to such minor parties, most of which were ill-funded. As the sums raised by the major parties rose after the Civil War, so this practice developed. In 1878 the Republicans underwrote the Greenbackers' electoral campaign in Indiana.[16] Then in 1884 the Republican national committee provided a $5,000-a-week subsidy to the Greenback-Labor-Antimonopoly Party, while the Prohibition Party was well subsidized by the Democrats in 1888, just as it had probably subsidized them previously in 1884.[17]

## The supply of funds from American society

The party-orientated, highly competitive electoral politics that had become established in America by the mid-1830s had developed in a society that consisted mainly of small towns and extensive rural hinterlands. Commercial firms and manufacturing industries were relatively small-scale enterprises, mostly family businesses. This placed quite tight limits on how much money the parties could hope to raise. Party supporters were approached for contributions, especially wealthier ones, and, as indicated earlier, relatively large numbers of people were probably involved in party funding. With industrialization, a process that accelerated rapidly from the 1860s onwards, the scale of party funding changed, and there were significant developments that eventually would transform the basis of party funding. For a start, the wealthy individuals of the 1880s were much richer than their predecessors of fifty years earlier, and there were many more of them. But it was not just a matter of individuals. Behind some of the wealthy people were business firms operating on a scale that was unknown in the earlier period. This was especially true of the railroad companies, and also of some banks, whose assets were huge and whose stake in certain aspects of national policy was great.

By comparison with the twentieth century, governments throughout the nineteenth century continued to do very little. This was especially true of the federal government. But there were key areas of public policy – such as tariffs, or the land grants to be made to railroad companies as incentives for opening up the west – in which various interests had a clear stake. The legislation that Congress passed, and, even more importantly, the judgements of federal courts both on that legislation and on state legislation, drew these interests towards party politicians. The railroads came to have their own people in Congress, and they also sought to influence appointments to the courts. Moreover, they had the resources the parties needed. With this development there is the beginning of a move away from money that was given mainly by partisans for partisan ends – a move that was highly significant for the future of party funding. Those interests, like the railroad magnates, who had a stake in what government did would take more instrumental decisions about whom to fund – and that might well include both parties. But while the railroads were the largest of the interests with a stake in national politics, and were forerunners of the large corporations that were to develop in the twentieth century, they were by no means the only interests that were funding parties on an instrumental basis by the last two decades of the nineteenth century. For example, in 1894 Henry O. Havermeyer was asked at a Senate hearing why his sugar trust supported Democrats in New York but Republicans in Massachusetts, and he replied that 'where there is a dominant party, wherever the majority is very large, that is the party that gets the contributions, because that is the party which controls the local matters'.[18]

Initially, the changing scale of American capitalism after the Civil War did not affect the balance between the parties so far as their access to funds was concerned. However, in 1896 the situation was transformed. Before then both Democrats and Republicans could be attractive to donors, depending on the circumstances. The Democrats' nomination of William Jennings Bryan changed this; the bi-metallic policy adopted at the 1896 National Convention was perceived as a threat to most Eastern business interests, and their money, most of it raised in New York, shifted heavily to the Republican Party. In 1896 the Republicans probably spent about five times as much as the Democrats, and, some contemporary observers believed that with equal funding Bryan would have won the election.[19] There had been a few similarly unbalanced contests previously – such as in 1872 – but 1896 was a watershed. It marked the beginning of an era of imbalance in party funding. Between 1896 and the introduction of public funding for presidential elections in 1976 the Republicans were outspent by the Democrats on only two occasions – 1912, when the party was split by Theodore Roosevelt running on the Progressive ticket, and 1948, when the incumbent Harry Truman won re-election. Bryan's nomination had two effects. Not only did it allow the Republicans to be identified firmly as the party of industry and commerce, but it also turned the Democrats into the minority party in much of the North, especially the North-East. Thus, after 1896, the Republicans had access to the biggest donors, and between 1896 and the New Deal they had the further advantage in attracting funds because they were the majority party in much of the country.

## The system of 'self-generated' funding

The primarily rural America of the 1830s in which a highly competitive party system developed was not one that could have sustained high-spending campaigns; yet the parties needed money every year for electoral contests. What they required, therefore, were ways of generating funds, and also 'in kind resources', on a regular basis that could consolidate appeals to partisan loyalty. And there was an obvious method on hand. The American colonies had inherited from their British colonial masters a method of appointment to public office that was based on favouritism. In Britain this system of patronage continued until the later part of the nineteenth century when the first Gladstone administration (1868–74) started to enact proposals for merit-based appointments that had been proposed by the Northcote-Trevelyan report of 1854. However, the key feature of earlier British administration had been that appointments were essentially the result of *personal* connections rather than *party* connections. In the era of elite partisan competition in the United States in the 1790s, however, appointments had come to be used for explicitly partisan ends. Most famously, the 1803 case of *Marbury v. Madison*, in which John Marshall asserted the Supreme Court's power of Judicial Review, was about party political appointments – in this case the refusal of the Democratic-Republican Secretary of State, James Madison, to deliver the commission of a federal judgeship to William Marbury, a Federalist who had been nominated just before the outgoing Federalist President Adams left office.

Thus, the 'spoils system' that was introduced by the Jackson-ian Democrats in the 1830s, and which was to be used just as extensively by their Whig opponents, drew on long-established practices in American politics. In part, what was new about the post-1830s patronage was that it was used systematically to provide parties with the electoral resources they needed. In many cities and states public employees were required to contribute money, as well as their time, to election campaign-ing. Usually this was a highly structured system that utilized well-established conventions about the basis of contributions, and which has been described as an 'extra-legal income tax'.[20] Yearley has noted:

> we know of a Philadelphia post office worker who in 1881–2 paid his party's national political tax of $16, a state assessment of $20, and a ward assessment of $5; on a salary of $800 a year, that is, he was taxed $41 or 5% of his income. Similarly, we hear of a New York letter carrier whose thousand dollar salary was taxed 3% by the National Republican Committee and another 3% by the party's New York State Committee.[21]

One of the interesting points about this description is that it illustrates just how much the funding system operated at dif-ferent, but complementary, levels of a party.

Candidates too were assessed a contribution for the party campaign. In New York in the 1880s this could run upwards from $10 for a single election district, with the total assess-ment for some offices, including judgeships, being as much as £15,000–$20,000.[22] New York City, though, was somewhat unusual in the naked use of power to extract money from can-didates; there it could be said to have almost amounted to a sale of offices and charges of corruption are not out of place.

One of the problems facing candidates in New York, and in many other localities, was the decentralization of the parties; in conjunction with the use of party ballots, this probably drove up the levels of their contributions. Before the introduction of the Australian Ballot in the late 1880s and 1890s, a party distributed its own ballot to its voters. This facilitated deals being concluded beween district captains, on the one hand, and unoffical party candidates and even candidates of the opposing party, on the other, to have their names substituted on the ballot for that of the official candidate. Often, therefore, official can-didates had to pay additional money to district captains to prevent 'treachery' as it was usually called.

Of course, control of government could generate resources in many other ways. While nineteenth-century governments may have spent relatively little by comparison with those in the twentieth century, much of their expenditure involved contracting with private firms. Not surprisingly, partisan considerations were usually paramount in the awarding of such contracts, and the businesses that benefited recognized their debt, to *their* party at election time, in the form of financial contributions.

Some of the resources a party obtained were ones for which in the next century they would have to pay – in a sense, therefore, the reciprocal nature of some intra-party relationships obviated the need for money. Good examples were parties' relations with newspapers and the consequent propaganda role of the papers: 'Across the country, loyal journals could count on receiving a contract for official county and city advertising when their party held local office'.[23] For their part most newspapers were fiercely partisan and determined propagandists for their party. However, as McGerr notes, the parties and the newspapers were not merely business partners.[24] At the very least the two were intertwined, and often there was an identity of interest: the editor-publisher of a newspaper, most of which were small operations, would be an active politician himself. A party, then, was an extensive system of institutions, comprised of intricate relationships between actors, so that disentangling a single aspect of its activities, such as its funding, inevitably draws a scholar into looking at a whole range of other activities that were crucial to it. Patronage was the 'glue' that held all these activities together. But it was a glue that also made it difficult, at least in the Northern states, to separate government and party.[25]

## Patronage and the late-nineteenth-century Canadian state

The importance of patronage in the United States provides a link with the very different experience of the democratizing Canadian regime during the first four or five decades after Confederation in 1867. In some ways Canada was a patronage regime *par excellence*; as Stewart observes,

> throughout the entire post-Confederation period from 1867 to 1910, both national parties used patronage as the cement of party . . . patronage was a preoccupation of the party leaders. This was a distinguishing characteristic of Canadian political culture. Patronage was the ballast which enabled the political ship to make headway.[26]

Even by 1914, when most of the higher echelons of the civil service were filled by non-political appointees, most of the lower positions were still occupied by party appointees.[27] Public appointments were made on partisan grounds not only at the federal level, but at the provincial level as well. For example, in Liberal-controlled Saskatchewan, highways inspectors and other public officials performed the party's organizational tasks.[28] In one province, Prince Edward Island, patronage remained the basis of appointment until well after the Second World War.[29] However, patronage operated in very different circumstances in Canada than in the United States, and this had important consequences for the funding of political parties.

The political institutions that were established in 1867 were highly centralized. Local government was unimportant – so unimportant that even today party competition is often absent from these elections. The provinces were not the equivalent of the American states, even though the political system was supposedly a federal one. As late as the 1950s Kenneth Wheare could describe Canada as 'quasi federal', and that description aptly summarizes just how many powers seemed to have been granted to the federal government.[30] (Of course, the federal–provincial relationship was to change dramatically in the mid-twentieth century.) Furthermore, within this federal-government-dominated regime Westminster-style parliamentarism was practised, and power was concentrated in the hands of the prime minister to a far greater degree than in Britain itself. Consequently patronage was a resource that was controlled hierarchically, with the prime minister at the apex of a much tighter hierarchy than existed in the American parties; it enabled them to consolidate their position against any potential rivals. Nevertheless, that consolidation was possible only by building up a party, so that Canada did develop a strong system of party politics, but with parties that were highly centralized and with leaders who thereby tended to remain in office for much longer than their British counterparts.

Thus, while power was much more centralized in parties in Canada than in the United States, successive Canadian Prime Ministers did not have the option of trying to build up purely personal machines. A party was essential for them to be effective at all, and party loyalty was encouraged, for example, in the way that patronage was deployed in appointments to judgeships:

> It was never enough for an aspiring lawyer to be an occasional contributor to party funds or to turn out only in the midst of an election campaign. Long years of hard work in good times and bad on behalf of the party was the prerequisite.[31]

As in the United States, then, party in the nineteenth century was more than a mere label, and, like the American parties, the Liberals and Conservatives in Canada were (and remained) cadre parties rather than mass parties. They did not enrol members whose dues could provide a major source of party finance. However, there were two main contrasts with the United States. First, at the constituency level the parties were skeletal organizations; they lacked both an extensive organization and a cadre of permanent officials who could provide experience and discipline.[32] In part, the second difference, the raising of money centrally, stemmed from this skeletal character of the Canadian parties as well as from the centralized character of the political institutions. In the early years locally-raised money was extremely important, and probably accounts for much of the difference in contemporary estimates of party spending. For example, Sir John A. Macdonald reckoned that the opposition Liberals spent $250,000 (Canadian) in Ontario alone during the 1872 campaign, while Liberals maintained that their central funds in the province hardly ever amounted to more than $8,000.[33] However, fairly rapidly it was the centrally-raised money that became crucial. Thus, while the candidates themselves still had to raise funds within their constituencies for their own campaigns throughout the pre-1914 era,[34] overall most of the money to cover the cost of an election seems to have been raised centrally.

In the early years after Confederation Sir John A. Macdonald, the first Prime Minister, raised the money himself for his party's election campaigns. And, as Paltiel notes, 'From the outset a relatively small number of business sources have been the main financial backers of the older parties.'[35] However, after a notorious episode in the early 1870s (the Pacific Railway scandal), involving acceptance of money by Macdonald from a railway magnate whose firm was bidding for a government contract, the personal involvement of party leaders declined. They were replaced by fund raisers whose task was to secure money from major financial interests in Toronto and Montreal; this did not eliminate scandals involving the parties, for they surfaced at regular intervals until well into the twentieth century, but it did help to protect the party leader. Unlike nineteenth-century America, therefore, party funding in Canada was rather narrowly based, in that relatively few people or firms contributed to the parties. In part, this was possible because the Canadian parties had so few elections to contest: between 1878 and 1917 the average time elapsing between federal elections was about four and a quarter years, and, in addition, provincial elections could be run fairly inexpensively. The Canadian model of party funding would have been entirely inadequate in a country, like the United States, in which there were significant partisan contests every year.

Nevertheless, it should not be assumed that Canadian elections were inexpensive affairs. As in pre-1883 Britain, there was considerable variation from one type of constituency contest to another. Although they were a distinct minority of the total, urban constituencies could be very expensive indeed. One candidate in the 1904 election estimated that in an urban Ontario seat that year the cost was never less than $3–4,000 (Canadian), and in some seats it was as high as $15–20,000; this meant that every vote cost a candidate at least one dollar and perhaps as much as six dollars.[36]

This leads on to other related contrasts between Canadian and American party financing. The first is that, while there were differences between the kinds of business interest that were likely to be drawn to each of the major parties in Canada, the relationship was always one of interests supporting that party which would most benefit them, rather than being a manifestation of the partisan commitments of particular individual business people. That is, the distinction between a party and interests is easier to make in the Canadian than in the American case, at least for the pre-Civil War period. Second, the weaker penetration of society by parties probably contributed to the greater problems Canadian parties had with funding after major electoral defeats. As Whitaker notes of a slightly later period (1930):

> whatever the motives of corporate donors to political parties, a party which sustained a major defeat was quickly abandoned. This was particularly crucial for the Liberal party, whose traditional links had been more to government contractors than to significant sections of big business whose interests closely related to party policy or ideology. A party which depends heavily on government contractors is in obvious difficulties when faced with a period out of office.[37]

As we have seen, in America the breadth of partisanship probably helped to sustain party funding after electoral defeat in the
nineteenth century, and there was actually a tendency for the
winning party's coalition to fall apart. There was no such tendency in Canada; indeed, Canadian politics from 1867 until the
1980s was characterized by extended periods in office for one
party – at both the federal and the provincial level. If money
flowed to the governing party, it was difficult for the opposition
party to retain its funding base and hence to remain competitive electorally.

## Problems of party funding in North America

Recognizing this point, that funding from business interests is
likely to flow disportionately either to a party that is considered
a likely winner or is likely to promote the particular interests
of the donors, leads back to two important considerations,
already mentioned, in relation to the United States. The first
is that, as the scale of economic enterprises increased after the
Civil War, so was there a growing tendency for political money
to be directed whence it would be most likely to be 'productive',
rather than to the entrepreneur's party. In other words, money
became more of an instrument, rather than simply an expression
of partisan solidarity. Second, when political conflict in the
United States moved in the direction of pitting the interests of
the industrial economy against those of other economic interests, as it did in the election of 1896, the pattern of party funding
changed fundamentally. The balance between the parties in
their ability to raise funds was shattered. Thereafter, while the
Democrats would do better when they were likely winners
rather than losers, the Republicans could nearly always raise
more money than the Democrats.

The overall imbalance in funding was perhaps not as great in
the United States as in Canada, partly because factors such as
mid-term congressional elections, the increasing role played by
seniority in Congress and the impact this had on the importance
of incumbency, tended to counteract some of the advantages
enjoyed by the Republican Party. But there is no denying that
the world of mid-to-late-nineteenth-century American politics,
in which neither party had a permanent advantage in funding
itself, had ended in 1896. Moreover, the growing financial link

between business and parties had consequences for the party systems – in both countries.

The dependence of Canadian parties on Toronto and Montreal corporations and the growing influence in the later nineteenth century of major East Coast financial interests in the American parties tended to produce a rather similar problem of party management. That problem was how to deal with those in the West who attributed their economic difficulties to 'eastern finance' and thus to the parties those interests supported. These territorially-based cleavages would have had political significance regardless of the system of financing political parties; but in both countries the perceived compromising of the major parties contributed to third party efforts, drawing on the West's problems, and also to shifts in support between the major parties that would make one of the parties temporarily the vehicle for western discontent (as, for example, in Bryan's support for bi-metallism).

Furthermore, to the extent that the system of funding was intimately connected to the patronage appointments system, it was affected by the limitations of this system and by growing public support in the twentieth century in favour of competence, rather than preferment, as the principle of appointment. Patronage systems can work, and work quite well, without engendering public discontent providing government is not required to do very much. Indeed, what is striking about the American patronage appointees is just how competent and dedicated many of them were; it is, perhaps, significant that Lord Bryce in his much-cited late-nineteenth century-study of the American polity was not critical of their performance.[38] But when there is a demand for greater and more complex public services, the issue of how well, and how efficiently, a service is delivered, is likely to come into the public domain because the potential tension between preferment and competence will be revealed. At the end of the nineteenth century just such demands were being placed on the American political system. The clamour for expertise in the public service, which was the rallying cry of American Progressives at the beginning of the twentieth century, came about because rapid urbanization had placed demands on government for remedies that party-based bureaucracies found it difficult to satisfy. As a result, from about 1900 to 1950, but especially between 1900 and 1916, much of the infrastructure which supported the

extensive American parties of the nineteenth century was dismantled. When the advent of television made it easier for individual candidates to appeal directly to mass electorates, from
the 1960s onwards, funding moved away from being party-
centred to being candidate-centred.

That development was not evident in Canada, and in an obvious sense it is still a party-based polity. Patronage has remained
sufficiently extensive to enable the party leadership to retain
strict control over their parliamentarians. In addition, the challenge of other parties, with very different funding sources to
those of the major parties, such as the New Democratic Party,
has not led to the supplanting of the older parties. Nevertheless,
there have been important consequences for these parties from
both their earlier reliance on patronage for party mobilization
and also their relatively narrow sources of party finance. They
failed to penetrate Canadian society very deeply, so that party
attachments among Canadians are rather weak; throughout its
history, there has been the possibility of relatively large swings
in electoral support in Canada from one election to another. A
much smaller proportion of legislative seats than in Britain or
the United States are safe, and, furthermore, a much higher
proportion of seats change hands against the tide of national
support. For new democracies in the late twentieth century
this experience may be instructive, for it may indicate the
consequences of failure by the parties to sink deep roots within
the society.

Yet, if in comparison with some of the older liberal democracies, Canada's parties did not penetrate its society that deeply,
arguably the reach of the parties was considerably greater than
that of parties in the new democracies of the late twentieth
century. That is, in the formative stages of democratization,
party control of patronage may well make it possible to manage
conflict. However, in the late twentieth century public attitudes
to patronage are rather different than they were a hundred years
earlier, and this has important consequences when assessing
the relevance of the earlier North American experience:

> The ability of the parties to be so culturally and socially significant
> and deliver rewards, and hopes of rewards . . . were some of the
> bases for successful democracy in Canada. Many of these methods
> would be frowned upon in the late twentieth century, certainly by
> the international community, and would lead to charges of corrup-
> tion and narrow partyism.[39]

It is very doubtful, therefore, that the experience of North America in the nineteenth century does provide a model that new democracies today could emulate. Whatever their advantages, such as support from the established democracies, the new democracies of the late twentieth century operate in a world where practices common in the nineteenth century are difficult to justify. Yet it was these very practices that played such a central role in the development of strong parties and of stable party systems in North America.

Moreover, there is also the question of whether in the context of the late twentieth century deep voter attachments to parties could ever be fostered in the way they were one hundred years ago. In the nineteenth century, party was a device for linking people in relatively isolated communities to each other. It provided a source of identity and of entertainment, and it had relatively few competitors – apart from other parties. The strength of party loyalty that developed among voters helped to stabilize the polity from the negative consequences of patronage. The party system could thereby withstand the frequent political scandals (in Canada), associated with the railroads' funding of the parties, and the irregularities and downright fraud that could, and did, occur in the informal system of party financing in the United States. Faced with similar scandals and irregularities in a world where information is more readily available to political opponents, it remains to be seen whether parties in the new democracies of the late twentieth century will be quite so resilient.

## Notes

1  R. D. Marcus, *Grand Old Party: Political Structure in the Gilded Age 1880–1896* (New York, Oxford University Press, 1971), pp. 48, 53 and 56–7.
2  H. E. Alexander, *Financing Politics* (Washington, DC, Congressional Quarterly Press, 1976), p. 20.
3  W. B. Gwyn, *Democracy and the Cost of Politics in Britain* (London, University of London, The Athlone Press, 1962), p. 55, cited in E. S. Wellhofer, *Democracy, Capitalism and Empire in Late Victorian Britain, 1885–1910* (Basingstoke, Macmillan, 1996), p. 35.
4  Data from D. Butler and G. Butler, *British Political Facts 1990–1994* (Basingstoke, Macmillan, 1994), pp. 213 and 240.
5  J. H. Silbey, *The American Political Nation, 1838–1893* (Stanford, CA, Stanford University Press, 1991), pp. 55–6.
6  K. M. Stemp, *America in 1857* (New York, Oxford University Press, 1990), pp. 72 and 73.

7 On Philadephia see P. McCaffery, *When Bosses Ruled Philadelphia* (University Park, PA, Pennsylvania State University Press, 1993), and for Chicago see K. Finegold, *Experts and Politicians: Reform Challenges to Machine Politics in New York, Cleveland and Chicago* (Princeton, NJ, Princeton University Press, 1995), pp. 29 and 163–8.

8 See M. Zelin, *The Magistrate's Tael* (Berkeley, University of California Press, 1984).

9 Marcus, *Grand Old Party*, pp. 4–5.

10 *New York Times*, 19 January 1887.

11 W. A. Swanberg, *Citizen Hearst* (New York, Bantam Books, 1971), pp. 26–7.

12 M. E. McGerr, *The Decline of Popular Politics: The American North, 1865–1928* (New York and Oxford, Oxford University Press, 1986), p. 33.

13 Stemp, *America in 1857*, p. 30.

14 Silbey, *The American Political Nation*, p. 55.

15 Alexander, *Financing Politics*, p. 20.

16 P. H. Argersinger, 'A place on the ballot: fusion politics and Antifusion Laws', *American Historical Review*, 85 (1980), p. 290.

17 Marcus, *Grand Old Party*, pp. 89 and 148.

18 Cited in G. Blodgett, *The Gentle Reformers: Massachusetts Democrats in the Cleveland Era* (Cambridge, MA, Harvard University Press, 1966), p. 107.

19 Alexander, *Financing Politics*, p. 65.

20 C. K. Yearley, *The Money Machines: The Breakdown and Reform of Governmental and Party Finance in the North, 1860–1920* (Albany, NY, State University of New York Press), 1970, p. 109.

21 Yearley, *The Money Machines*, p. 109.

22 H. J. Bass, *'I am a Democrat': The Political Career of David Bennett Hill* (Syracuse, Syracuse University Press, 1961), p. 97.

23 McGerr, *The Decline of Popular Politics*, p. 16.

24 *Ibid.*

25 Yearley, *The Money Machines*, p. xiii.

26 G. T. Stewart, *The Origins of Canadian Politics* (Vancouver, University of British Columbia Press, 1986), p. 74.

27 J. English, *The Decline of Politics: The Conservatives and the Party System 1901–20* (Buffalo and Toronto, University of Toronto Press, 1977), p. 27.

28 K. Z. Paltiel and J. B. VanLoon, 'Financing the Liberal Party, 1867–1965', in Committee on Election Expenses, *Studies in Canadian Party Finance* (Ottawa, The Queen's Printer, 1966), p. 161.

29 F. MacKinnon, *The Government of Prince Edward Island* (Toronto, University of Toronto Press, 1951), pp. 198–201. A good discussion of how patronage could operate at the provincial level is D. E. Smith, *Prairie Liberalism: The Liberal Party in Saskatchewan 1905–71* (Buffalo and Toronto, University of Toronto Press, 1975), chapter 2.

30 K. C. Wheare, *Federal Government* 3rd edn (London: Oxford University Press, 1953).

31 Stewart, *The Origins of Canadian Politics*, p. 79.

32 English, *The Decline of Politics*, p. 14.

33 Paltiel and VanLoon, 'Financing the Liberal Party', pp. 149–50.

34 English, *The Decline of Politics*, p. 21.

35 K. Z. Paltiel, 'Contrasts among several Canadian political finance cultures', in H. E. Alexander and A. J. Heidenheimer (eds.), *Comparative Political Finance* (Lexington, MA, D.C. Heath, 1970), p. 112.

36 English, *The Decline of Politics*, p. 21.

37 R. Whitaker, 'Party and state in the Liberal era', in H. G. Thorburn (ed.), *Party Politics in Canada* 5th edn (Scarborough, Ont., Prentice-Hall, 1985), p. 143.

38 Yearley, *The Money Machines*, pp. 101–2.

39 G. T. Stewart, 'The poverty of Canadian politics?', *Democratization*, 3 (1996), 41.

# 3

# Financial uncertainties of party formation and consolidation in Britain, Germany and Italy: the early years in theoretical perspective

ROSA MULÉ

This chapter explores the role of funding arrangements in shaping the internal life of some major political parties in Britain, Germany and Italy, covering a period from the mid-nineteenth century to the mid-twentieth century. One major left wing and one major right wing party is chosen from each country, drawn from parties that have experienced some continuity from the nineteenth century to the mid-1950s. For this reason the Italian case focuses on the Socialist Party rather than on the Communist Party. The selection of Britain, Germany and Italy reflects a methodological choice of using Britain as a control case in the comparative analysis. Problems related to the maintenance of party organizations emerged much earlier in Britain and funding practices evolved within uninterrupted democratic rules; by contrast, in Italy and in Germany the collection of money was discontinued when the totalitarian regime disrupted the traditional party system and banned political parties in the 1920s and 1930s. It is therefore instructive to look at the similarities and differences in funding arrangements between the three countries.

Until the early twentieth century none of the three countries met all the criteria that would be regarded as necessary for a fully fledged democracy. Similarly to North America, the requirements of the *régime censitaire* (suffrage based on property or taxation) were strict and large sections of the electorate were disenfranchised.[1] In such circumstances political parties sought to secure political rights for less privileged groups and became the principal protagonists of transition to democracy.

During this transition political parties evolved from amorphous groupings composed of local notables to large, tightly knit organizations supported by millions of adherents. Such a remarkable change was achieved primarily through the invention and diffusion of fund-raising techniques. However, the new methods of gathering funds often impinged on the bargaining power of party elites. The survival and functioning of the party delicately hinged on the collection of money and so the possibility that this vital activity could be either denied or halted constituted an uncertain situation for party leaders. This uncertainty meant that party actors could swing power games to their advantage by controlling the flow of income to the central apparatus.[2] Hence the way in which the parties were funded often shaped their structure and policy.

Despite the key role of funding operations in the internal life of parties, important questions regarding their impact on the structure of political parties, and the manner in which contributors tried to target different wings within a party in order to promote their particular interest, have found almost no answer.[3] The aim of this chapter is to fill a gap in the literature by examining the implications of funding methods for elite recruitment, party structure, cohesion of party leadership and autonomy of the party from its environment.

In tracing the patterns of party funding over the nineteenth and twentieth centuries it proved useful to merge Heidenheimer's developmental approach[4] with the classical models of party organization elaborated by Ostrogorski, Duverger and Kirchheimer.[5] A developmental approach has advantages over an evolutionary view because it does not postulate a necessary progression from one stage to the next; instead it productively allows for the coexistence of different types of parties and funding methods.

In one of the very few attempts to develop a theoretical understanding of party finance, Heidenheimer provides us with the rudiments of a general model. He posits the establishment of four phases of political financing, encompassing historical evolution and political development. Phase A is characterized most predominantly by a limited politicization of the electorate and so campaign costs are quite low on a per capita basis. In phase B of political financing the expansion of communication techniques and the diffusion of professional agents bring about rising campaign costs. In contrast phase C is marked by lower campaign expenditures because much of the effort is of a voluntary or institutional kind. Finally, in phase D there is a wider gap between the material resources needed for political persuasion and the resources available in terms of voluntary work and institutionalized support, and thus campaign costs are higher.

What Heidenheimer neglects is the fact that each of those phases is associated with specific funding arrangements in party organizations. As he is more concerned with financial operations in the political system, he ignores their impact on the structuring of party organizations. In this chapter it will be shown how the different phases of political financing coincided historically with the formation of specific types of party organizations. The first section briefly looks at phase A and the evolution of amorphous party groupings; it then shows how phase B involved higher campaign costs and the emergence of the cadre party with an irregular system of money collection. The second section highlights the gradual development of collective funding and the way in which the balance of power within left wing parties hinged on trade union financial support. The third section examines the shift to phase C and the reduction in campaign costs brought about by the diffusion of the mass party technique. The last section looks at the higher costs of phase D and the role of pressure groups as a main source of party income. The conclusion argues that the theoretical perspective endorsed in this chapter can be viewed as an ideal-type model, and finally points to some possible implications of the findings for today's new democracies.

## From personal wealth to patronage

In phase A of political financing the requirements of the *régime censitaire* limited the politicization of the electorate and contributed to low campaign costs. As the process of democratization evolved, the diffusion of literacy, the expansion of communication techniques and the professionalization of election agents signalled the beginning of phase B of political financing marked by rising campaign costs. In Britain the constitutional barriers of the *régime censitaire* were lowered earlier than in the other two countries, so that party leaders were forced to find new methods to solicit votes. The introduction of the limited vote spurred the formation in 1865 of the Birmingham Liberal Association, also known as the Liberal caucus, an exclusive committee of wealthy individuals, whose name, prestige and connections provided a financial backing for the candidates and secured them votes. The Second Reform Act (1867) gave the caucus a chance to show its efficacy and thus to became the basic unit of the cadre party, characterized by an irregular system of funding collection and a skeletal organization.[6] Party funding relied on the candidates' personal assets, on large donations from landowners, industrial magnates and bankers and on the benefits derived from easy access to important channels of communication, including the commercial press. Status and economic position enabled local notables to engage in politics at a time when the salaries for MPs were not paid by the public purse and parliamentary seats could be purchased.

Personal wealth and occasional donations soon proved to be inadequate to pay for the rising campaign costs of a democratizing society, and thus party leaders were encouraged to integrate donations from aristocrats and the business community with income accruing from patronage. To this end, cadre parties availed themselves of the opportunities offered by their parliamentary origin. They could deploy governmental resources to lure voters and distribute material incentives, such as money, status and jobs in exchange for political participation. In Italy for example it is well documented that in the 1890s Socialist MPs lobbied state bureaucrats for commissions on public works awarded to members of Socialist cooperatives.[7] A typical example was what Sivini dubbed 'municipal socialism' which consisted in the distribution of local government resources to party members and sympathizers. The penetration of the Italian Socialist Party (PSI) in a great number of local administrations provided a major source of income to the party and continued relentlessly in the twentieth century.[8]

Funding operations moulded the structure of the PSI. The advantages obtained from patronage jobs persuaded many voters to re-elect the same representative several times, helping local leaders to conduct personal feuds. With independent financial means peripheral groupings evolved in complete independence from the central apparatus. In this way local associations institutionalized into strong factions which turned into real centres of organizational power.

In Britain as well patronage was widely practised. Concern with corruption habits reached a peak during the 1880 parliamentary election campaign, which was considered one of the most expensive in British electoral history.[9] In 1883 the government passed the Corrupt and Illegal Practices Prevention Act which introduced a ceiling for campaign expenditure by candidates in a constituency and placed limits on the sorts of expenditure allowed. Britain was the first country to carry out legal regulations for the expenditure of political parties and all successive legislation controlling campaign spending has been based on this Act.[10]

The anticorruption bill immediately affected electoral costs. From 1883 to 1885 the total declared expenses of parliamentary candidates declined by approximately 40 per cent. However, it would be naive to attribute this drop exclusively to the implementation of the law. Experience suggests that anticorruption laws can be easily avoided or evaded. It is more reasonable to assume that reductions in campaign costs were caused by economic and political circumstances. Towards the end of the nineteenth century Britain underwent a severe economic recession that eroded the power of the landed aristocracy and discouraged local notables from purchasing seats in the House of Commons. This tendency was reinforced by the gradual emergence of well-disciplined parties which meant that individual MPs could no longer use their power independently to obtain and allocate material rewards. Finally, opportunities for patronage jobs shrank with the introduction and extension of the merit system in the public bureaucracy after 1854. All these factors account for the lasting effect of the anticorruption law and the declining cost of political financing.

Reduced opportunities for patronage and the limits to campaign expenditure increased the importance of voluntary work as a source of in-kind revenue; but recruitment of volunteers and helpers required the existence of an organizational basis. For this reason Pinto-Duschinsky claims that the Corrupt and Ilegal Practices Prevention Act of 1883 stimulated the development of constituency organizations operating on a permanent basis between elections.[11] The Conservative Party sought to expand local associations in order to collect funds by soliciting membership dues, organizing recreational activities and distributing the party press. Panebianco observes that the British Conservative Party represents an exception in the theory of party formation because it acquired a powerful bureaucracy, although it developed during a long period in government.[12] The key to understanding this anomaly lies in funding arrangements based on a regular revenue system, which led to a precocious construction of a solid apparatus at the local and national levels. Because party leaders were unable to benefit from a spoils system to obtain and distribute material rewards they concentrated on strengthening independent funding arrangements.

As mentioned earlier, in Italy the weakness of the state administration had a dual effect. It allowed the PSI to enjoy the advantages of patronage but prevented the party organization from developing a stable revenue system. In Germany, by contrast, patronage was hampered by the fact that Bismarck succeeded in imposing the Prussian pattern whereby the monarch exercised his power through a loyal administrative and military elite.[13] In such circumstances, the legislative assembly was more an advisory than a decision-making forum, relegating parties to the role of outsiders in the political system.

Yet some party groupings did slowly develop. Under Bismarck the Zentrum firmly established itself as the party of the overwhelming majority of German Catholics. The suppliers of funds were a plurality of Catholic associations, including the Christian working class organization, the Union of German Catholics and the so-called electoral unions, which were enlarged committees of Catholic notables.[14] Financial reliance on Catholic associations entailed the recruitment of most party leaders from the clerical elite. Furthermore, because the Zentrum drew on funding from pre-existing peripheral groups the organization retained the features of the cadre party, characterized by the lack of a regular revenue system and by a loose structure devoid of central direction.

Cadre parties were the first form of party organization endowed with a system of money collection. We have seen that over the nineteenth century political parties in the three countries received funding from the candidate's personal assets, from a few large donations and from patronage. Whether one or the other source of funding prevailed depended on the permeability of the state bureaucracy and on the extension of the franchise. Members of Parliament were expected to self-finance their campaign expenditures and to reward followers and voters with material incentives. During phase B of political financing party income was irregular because restrictive suffrage requirements made a constant flow of income to support permanent organizations superfluous.

## From large donors to a multitude of small subscriptions

This situation gradually changed as liberal democracy established itself. With the further extension of the franchise a substantial amount of income was needed to solicit votes from larger sections of the masses. New forms of political organization were necessary to canvass, mobilize and organize the masses. Party competition aimed at capturing the newly enfranchised voters intensified, prompting ceaseless agitation and propaganda which required both a permanent structure and committed party workers.

Moreover, the process of industrialization meant that the bourgeois state was unable to prevent the working class from organizing and taking action in the political sphere. Less privileged groups, however, had no personal wealth to finance their campaign expenses. Most of their members worked between twelve and fifteen hours a day, precluding the possibility of engaging in honorary, non-salaried commitments. The implication was that an income for working class leaders had to be provided. In such circumstances the irregular financial operations of cadre parties were insufficient to pay for the administrative costs of a mass organization and the caucus was eventually replaced with the branch, a permanent organization aimed at collecting funds.[15] While the caucus was narrowly recruited, decentralized and semi-permanent, the branch was more widely based, tightly knit and permanent. The branch was financially reliant upon the subscriptions paid by party members; accordingly, the first duty of the branch was to ensure that membership fees were regularly collected. In order to offer an income to working class MPs party organizations adopted the mass party technique of collective funding. The mass party counted on the fees of its adherents and exerted an increasing influence over all spheres of a member's daily life.

It is important to note that the transformation from cadre to mass party was triggered by the introduction of different funding procedures. Instead of collecting large amounts of funds from a few donors the mass party relied on small fees paid by many members. In Duverger's words, 'the mass-party technique in effect replaces the capitalist financing of electioneering by democratic financing'.[16] Membership dues financed election campaigns, paid the costs of educating the working class and provided a salary for party leaders.

Besides paying membership fees, activists contributed to party life by means of voluntary work. They invested a considerable amount of time and energy in attending local party meetings, fund raising and maintaining the grass-roots organization. Rewards of such labour were largely purposive. Solidary incentives encouraged membership subscriptions while doctrine and ideology nourished political participation. Mass organizations offered an avenue for activists' input into the party by allowing them a say in the internal decision-making process.

Against this background it is not surprising that the funding techniques of mass organizations were initially adopted by left wing parties to secure working class representation in Parliament. The paradigm case of the mass party is the German Social Democratic Party (SPD). The SPD emerged out of the fusion of the General Association of German Workingmen and the Social Democratic Workingmen party in 1875. Both organizations had an established membership, and so the SPD could immediately benefit from 24,443 subscriptions. From these membership fees the party paid its officials, supported professional agitators and subsidized the publication and distribution of newspapers.[17]

Between 1878 and 1890 when the Social Democratic organization (but not the parliamentary party) was outlawed, the party networks were diffuse, informal and often transitory. There is no published information on funding practices during this period. Historical accounts suggest that the party organization relied on underground activities, mostly undertaken by volunteers.

> Perhaps nothing in the twelve-year history under the Socialist Law highlighted the loyalty of the party members as much as the innumerable risks they took to distribute the *Sozialdemocrat*, the party's major newspaper published in Switzerland under the direction of Bebel.[18]

By 1884 some 9,000 copies of the paper were being sent into Germany. Other sources of funding were obtained from abroad. Lidtke reports that in 1886 Liebknecht was in the United States collecting about 16,000 marks for the party's election fund, which at the time was a considerable amount.[19]

When the anti-socialist laws elapsed in 1890 the SPD entered a period of rapid growth. The earliest figures show that the party enrolled 400,000 members in 1905; by 1914 membership rose to 1,085,000 and in the same year there were 91 daily newspapers with 1.5 million subscribers.[20] There was also a tremendous growth in the size of affiliated organizations. The Socialist movement founded in 1904 enlisted over 10,000 members four years later; the Volksfürsorge, created in 1912 as an insurance company owned and operated by the labour movement, had one million insured by 1922; women's organizations also flourished. These ancillary organizations were an important source of party income.

Another major source of income originated from trade unions. The history of the changing relationship between the trade unions and the SPD over the nineteenth and early twentieth century is a telling example of how the internal life of parties hinges on funding arrangements. Over the nineteenth century German trade unions were organized on a local rather than a national basis, and were numerically weak. For a long time the SPD retained almost a monopoly of workers' representation; it also engaged in mobilizing the union movement until the economic boom of the late nineteenth century boosted the number of unionized workers. Union membership grew concomitantly with the increasing demand for labour. In 1906 there were 1,689,709 unionized workers and 384,327 SPD members.

This asymmetry in size increased the financial dependence of the SPD on trade unions. To protect the vulnerability of the party organization Socialist leaders sought a mutually supportive alliance with the unions that was sanctioned at the Mannheim Congress in 1906. The Mannheim resolution stated that the selection of party policies required prior consultation with the unions, thus accepting the unions' influence in the decision-making process.[21] It therefore represented a landmark in the history of German Social Democracy because it ratified the fact that the party elite was effectively composed of a coalition of SPD leaders and union representatives. Heavier financial reliance on the trade unions was therefore reflected in a new balance of power within the SPD.

Similarly to the SPD, the British Labour Party derived financial support from trade unions. The main difference in funding arrangements between the two parties was that membership dues were paid directly to the SPD while Labour collected funds on an institutional basis, primarily from trade unions. Labour received funds from fees paid by each affiliated body according to its membership. In Duverger's terms funding practices accounted for the evolution of a direct structure in the SPD and of an indirect structure in the Labour Party.

Formal rules regulating funding to the Labour Party changed several times in the course of the decades. In 1913 the Trade Union Act introduced a 'political levy'. Union members could 'contract out' of the political levy by signing an express declaration. Every member who did not protest was automatically included in the party. Because of automatic fund raising the sums that could be raised were very substantial for a new political force. Partly the reason was that the number of trade unionists grew steadily at the beginning of the twentieth century. Total union membership rose from about 2.5 million in 1910 to around 8.25 million in 1920.

The 1927 Trade Union Act abolished the automatic element in the payment of the political levy by introducing the clause of 'contracting in'. Only those members who formally accepted to pay the political levy became party members. With the coming to power of the Labour government in 1945 the law was repealed and 'contracting out' reintroduced. The effects on party funding of such simple changes in formal regulations can be gauged by examining the trend in party membership. Between 1912 and 1913 the number of members dropped by almost 15 percentage points and between 1926 and 1928 membership declined by 32 per cent. In contrast, the repeal of contracting in after the Second World War raised membership figures from 3,038,697 in 1945 to 5,040,299 in 1948, a rise of 65 percentage points.[22] This example highlights the importance of psychological factors such as apathy in determining the amount of membership fees accruing to political parties.

· Affiliation fees were only one channel of trade union financial support to the Labour Party. During election times at least 90 per cent of elections funds was drawn from large extra payments made by unions. Union funds served several purposes. They covered Labour's administrative costs and contributed to the life of affiliated bodies such as the Fabian Society. Heavy reliance on trade union political levies had far-reaching consequences for Labour. The ease with which the party received money hampered the search for additional sources of income, thwarting the growth of constituency organizations. A manifestation of the organizational weakness of the Labour Party was the small number of local associations as compared with the Conservative Party. A further implication was that party wings were able to consolidate into stable factions dependent on funding from external organizations.

The constitution of the Labour Party endowed unions with a considerable amount of power. Affiliation fees entitled unions to representation in the general management committees of the Constituency Labour Parties (CLP) and qualified them for 90 per cent of the votes at the annual conference. Unions sponsored over half of Labour MPs and controlled a majority of seats in the National Executive Committee (NEC). Their predominant position enabled unions to influence the selection of MPs. Candidate recruitment was based on two lists compiled by the NEC where unions had the majority vote. One list included union-sponsored candidates who would officially represent unions in Parliament if elected; the second list was made up by the delegates of local associations at the General Management Committee, itself controlled by the unions. Members of the main decision-making committees were thus selected from affiliated groups. Hence by controlling the bulk of funding to the party, unions were often able to swing bargaining power to their advantage. This imbalance was reflected in the subordination of the Parliamentary Labour Party to the unions, in sharp contrast to the position of superiority enjoyed by the SPD *vis-à-vis* German trade unions.

Over the years, however, the rationale for union funding was weakening. In 1911 MPs were granted public funding which removed a major financial burden form the party. The Representation of the People Act in 1918 continued the spirit of the 1911 Act by increasing state subsidies for campaign costs. Both these measures released substantial amounts of money to finance other party activities. From 1918 onwards the party constitution was amended to allow individual membership alongside collective membership. Labour leaders could now draw on a pool of individual members to mould a party image detached and distinct from trade union identity. The party also sponsored membership drives to invigorate constituency Labour parties. But these efforts were only marginally successful because local parties could easily attract union funds without stimulating organizational growth. In this way the Labour Party remained financially dependent on trade unions.

Contrary to the German and British experience, the Italian Socialist Party (PSI) was financially neither subordinate nor superior to the unions. The alliance stipulated between the General Confederation of Workers (Confederazione Generale dei Lavoratori) and the PSI was based on an equality of powers.[23] Unlike the British Labour Party, the PSI was not funded by a single external group but by many socialist bodies, including affiliated cooperative societies and individual members. Yet unlike the SPD, the Italian Socialist Party was unable to collect a vast number of membership subscriptions. It appealed to the rural communities of central Italy and to liberal, middle class anti-clerical groups who were not amenable to modes of mass mobilization. A further consideration is that industrialization took off relatively late in Italy, delaying the emergence of a working class movement.[24] The widely held view of a sequential link between industrialization and formation of Socialist parties through the mobilization of the working class must be amended in the Italian case.

The main point, however, is that the heterogeneity and fragmentation of its social bases hindered the transformation of the PSI into a mass party funded through fee-paying members. Lack of centrally controlled funding strengthened the autonomy of affiliated associations and fostered strong centres of power, including the Confederazione Generale dei Lavoratori (CGL), professional unions, chambers of commerce and the parliamentary group. These party groupings were organized into factions with independent financial means. Overall, the bargaining equilibrium between the PSI and sponsor associations was based on funding arrangements which limited the organizational development of the party. Therefore when the union movement grew stronger it was not confronted with a powerful Socialist Party.

Funding arrangements had profound implications for the internal distribution of power within the party. First, the influence of the centre on local associations was extremely limited. Second, the development of a solid organization able to dominate the trade unions was precluded. Third, affiliated associations influenced the selection of leaders, although their impact was less extensive than the one exerted by British unions on the recruitment of Labour MPs. Finally, the financial weakness of the central apparatus precluded the payment of salaries to Socialist MPs and consequently elite recruitment took place principally among the ranks of professional groups and intellectuals.

In the PSI funding arrangements hindered the development of the party into a tightly knit mass organization and impeded the selection of working class MPs. Similarly to the German SPD and the British Labour Party, the dependence on trade union funds impinged on the internal balance of power and moulded the structure of the party organization. In the three countries this dependence became less problematic when parliamentary salaries and indemnities were introduced in the early twentieth century.

## The diffusion of the mass party technique

After the First World War the political mobilization of the electorate as well as social class distinctions developed to a higher degree. Political parties evolved into fully fledged mass organizations with a dues-paying membership. Under the Weimar Republic the Zentrum and the SPD tightened the links with mass electorates through their members. The Zentrum was the only bourgeois party in Germany able to make the transition to a mass party, thanks to the support of the Union of German Catholics which numbered 800,000 members.[25] In the early 1920s party membership increased to 200,000 in the PSI and peaked to 4,359,807 in the British Labour Party.

The fast-growing strength of left wing parties posed a serious threat to established middle class/cadre parties, intensifying party competition. The translation of the class cleavage into the electoral arena sharpened campaign struggles. Some of the old-style parties responded with heavy investment in professional publicity techniques and political propaganda. A further advantage of propaganda techniques in Britain was an evasion of the legal penalties imposed for breach of expenditure ceilings because the law covered spending only by candidates.

In the developmental approach, phase C of political financing is marked by lower campaign expenditures than the preceding phase because much of the effort is now of a voluntary or institutional kind. Empirical evidence for the British case supports this point.[26] In Britain after the First World War the total declared expenses of parliamentary candidates in general elections declined sharply at constant prices.[27] With the

institutionalization of social cleavages, political parties capital-
ized on the loyalty of their members to elicit voluntary work
and political propaganda.

Following these developments, in the 1920s the Conservative
Party gradually became less reliant on a small number of large
donations and more dependent on contributions from individual
corporations. The reason was partly that in 1925 the Baldwin
government made sales of titles illegal. Towards the end of the
nineteenth century the bulk of funding to middle class parties
came from the sales of honours to business people. When this
system was dismantled by the Baldwin government, the Conservative Party enacted a vigorous membership drive to minimize
the role of rich local backers as sources of money and to enhance
the position of constituency associations. Tougher party competition prompted the Conservative Party to strengthen peripheral groups in order to implement predatory strategies against
the Liberals and Labourites. There was a conscious move in
the 1920s and 1930s to make local associations financially less
dependent on their candidates and more reliant on the distribution of services from the Central Office.[28]

By the outbreak of the Second World War, the main patterns
of modern British political finance were already established. The
Labour Party drew on income from both individual members
and affiliated unions while the Conservative Party relied on a
substantial amount of membership fees and contributions from
the business community.[29] Thanks to its organizational efforts,
the Conservative Party turned into one of the largest and most
successful bourgeois parties of the twentieth century anywhere.
By contrast, the failure of the Liberal Party to stimulate the
growth of its constituency associations and build a solid revenue
system was a major determinant of its marginality in post-war
party competition.[30]

Whereas in Britain the Conservative Party emulated the techniques of collective funding to respond to growing left wing support, in Italy and Germany the socialist challenge triggered the
political participation of denominational and business groups.
In Italy, the rise of socialism spurred Catholic groups to organize
politically and in 1919 Luigi Sturzo, a southern priest, formed
the Partito Popolare. Previously, Catholics had thrown the
weight of their support behind liberal groupings. The church
had barred Catholics from direct political participation after
the unification of the Italian state. Following the success of

socialism, this inflexible stance was abandoned in the 1920s when the church authorized Catholic support for the Popolare. Although the church did not overtly commit itself to the party, the financial dependence of the Popolare on clerical associations was blatantly revealed when the party ceased to exist as soon as the Vatican decided to interact directly with the Fascist regime.[31]

In Germany, the perceived threat of socialism raised the concern of the business community. It prompted the creation of Conveyers – organizations specializing in channelling funds from firms to several non-socialist parties. In 1905 industrial associations founded the Reich Association against Social Democracy (Reichsverband gegen die Sozialdemocratie) which developed a professionally staffed organization to supplement the campaigns of the right wing parties in the election of 1907. Conveyers flowered extensively during the Weimar Republic, although the replacement of the pre-1918 single-district electoral system by a proportional representation system reduced their ability to sponsor specific candidates. Funds were allocated in relation to the number of 'pro-industry' candidates nominated in the party lists. In 1924 Conveyers' funds were distributed in a ratio of three parts to the German Peoples' Party, two parts to the German Democratic Party and German National People's Party and one part to the Zentrum.[32]

In the three countries the intensity of left wing competition provoked a reaction from right wing parties and their sponsor associations. Collective funding proved so successful for the consolidation of working class organizations that middle class parties quickly imitated the technique. By the 1930s membership fees became the dominant form of revenue system.

### Expanding the range of financial sources

After the Second World War advances in communications technology significantly influenced funding arrangements. By participating in televised campaigns and radio programmes party leaders could reach large audiences more efficiently. Political parties were entitled to free radio and TV broadcasting. In Britain, the costs of transmission were met by the broadcasting company provided the party paid for the production of its broadcast. In the three countries access to mass media was decided by each party's share of the vote in the previous general election. Paid political advertising has never been permitted.[33]

One consequence of the communication revolution was the appearance of professional political consultants trained in image building and image protection, which marginalized the importance of older skills of personal contact and public speaking. Television broadcasting was far more effective in terms of speed of transmission and breadth of coverage than door-to-door canvassing or the organization of local meetings. Communication between leaders and supporters was established increasingly through mass media.

These changes were compounded by the rise in the general level of socio-economic well-being. With the expansion of the welfare state many individuals felt more secure and no longer required to be politically educated or to be protected from the 'cradle to the grave'. Social stratification became less rigid and pressure groups representing sectional interests proliferated. Accordingly, party leaders turned to the electoral scene to try and exchange 'effectiveness in depth for a wider audience'.[34] The transformation of mass parties into catch-all parties involved a drastic reduction of the ideological baggage, a downgrading of the role of the individual party member and, most significantly, greater access to a variety of interest groups. For Kirchheimer the implications for funding methods were obvious. Political parties were progressively less reliant on a fee-paying membership and more dependent on other funding sources, such as interest groups. Thus, in the developmental approach, phase D of political financing is characterized by a wider gap between the material resources needed for political persuasion and the resources available in terms of voluntary work and institutionalized support. In such circumstances pressure groups acquire a privileged position as suppliers of funds.

When the party organization became increasingly independent from membership dues the ties between leaders and rank-and-file loosened. Party survival did not depend on the grass-roots fees. Freed from the straitjacket of the *classe guardée*, the catch-all party enjoyed greater strategic flexibility to design policies aimed at achieving immediate electoral success.

This evolution was faster in Germany and Italy when party organizations were reconstructed after the totalitarian experience. Some of the newly established parties, such as the German Christian Democratic Union (CDU) more clearly exhibited the politics of de-ideologization. In sharp contrast to the Zentrum, the CDU had an all-embracing and conveniently vague ideology, which attracted both Catholic and Protestant voters.

Observers have noted that the development of the CDU into Germany's first majority party was significantly linked to the sources of financial support which permitted campaign styles that maximized the electoral appeal of its leaders.[35] The CDU had no system of national membership dues and money collected at the local and regional levels was insufficient to finance the organization. Limited membership enrolment encouraged the CDU to approach business associations in order to cover about 90 per cent of its administrative and campaign costs. Rewards for such donations included both ideological deradicalization and accommodating programmatic commitments.

The financial dependence of the CDU on pressure groups was formalized in 1952 when CDU leaders and business executives created sponsors' associations (Förderergesellschaften) which acted as a transmission belt from business donations to the party. Sponsor associations differed from the Conveyers mentioned earlier in that they supported only one party. The Federation of German Industry collected funds from about half of all employers and from more than 70 per cent of the large corporations. Other contributions were given by promotional groups, such as Die Waage (the balance wheel), composed of supporters of free trade and free competition without cartels. More generally, donations to political parties in West Germany were encouraged in 1954 when the national coalition government ratified legislation providing tax benefits for membership dues and contributions for political purposes.[36]

The CDU rewarded donations from pressure groups by offering them privileged channels of access to party life. Consequently, at local, regional and national levels the party leaders were often recruited from groups external to the party, usually among industrialist, local notables or representatives of interest groups. In this way the business community was able to press for economic and social policies consistent with its goals and to request that coalitions with the SPD be avoided.

A second crucial element explaining the impact of funding on the structure and policy of the CDU was that it developed while in power. The inaugural congress of the federal party in Goslar was held in 1950, one year after the CDU formed the government. The possibility of drawing on the expertise of the German bureaucracy coupled with the generous funding accruing to the party from sponsor associations hampered the organizational growth of the CDU. During electoral campaigns the party was very active thanks to large sums of money from financial and business circles, but ceased most of its activities in periods between elections. Thus it retained the structure of an electoral organization composed of a plurality of heterogenous groups. This characteristic was in stark contrast to the revenue system of Britain's Conservative Party which allowed the organization to operate on a regular basis. The difference was reflected in a far greater autonomy of the Conservative organization with respect to the environment and in the subordination of the CDU to interest groups.[37] Moreover, central control of funds in the Conservative Party cemented the cohesion and stability of its leadership while the dispersion of control over the sources of income in the CDU generated a divided and fragmented elite.

The Italian Democrazia Cristiana (DC) differed from the CDU in that it grew out of the deliberate will of the Vatican.[38] Founded in 1943 from an alliance between De Gasperi and the church, the purpose of the DC was to shape the Italian polity in a way consistent with the church's interests. Because the church was the only institution allowed to engaged in social organization under the Fascist regime, Catholic Action had 3 million members by 1945. Drawing on this pool of individuals the DC enrolled 1,099,682 members in 1948.

The organizational growth of the DC was prompted by the initiative of the local clergy under instructions of the central church. Local organizations were controlled by church-related associations especially in the north-east region where the Catholic movement had been traditionally very strong. In-kind benefits were the primary source of church funding. A network of Catholic associations, such as the local parish, acted as electoral committees or simply as replacements for local party organizations. Catholic associations offered an elaborate local network which encapsulated, orientated and directed a vast number of voters.[39] The inflow of leaders from Catholic organizations into the party, or working as electoral agents for the DC were the most explicit manifestations of the influence of the church. Party leaders were recruited among the young members of Catholic Action and among the former Popolare, both intimately connected with the church.

The financial dependence on Catholic associations hindered the growth of the DC. Party leaders had little incentive to build a solid and autonomous organization because the vital resources for its functioning were readily available from the external sponsor, including money and ideology. The DC retained an electoral structure, with blurring borders with the environment and with party functionaries paid by Catholic associations.

In the South where Catholic associations were weak, local notables with a clientelistic following activated the development of peripheral organizations. Hence the DC was controlled either by Catholic associations in the North or by local notables in the South. In both cases the external sponsor participated in party life by influencing elite recruitment. MPs and party leaders were typically selected from the top ranks of the ancillary organizations because the organizational weakness of the DC militated against the formation of an internal pool of candidates.[40]

In addition to in-kind benefits received from the church, the DC was generously financed by the Confederation of Industrialists (Confindustria) which had legitimated it as the party of free market principles.[41] Contributions from the Confindustria were not directly channelled to the party but were often given to local auxiliary organizations. These funding methods had profound implications for the distribution of power within the DC because they strengthened the power of peripheral associations with respect to the centre. Consequently no strong internal group was able to impose direction and discipline on the party.

From the late 1940s the DC slowly asserted its independence from external sponsors. Between 1951 and 1955 membership went up by 40 per cent, in 1956 the party maintained 11,525 centres and the number of federations was around 100. In 1953 support was given to the creation and expansion of the Coldiretti, a farm organization which rapidly developed into a powerful satellite organization. Under the leadership of Fanfani (1954–59) the DC established independent power bases in the state-owned enterprises and banks. This strategy began the implacable colonization of the state administration by the DC during its long-lasting domination of national coalition governments from 1946 to 1993. By 'occupying' the public bureaucracy Fanfani multiplied the centres of power and sought to acquire direct control over them, bypassing the parliament. Ministries were staffed with large numbers of clientelistic appointees. Other sources of money not related to the Confindustria were found by expanding the state sector of the economy, in particular by reviving the Istituto di Ricostruzione Industriale (IRI), and by creating the Ente Nazionale Idrocarburi (ENI) (oil and methane). Public corporations enjoyed a considerable degree of autonomy and provided financial contributions to factional leaders.[42]

Given the absence of any law on state subvention and of any rules regarding campaign financing, it is not possible to determine the amount of money devoted to party activities. Bardi and Morlino suggest that the main sources of DC party financing were the 'black funds' which derived from the public sector and from private contribution of entrepreneurs.[43]

Money income, however, does not tell the whole story. Some of the largest daily newspapers, such as *Il Mattino*, *Il Corriere di Napoli*, *La Gazzetta del Mezzogiorno* and *Il Giorno*, totalling a circulation of 430,000 copies in the early 1960s, were also controlled by the state. Radio and television programmes were another source of powerful support. The DC created the RAI-TV, the state-controlled television channel which produced enormous consensus for the party.

State penetration intensified internal strife because party factions competed for the appropriation of state resources to reward funding bodies and voters. The result was the institutionalization of factional politics through patronage and the 'spoils system'. One consequence of internal fragmentation was to prevent the DC from designing coherent policy programmes, and thus its governing style was marked by disjointed and ambiguous policy-making.

Both the CDU and the DC provide good case studies to investigate the impact of funding on the internal structure of parties. In the reconstructed democratic regimes of West Germany and Italy these parties enjoyed a dominant position in governmental coalitions. They could thus benefit from the financial support of the business community and of other pressure groups eager to reap the benefits of favourable policy-making. Both parties, therefore, had no reason to stimulate the growth of the bureaucratic apparatus and retained a decentralized and loose structure. Furthermore, the direct links between party factions and external sponsors increased the autonomy of peripheral associations, preventing the formation of strong and cohesive leaderships. Finally, auxiliary organizations which funnelled income to the party influenced the selection of MPs and sponsored certain wings of the party in order to secure advantageous policies.

## Conclusion

Over the decades party funds stemmed from a variety of sources including plutocratic donations, grass-roots fees, pressure groups and the spoils system. Some of these funding operations were associated with a specific type of party organization and with a distinct phase of party financing. Table 3.1 outlines some of the arguments developed throughout this chapter. In phase A of political financing the *régime censitaire* entailed low campaign costs and amorphous political parties funded from the candidate's personal wealth. Political behaviour was shaped by traditional centres of power. The shift to phase B was marked by the gradual extension of the franchise, higher campaign costs and the formation of cadre parties funded from personal wealth and patronage. Campaign costs were lower in phase C because the financial survival of mass parties was ensured by a large

**Table 3.1** Western Europe: phases of political finance and party funding

| developmental phase | *phase A* | *phase B* | *phase C* | *phase D* |
|---|---|---|---|---|
| campaign costs | low | high | lower | higher |
| funding method | personal wealth | personal wealth and patronage | membership dues | membership dues and pressure group contributions |
| party type | parliamentary groupings | cadre | mass | catch-all |
| organization | amorphous | loose, semi-permanent | tightly knit, permanent | loose, permanent |

number of membership fees. Finally, in phase D the revolution in communication technology raised election costs and increased the amount of material resources required for political persuasion. Funding arrangements became more diversified and catch-all parties turned to pressure groups to gather money to pay for higher expenditure.

Table 3.1 represents an ideal-type model, a useful device to examine the similarities and differences between countries both synchronically and diachronically considered. As noted at the beginning of this chapter, underpinning this model is a developmental view which rejects the idea that one phase necessarily evolves into the next. This flexibility allows the approach suggested here to throw some light on the current situation in new democracies. For example, the fact that party organizations evolved primarily to collect funds may be one reason why there is a reluctance to invest energies in building those organizations where new parties have access to state funding. In Hungary and Poland where democratization was achieved by elite initiatives and campaign expenditures have been indirectly paid by state subventions there is a general hesitancy with regard to the idea of a party-based democracy.[44]

For some other new democracies such as Brazil,[45] the approach suggested here indicates that they are experiencing phase D of political financing with high campaign costs while party organizations retain a cadre structure typical of phase B. In other countries undergoing democratization the picture is more fragmented. In the Arab world, for instance, Islamist parties are closer to phase C. They can afford low campaign costs because they are able to elicit a vast amount of voluntary work by distributing collective incentives in the form of religious beliefs.[46]

From these brief comments it is clear that the ideal-type model represented in Table 3.1 is a powerful analytical tool. Yet the evidence assembled in this chapter also implies that funding practices have impinged on the internal dynamics of political parties in ways not captured by Table 3.1. In particular, the cohesion of mass parties was deeply influenced by funding possibilities. If the central apparatus controlled the flow of income to the organization, party leaders preserved cohesion and stability. This was the case of the Conservative Party and the German SPD. In contrast, the control of financial resources by external associations often produced divided leaderships, as in the case of the PSI or the DC. The recent collapse of these two parties indicates that the survival of party organizations is at risk if the external environment becomes suddenly hostile. Such events could be a warning sign for South African parties where leaders resort to external (extra-national) funds rather than, or in addition to, building their own resources. If foreign countries halt their financial contributions South African parties might face the sort of critical situation which the PSI and the DC encountered.[47] A fragile financial revenue system may affect the destiny of political parties. The argument is supported by the marginality of the Liberal Party in Britain which reflects its persistent inability to enhance the role of constituency organizations in the collection of funds since the First World War.

In addition to the role of sources of income, this chapter has shown that the development of political parties while in government and in opposition has affected funding arrangements. Except for the Conservative Party, the opportunity to draw on the resources of the state bureaucracy and on the funds received from pressure groups hampered the search for independent sources of income in the CDU and the DC, rendering party leaders more vulnerable to external demands.

In recent years this vulnerability has aroused lively debates. Proponents of state funding claim that the dependence of political parties on powerful financial backers affects their ability to formulate and select public policy-making. In some countries escalating campaign costs leave no alternative to party leaders but to rely on the goodwill of those groups that marshall and distribute campaign resources. In a small number of other countries, like Britain, not only have legally imposed ceilings on campaign expenditures restrained electoral costs but the parties continue to rely almost exclusively on private funds.

In Germany and Italy rising costs have been the direct consequence of having no spending limits. In 1959 the German government approved overt subventions to political parties which were distributed according to the party's strength in the Bundestag. Public subsidies for secretarial and advisory assistance to parliamentary parties had already been introduced after the war. The Italian government ratified public funding to political parties in 1974.[48] Public subventions have been highly controversial ever since. In 1993 the law was repealed after the majority of the electorate voted against it in a public referendum; yet on 2 January 1997 a new bill introduced tax concessions for donations and stated that political parties will receive public funding according to the proportion of seats gained in parliament. The bill reflects the logic of the electoral law of 1993 which was an odd combination of plurality and proportional elements.[49]

The full implications of state funding for the distribution of power within the party organization are not entirely clear and are the subject of considerable debate. In theory public subventions have been introduced to protect elected representatives from the pressures of sponsor associations and to increase the responsiveness of party leaders to voters and followers. In practice, however, public party funding seems to have contributed to the concentration of power in the hands of the national leaders, enabling them to become less sensitive to the needs of the grass-roots and the general electorate.[50] Indeed there is a possibility that state funding is generating yet a new form of party organization, perhaps based on a cartel alliance among party elites.[51]

## Notes

1 See A. Ware in this volume.
2 A. Panebianco, *Political Parties: Organization and Power* (Cambridge, Cambridge University Press, 1988).
3 This point has also been raised by P. Lösche, 'Problems of party and campaign financing in Germany and the United States – some comparative reflections', in A. B. Gunlicks (ed.), *Campaign and Party Finance in North America and Western Europe* (Boulder, CO, Westview, 1993), pp. 219–30. However, Lösche does not investigate these matters.
4 A. J. Heidenheimer, 'Comparative party finance: notes on practices and toward a theory,' *Journal of Politics*, 25 (1963), 790–811.
5 M. I. Ostrogorski, *Democracy and the Organization of Political Parties* (Cambridge, Cambridge University Press, 1902); M. Duverger, *Political Parties* (London, Methuen, 1951); O. Kirchheimer, 'The transformation of Western European party systems', in J. LaPalombara and M. Weiner (eds.), *Political Parties and Political Development* (Princeton, Princeton University Press, 1966), pp. 177–200.
6 For the development of the caucus in Britain see A. McMillan, 'The Limited Vote in Britain', M. Phil. thesis, University of Warwick, 1995, pp. 87–9.
7 See G. Sivini, 'Socialisti e cattolici in Italia dalla società allo stato', in G. Sivini, *La Sociologia dei Partiti Politici* (Bologna, Il Mulino, 1971), pp. 72–105.
8 S. Passigli, 'Italy', *Journal of Politics*, 25 (1963), 718–36.
9 J. O'Leary, *The Elimination of Corrupt Practices in British Elections* (Oxford, Oxford University Press, 1962), p. 156.
10 M. Pinto-Duschinsky, *British Political Finance 1830–1980* (Washington and London, American Enterprise Institute for Public Policy Research, 1981); R. J. Johnston and C. J. Pattie, 'Great Britain: twentieth century parties operating under nineteenth century regulations', in Gunlicks, *Campaign and Party Finance*, pp. 123–54.

11 Pinto-Duschinsky, *British Political Finance*, p. 50.

12 Panebianco, *Political Parties*, pp. 138–9.

13 A. J. Heidenheimer, *Adenauer and the CDU* (The Hague, Martinus Nijhoff, 1960), p. 2.

14 F. Neumann, 'Nascita e sviluppo dei partiti politici', in Sivini, *Sociologia dei Partiti Politici*, pp. 47–69.

15 Duverger, *Political Parties*, p. 63.

16 *Ibid.*

17 V. Lidtke, *The Outlawed Party. Social Democracy in Germany, 1878–1890* (Princeton, NJ, Princeton University Press, 1966), p. 54.

18 *Ibid.*, p. 93.

19 *Ibid.*, p. 225.

20 D. Chalmers, *The Social Democratic Party of Germany* (New Haven, CT, Yale University Press, 1964), p. 11.

21 C. E. Schorske, *German Social Democracy* (New York, John Wiley & Sons, 1955) p. 49.

22 Duverger, *Political Parties*, pp. 68–9.

23 H. Hesse, 'Il gruppo parlamentare del Partito Socialista Italiano: la sua composizione e la sua funzione negli anni della crisi del parlamentarismo italiano', in L. Valiani and A. Wandruszka (eds.), *Il Movimento Operaio e Socialista in Italia e in Germania dal 1870 al 1920* (Bologna, Il Mulino, 1978), pp. 179–220.

24 Sivini, 'Socialisti e cattolici in Italia dalla società allo stato'.

25 Neumann, 'Nascita e sviluppo dei partiti politici', p. 59.

26 It is believed that there is no published information on election expenses in Germany and Italy for this period.

27 Pinto-Duschinsky, *British Political Finance*, p. 27.

28 J. Ramsden, *The Age of Balfour and Baldwin* (London, Longman, 1978), p. 68.

29 In the post-war period there were minor changes in the formal rules regulating the revenue system. For a detailed summary see M. Harrison, 'Britain', *Journal of Politics*, 25 (1963), 664–85.

30 See Pinto-Duschinsky, *British Political Finance* and Panebianco, *Political Parties*.

31 G. De Rosa, *Il Partito Popolare Italiano* (Bari, Editori LaTerza, 1974).

32 A. J. Heidenheimer and F. C. Langdon, *Business Associations and the Financing of Political Parties* (The Hague, Martinus Nijhoff, 1968), pp. 27–37.

33 A. Smith, 'Mass communications' in D. Butler, H. R. Penniman and A. Ranney (eds.), *Democracy at the Polls* (Washington and London, American Enterprise Institute for Public Policy Research, 1981), pp. 173–95.

34 Kirchheimer, 'The transformation of Western European party systems', p. 184.

35 U. Duebber and G. Braunthal, 'West Germany', *Journal of Politics*, 25 (1963), 774–89.

36 The law was repealed in 1958 but reintroduced in a different form in 1967. Von Arnim notes that federal tax concessions in Germany are in the lead and that provisions in other western democracies do not come anywhere close. Von Arnim also provides a descriptive account of the laws regulating public financing of party groups and party foundations. See H. H. von Arnim, 'Campaign and party finance in Germany', in Gunlicks, *Campaign and Party Finance*, pp. 201–18.

37 Panebianco, *Political Parties*, pp. 138–9.

38 A. Cavazzani, 'Organizzazione, iscritti, elettori della Democrazia Cristiana', in G. Sivini (ed.), *Partiti e Partecipazione Politica in Italia* (Milano, Giuffre' Editore, 1971), pp. 169–88.

39 G. Poggi, Gianfranco (ed.), *L'organizzazione Partitica del PCI e della DC* (Bologna, Il Mulino, 1968), p. 298.

40 *Ibid.*, pp. 306–8.

41 G. Pasquino, 'Crisi della DC e evoluzione del sistema politico', *Rivista Italiana di Scienza della Politica*, 3 (1975), 443–72.

42 S. Passigli, 'Italy', *Journal of Politics*, 25 (1963), 718–36.

43  L. Bardi and L. Morlino, 'Italy: tracing the roots of the Great Transformation', in R. Katz and P. Mair (eds.), *How Parties Organize* (London, Sage Publications, 1994), pp. 242–77.

44  There are obviously other reasons for the reluctance to appreciate a party-based democracy. See P. Lewis in this volume.

45  See M. Kinzo in this volume.

46  This point has been made by Azza Karam at the workshop 'Funding political parties in emerging democracies', held at the University of Warwick, on 25 January 1997.

47  See R. Southall and G. Wood in this volume.

48  For a detailed description of public funding in Germany see H. Oberreuter, 'Politische Parteien: Stellung und Funktion im Verfassungssystem der Bundesrepublik', in A. Mintzel and H. Oberreuter (eds.), *Parteien in der Bundesrepublik Deutschland* (Opladen, Leske & Budrich, 1992, 2nd edn), pp. 15–40; for Italy see G. Ciaurro, 'Public financing of parties in Italy', in H. E. Alexander (ed.), *Comparative Political Financing on the 1980s* (Cambridge, Cambridge University Press, 1989), pp. 153–71.

49  A. Panebianco, 'La compagnia dei nostalgici', *Corriere della Sera*, 27 December 1996, 1 and 5.

50  J. Mendilow, 'Public party funding and the schemes of mice and men: the 1992 elections in Israel', *Party Politics*, 2 (1966), 329–54.

51  See R. Katz, and P. Mair, 'Changing models of party organization and party democracy. The emergence of the cartel party', *Party Politics*, 1 (1995), 5–28.

# 4

# Party funding in a new democracy: Spain

RICHARD GILLESPIE

The post-Franco experience of party funding in Spain is of interest for a number of reasons. First, Spain's transition to democracy is generally regarded by observers as a success story, and a foundation for the country's re-emergence as a much more effective player on the international scene.[1] Second, and somewhat paradoxically, the quality of Spanish democracy has been the subject of much criticism, some of it relating to the illicit funding of political parties.[2] And third, although state subsidization of a multi-party system is only twenty years old, it has already been the subject of reform on two occasions, in the mid-1980s and mid-1990s. This fact immediately casts doubt on the effectiveness of the early post-Franco provisions, yet confirms Spain's value as a laboratory for examining the differential effects of alternative funding arrangements.

In this chapter, the main focus is upon the system of funding adopted during the transition to democracy and thus it is the arrangements introduced between 1976 and 1978 that are of prime interest, together with the experience of their practical consequences, prior to the first round of reform (1985–87). The first two sections of the chapter are therefore devoted to the system itself and its effects. However, it is also important to consider the long-term effects of the funding model. These were appreciated fully only during the ensuing decade, when criticisms of the quality of Spanish democracy emphasized an excessive concentration of power in the hands of party oligarchies and inadequate civil control over the state.

### Improvisation during the transition

Spain's transition to democracy took some three years to achieve, if one understands this process to embrace the initial reform of the Francoist political system by Adolfo Suárez in 1976, the first competitive general election in forty-one years in 1977, the introduction of a new constitution in 1978 and the first general and municipal elections held under that constitution in 1979. 1979 was also the year in which new autonomy statutes for Catalonia and the Basque Country further clarified the type of new state that was emerging. Controlled throughout by political elites, and never quickened by an external catalyst as the Greek and Portuguese transformations were, the Spanish transition has the appearance (especially when viewed in retrospect) of a sedate, gradual, evolutionary process, during which firm democratic foundations were laid amid cross-party demonstrations of moderation and cooperation.

However, while elite pacts certainly helped impose order during the Spanish 'transition by transaction', there was much improvisation of the new arrangements, which were introduced expeditiously under pressure from looming general elections – first, in the run-up to the 1977 (constituent) general election and, second, as a further election approached just two years later, based on the new democratic constitution. With the democratic parties sharing a common interest in avoiding confrontation, the new political system was defined only in outline (and occasionally in a blurry one at that); quite substantial issues were deferred to a later date when they could be addressed in more secure circumstances. This was true of the system of party funding and of other major questions (most notably the future political status of the regions in relation to the Spanish state). Agreements and compromises were reached in this period among a relatively small number of politicians, with very little consultation of 'experts' (democratic expertise being in short supply anyway after four decades of permanent authoritarian rule).

The provisions on party funding began to be defined in March 1977 through a decree announcing supposedly *ad hoc* arrangements to subsidize the participation of parties in the forthcoming general election in June;[3] and they were added to in the following year with legislation concerning state support for 'ordinary' (that is, non-electoral) party activity. Never considered comprehensively by legislators, nor consciously imitating the system employed in another country,[4] the party funding arrangements can hardly be regarded as the adoption of a 'model', whether a 'mixed public/private model'[5] or some other. Rather, the new arrangements were improvised piecemeal in response to pressing political exigencies of the moment, and then were retained much longer than expected because (a) the parties had other priorities and (b) the new arrangements helped entrench the positions of those parties that had enjoyed immediate electoral success and thus now had little desire to alter the system.

One must pause briefly here to note some relevant historical points of reference for Spain's new political elite. A long authoritarian political tradition had left contemporary Spain with comparatively under-developed democratic associations, some strong enemies of democracy (based chiefly in the military) and widespread public reservations about political involvement. While the Second Republic of 1931–36 had hardly provided an ideal model of democracy, with its heavily fragmented party system, acute governmental instability and inability to ensure public order, the ensuing Franco regime had instilled in Spanish minds the message that involvement in political parties and pro-democratic associations was a dangerous, subversive activity. Spain had never enjoyed a period of stable unhindered party development, leading to the emergence of mass political organizations. Its most successful party in historical terms, the Partido Socialista Obrero Español (PSOE), had reached a peak affiliation figure of only 90,000 members by the eve of the Civil War of 1936–39,[6] before being undermined for decades thereafter by internal factionalism and political repression.

More recently, the emergence of mass opposition to Francoism during the 1960s had led to some growth among opposition parties operating within the country and also brought into being substantial new associations based on workers and students. Collectively, while they began to exert constant mass pressure for a change of regime, they were never strong enough to overthrow the old one. Eventually, in 1976–77 anti-Franco parties had to suffer the indignity of submitting themselves to the still basically Francoist authorities for registration as legal parties in order to participate in the new political system that had begun to emerge, thanks in part to the actions of former Francoists such as Suárez. Some political parties, whether old or new, then experienced rapid growth, while others were exposed as little more than coteries when submitted to the full glare of publicity. Yet even those that showed themselves to have a genuine rank and file in most parts of Spain remained weak in comparison with equivalent organizations in other parts of Europe. In no case did party membership during the 1970s exceed 200,000 – the figure claimed by the Partido Comunista de España (PCE), which had been the most strongly organized illegal anti-Franco party – and even among the parties of the Left, rapid growth gave way to membership loss by the time of the third post-Franco general election in October 1982.[7]

Faced with numerically weak parties, which enjoyed only a few weeks or months as legal entities before having to compete with one another in the general election of 1977, Suárez initially came up with a funding formula designed to enable the electorally successful parties to gain partial reimbursement for their expenditure in that contest. Taken together with an electoral system calculated to favour the front runners and to eliminate the smaller parties (other than those with concentrated support in particular provinces), the intention was clearly to simplify a political field in which over 100 groups sought to compete, and to reinforce the position of those parties that managed to gain parliamentary representation in this crucial first election. Both in the scheme announced in March 1977 to defray party election expenditure and in the law of December 1978 introducing subsidies of the parties' ordinary activities, the formula chosen rewarded only those parties that had won parliamentary seats, while making this criterion more significant than the number of votes that each party had obtained.[8] Given the lack of a national tradition of donations to parties, a certain public wariness of political parties, and the legal restrictions that were placed on foreign and public sector donations,[9] parties inevitably had to turn to the banks for credit, hoping to repay their loans with the aid of state subsidies following success in the coming election.

Just as important as the provisions affecting party income was the lack of regulation of party expenditure, for no maximum limit was placed on election campaign spending, which grew precipitously. The lack of regulation of party finances prevents one from knowing the real extent of this growth, although undoubtedly it exceeded the 200 per cent increase in election spending between 1977 and 1982 that was reported by the parties themselves. While parties could fix their own election budgets, there was no public control of party finances in general. For the Junta Electoral Central lacked the resources to scrutinize party accounts effectively and the fines that could be imposed on parties for infringements were ridiculously low.[10] Beyond all the debates about the respective merits of public and private funding, the system has been criticized precisely on these grounds, for being excessively permissive and failing to enforce the restrictions that were nominally in force.[11]

Such criticisms came mainly from academics, while the parties (or to be more exact the leadership bodies of parties receiving state subsidies) indicated their conformity with the system and even maintained a high level of inter-party consensus as reform of the system was undertaken in the mid-1980s. For a while, parties across the political spectrum seemed reasonably content with the initial funding system: the parties of the Left saw state subsidies as a means of counteracting the risk of large corporate donations subverting fair electoral competition; Suárez's Unión del Centro Democrático (UCD) stood to secure the lion's share of state support as the most successful electoral force; and the right wing Alianza Popular led by Manuel Fraga, although the main beneficiary of private funding, was in no position to support itself exclusively from non-state sources, nor was it strong enough in Parliament to contemplate pushing for an alternative funding formula (see Table 4.1). All the parliamentary parties were weak in European terms, yet lived way beyond the resources that their members and supporters could generate. Moreover, they were united by a general spirit of consensus that accompanied the Moncloa pacts of 1977, the drafting of the new constitution and party responses to the regional question. The only hint of early disagreement over the system of party funding thus emanated from minor parties: specifically, from the parliamentary group in the Senate formed by Progressives and Independent Socialists, which called for state subsidies to be based exclusively on votes won, without reference to seats. Their amendment to the Political Parties Law of 1978 attracted only their own ten votes in the Senate, after Congress had approved the bill unanimously.[12]

**Table 4.1** General election results, 1977–96 (Congress of Deputies)

| Party | 1977 votes | 1977 seats | 1979 votes | 1979 seats | 1982 votes | 1982 seats | 1986 votes | 1986 seats | 1989 votes | 1989 seats | 1993 votes | 1993 seats | 1996 votes | 1996 seats |
|---|---|---|---|---|---|---|---|---|---|---|---|---|---|---|
| PSOE | 29.3 | 118 | 30.5 | 121 | 48.4 | 202 | 44.3 | 184 | 39.6 | 175 | 38.8 | 159 | 37.6 | 141 |
| PP (AP, CD, CP) | 8.3 | 16 | 6.0 | 9 | 26.5 | 107 | 26.1 | 105 | 25.8 | 107 | 34.8 | 141 | 38.7 | 156 |
| IU (PCE) | 9.4 | 20 | 10.8 | 23 | 4.1 | 4 | 4.7 | 7 | 9.1 | 17 | 9.6 | 18 | 10.5 | 21 |
| CiU | 2.8 | 11 | 2.7 | 8 | 3.7 | 12 | 5.0 | 18 | 5.0 | 18 | 4.9 | 17 | 4.6 | 16 |
| PNV | 1.6 | 8 | 1.5 | 7 | 1.8 | 8 | 1.5 | 6 | 1.2 | 5 | 1.2 | 5 | 1.3 | 5 |
| HB | – | – | 1.0 | 3 | 1.0 | 2 | 1.1 | 5 | 1.1 | 4 | 0.9 | 2 | 0.7 | 2 |
| EE | 0.3 | 1 | 0.5 | 1 | 0.5 | 1 | 0.5 | 2 | 0.5 | 2 | – | – | – | – |
| EA | – | – | – | – | – | – | – | – | 0.7 | 2 | 0.6 | 1 | 0.5 | 1 |
| UCD | 34.4 | 166 | 35.0 | 168 | 6.7 | 11 | – | – | – | – | – | – | – | – |
| CDS | – | – | – | – | 2.8 | 2 | 9.2 | 19 | 7.9 | 14 | 1.8 | 0 | – | – |
| Others | 13.9 | 10 | 12.0 | 10 | 4.5 | 1 | 7.6 | 4 | 9.1 | 6 | 7.4 | 7 | 6.1 | 8 |
| Total | 100.0 | 350 | 100.0 | 350 | 100.0 | 350 | 100.0 | 350 | 100.0 | 350 | 100.0 | 350 | 100.0 | 350 |
| Turnout | 78.1% | | 68.0% | | 79.9% | | 70.4% | | 69.9% | | 76.4% | | 77.1% | |

*Source*: Author's compilation from official results published in the Spanish Press.

*Notes*: PSOE (Socialist Party), PP (People's Party), AP (Popular Alliance), CD (Democratic Coalition), CP (People's Coalition), IU (United Left), PCE (Communist Party), CiU (Catalan centre-right nationalists), PNV and EA (Basque centre-right nationalists), HB (pro-ETA Basque nationalists), EE (Basque Left), UCD (Union of the Democratic Centre), CDS (Democratic and Social Centre).

## The effects of funding arrangements

The funding system adopted during the transition to democracy must be evaluated first in terms of its capacity to generate sufficient finance to maintain competitive party politics. Here, the very fact that the leading Spanish political parties became increasingly indebted to the banks, while minor ones struggled to survive, often without success, immediately casts doubt on the adequacy of the mixed public-private system. Funding from private sources proved impossible to mobilize overnight, apart from bank support which tended to favour small right wing parties and individual conservative politicians. The parties inevitably had a weak capacity to generate finance internally through membership dues and other contributions; and the state subsidies to the parliamentary parties proved insufficient to satisfy their financial appetites. Even the best electoral performance of the post-Franco era – the PSOE's landslide victory in the general election of 1982 – did not produce sufficient electoral subsidies to meet the full costs of the party election campaign.[13] State funding came to contribute a much higher proportion of total financing in the case of some parties (on the Left) than had been expected, up to 90 per cent of the total income of the Socialists,[14] yet the parties collectively sank further and further into debt.[15] While the subsidies for ordinary party activities were increased on an annual basis, usually in direct response to inflation, the level of electoral subsidies remained constant into the 1980s, notwithstanding mounting expenditure on general election campaigns.

The party elites themselves were partly responsible for this situation, for living beyond their means and devising legislation that allowed themselves to do so. With the exception of the Communists, the parties betrayed little fear of indebtedness, which in theory could be tackled by increasing the level of subsidy through the annual budget or by asking 'Parliament' to assume bad debts. The lack of effective monitoring and control of ordinary party finances by the state hardly encouraged a commitment to balanced budgets. Indeed, the Popular Alliance (AP) – the party most favoured by private sector donations – did not begin to organize its finances properly until after the general election of 1982.[16]

However, party irresponsibility offers only a partial explanation of the growing financial difficulties in which political forces found themselves. Determined to establish a public presence after forty years of dictatorship, the parties had to devote substantial resources to the building of infrastructure, although it must be said that most of them opted for a particularly costly model of party building, based on establishing a network of local party headquarters throughout Spain, often with paid officials.[17]

Electoral competition was another major cost factor too. With relatively small memberships, parties scarcely had the option of using their members as their chief electoral campaigning resource, except momentarily the Communists, who had a genuinely active membership, although one riven by factionalism by the end of the 1970s.[18] In any case, the newcomers to the Spanish political class were modernizers, keen to use the campaign techniques employed by their counterparts in northern Europe and the United States. It may well be that the European parties, with the Germans in the forefront, unwittingly encouraged a high-cost style of electioneering purely as a result of the exceptionally high level of external support for the Spanish parties during the transition to democracy.[19] Once lavish election campaigns had become the norm, it was difficult to countenance more austere electoral contests thereafter.

Party expenditure as a topic has been less extensively researched than party income, and Spanish political scientists themselves venture different opinions as to why national election campaigns have been comparatively costly in international terms. While some have related the cost of general election campaigns to an *insufficient* use of modern 'American' techniques (few televised debates are held, in contrast with a large number of public meetings), others have associated the escalating costs with *excessive* US influence (saturation marketing).[20] In fact, the expense is generated by a combination of traditional and modern electioneering methods, both costly, with an increasing tendency in recent years to use party-produced videos and even satellite link-ups (as when the actor Antonio Banderas addressed a PSOE rally from afar during the 1996 election campaign).

Elections in Spain are also costly as a result of their frequency; for since 1980, in addition to general and municipal elections, the parties have had to contest four-yearly regional elections in the seventeen 'autonomous communities' (whose electoral agendas do not invariably coincide). There have also been various referenda – on the Constitution, on regional autonomy statutes and on Spain's membership of the North Atlantic

Treaty Organization (NATO) – for which no equivalent of election subsidies has been available.

Thus the initial funding regime proved inadequate for its own purposes. But what of its influence on the political system under construction? Here the line of causation is complex and it is difficult to separate the influence of the party funding arrangements from that of other variables. What is clear is that, together with the electoral system and the preferences of the electorate, the system of party funding exerted an important influence on the number of parties that survived and on the nature of the party system more generally. For one thing, the decision to go for a reimbursement approach to funding meant that the banks were influential in determining which parties would be able to mount expensive election campaigns in 1977. This was done quite openly in the late 1970s when the representatives of the big banks (known popularly as 'The Seven Sisters') met quite ostentatiously in advance of the elections to decide upon the extent of credit and its distribution – in 1977 without any previous election results available as a guide to performance. Although parties could seek additional credits, most of the campaign funding depended on the quota fixed for each of the parties deemed promising by the bankers.

In fact, as things turned out, there was no clear correlation between the volume of pre-electoral credit and the electoral performance of the more successful parties. AP, the party most favoured by the bankers, ended up in fourth place, behind even the Communist Party.[21] However, it is obvious that the early procedures were open to bias, with relatively little credit going to parties judged by the bankers to lack credibility or respectability.

Immediately after the first general election, the dual impact of the electoral system (especially the 3 per cent threshold for gaining parliamentary representation, the small size of the electoral districts and the d'Hondt system's distortion of proportionality in the translation of votes into seats) and the funding system (based on seats won, more than votes) became obvious. Together, the two influences conspired to ensure that, whereas there would almost certainly be a multi-party system to sustain political pluralism, certain political options would not be available to the Spanish electorate after 1977. They ensured that the party system, which experienced a process of organizational mergers, would become consolidated around the front

**Table 4.2** Party performance and share of state subsidies, 1977 and 1979

| Party | % valid votes | % seats | election subsidies (million ptas) | % of total received by four main parties |
|-------|--------------|---------|-----------------------------------|------------------------------------------|
| *1977* | | | | |
| UCD | 34.4 | 47.4 | 698 | 50.9 |
| PSOE | 29.3 | 33.7 | 543 | 39.6 |
| PCE | 9.4 | 5.7 | 89 | 5.4 |
| AP | 8.3 | 4.6 | 83 | 4.0 |
| *1979* | | | | |
| UCD | 35.0 | 48.0 | 753 | 49.6 |
| PSOE | 30.5 | 34.6 | 594 | 39.1 |
| PCE | 10.8 | 6.6 | 137 | 9.0 |
| AP | 6.0 | 2.6 | 35 | 2.3 |

*Sources:* Subsidy figures derived from R. Gunther, G. Sani and G. Shabad, *Spain after Franco: The Making of a Competitive Party System* (Berkeley, CA, University of California Press, 1986), p. 131; and P. del Castillo, *La financiación de partidos y candidatos en las democracias occidentales* (Madrid, Centro de Investigaciones Sociológicas/Siglo XXI de España, 1985), p. 206.

runners in a manner that was clearly discriminatory against the smaller parties (see Table 4.2). The small parties lost out in the distribution of seats and public money, and there were also anomalies among them, as the following examples illustrate:

1 The Partido de los Trabajadores de España won just over 1 per cent of the total vote, yet gained no seats, and thus received no state subsidies, because its vote did not reach the 3 per cent threshold in any of the provinces/electoral districts. However, the geographically concentrated support for the Partido Nacionalista Vasco (1.54 per cent of the total vote) enabled it to obtain seven seats and thus receive subsidies.

2 The Equipo Demócrata Cristiano was another victim of the system, gaining no seats despite receiving 250,000 votes (1.4 per cent of the total), a result that led it to be 'wiped out' . . . 'Burdened by debts and defeat, it decided to dissolve . . .',[22] the UCD being the main beneficiary.

3 The Partido Socialist Popular (PSP) of Enrique Tierno Galván, a party that did quite well in the first general election, also found itself under huge financial pressure to surrender its independence. Left with 'an enormous and unpayable debt'

after the election, its tally of six deputies falling well short of the fifteen seats required to qualify for a separate parliamentary group subsidy, the party leadership opted for a merger with the PSOE, not least because the latter offered to assume its campaign debt.[23]

4 Even the party most strongly backed by capitalist interests was not immune from the financially and electorally induced process of political mergers in 1977–79 which helped shape the new party system. AP, led by former Francoist minister Manuel Fraga, may have spent between $7 million and $30 million on its 1977 election campaign, having received donations from some sixty-one business firms and banks.[24] However, its disastrous result meant that it recouped just 5 per cent of its campaign expenditure from state subsidies. This caused the original AP to break up and its leader to regroup his remaining supporters in an alliance with two politicians, José María de Areilza and Alfonso Osorio, who counted for little in electoral terms but whose links with business and banking were calculated to attract even more donations and bank credits. Thus, financial considerations were central to the creation of the Coalición Democrática in time for the next election.[25]

5 Another party to feel the harsh impact of electoral failure was the Communist Party. The PCE's very poor result in 1982 meant that it recouped from the state only 3 per cent of the 506 million pesetas spent on its campaign.[26] Never one to live beyond its means, the party resorted to the drastic solution of selling the central party headquarters in Madrid in order to clear its debts.[27]

Parties that failed to secure representation in the first election would in future be up against parties that were recipients of state funding as a result of past electoral success; this made it very difficult for new parties to enter the electoral arena. The new party system did not become so ossified as to preclude evolution – indeed, there was a shift from multi-partyism in the late 1970s to one-party dominance in the 1980s, before reverting to multi-party form in the 1990s – but the party system became a most exclusive club which new aspiring members could not afford to join. The discrimination practised against non-parliamentary parties is difficult to reconcile with liberal democratic notions of fair electoral competition. Even parties that gained some parliamentary representation in 1977 in several cases found themselves in a highly precarious situation because they fell short of a second threshold, that for the formation of a parliamentary group (which affected a party's legislative rights as well as its funding). Yet it was not that the 'rich got richer and the poor were driven to bankruptcy', as some have claimed:[28] the system generated a growing burden of debt even for the successful parties which received a disproportionate share of state subsidies. However, the parties that managed to consolidate their parliamentary position did have one major advantage over the electorally unsuccessful parties. Namely they could alleviate their problems simply by increasing the sums allocated in annual budgets to the reimbursement of ordinary party expenditure, so long as there was sufficient agreement among the parliamentary forces.

The significant role played by state subsidies also affected the nature of political parties, for those that survived tended to be 'top-down' parties with strong leaderships, closer to the state than to society. In parties with good electoral prospects (such as the Socialist Party), leadership dominance was buttressed both by the electoral system (which gave leaders leverage over their rank and file, as dispensers of patronage able to determine the final place of candidates in electoral lists) and by the funding system, under which an overwhelmingly large proportion of a party's income usually came from the state. The proportion for which leaders were beholden to their own rank and file was at times as little as 2 to 4 per cent (in the case of the PSOE). Under these circumstances, parties tended to be internally authoritarian, notwithstanding an insistence upon internal democracy in the Political Parties Law of 1978.[29]

The level of state funding was not so great as to serve as a discouragement to party affiliation drives and indeed most parties did make strenuous efforts to recruit in the late 1970s. However, fast growth provided such a stimulus to internal party factionalism (particularly on the Left where notions of internal party democracy were most influential) that leaders became concerned about internal threats to party progress; in response they proved ready to deal with factional challenges through exclusion, even if the price of control was (for a while at least) a smaller party. In contrast to the experience of the northern European countries, Spain (together with other new southern European democracies) moved very rapidly into the world of cartel politics, characterized by a heavy party reliance on state resources,[30] without first witnessing the development of real mass parties. The model of party funding contributed to this trend, brought about by technological change, widespread recognition of the need for strong parties as bulwarks of the new Spanish democracy, the imitation of external examples, and the persistence of a traditional political culture that remained deeply suspicious of political parties and inimical to political participation.

## The need for reform

The inadequacies of the initial funding regime led to its reform before a decade of democracy had elapsed. Reform was deemed necessary for two reasons: the Flick case of 1984 provided the first substantial indication that the official system might not be operating efficiently, either in terms of generating adequate funding or of commanding respect among the parties; and there was also the growing indebtedness of the parties. That reached particularly serious proportions as a result of the high costs associated with the campaigns that preceded the NATO referendum and the fourth post-Franco general election, which came within three months of one another in 1986. The Flick case involved allegations that German Social Democratic Party (SPD) money had been donated to the PSOE's electoral coffers, despite legislation that only permitted foreign contributions towards ordinary, non-electoral, party expenditure. On the NATO referendum campaign, the Socialists claim to have spent 5,000 million pesetas ($36 million) trying to convince voters that Spain should stay in the Alliance, and not a single peseta of this was recoverable.[31] One of the aims of reform was thus to reconsider the question of donations, while another was to increase the level of state subsidies in order to alleviate the party debt problem.

Successive reforms introduced in the Electoral Law (LOREG) of 1985 and the Financing of Political Parties Law (LOFPP) of 1987 brought the following changes:[32]

*(1985)*

1 The level of subsidy for electoral expenses was increased (to 60 pesetas per Congress vote, 20 pesetas per Senate vote and 0.5 million pesetas per seat), and in future the amounts would grow automatically in line with inflation.

2 In future, parties could receive an advance payment a month before the election, this being the equivalent of up to one-third of their total subsidy in the previous election.

3 The existing ban on electoral donations from foreign sources was retained, and stricter limitations were imposed on donations from individuals and companies, such that no donation of more than 1 million pesetas (the equivalent of $7,000 in 1986) could be contributed to a general election campaign.

4 In a bid to reduce electoral costs, and for the first time, a limit (related to the number of voters, but adjustable in line with inflation) was placed on the amount that parties could spend in each district where they presented candidates.

5 The parties were required to submit their accounts to the Tribunal de Cuentas and stiffer penalties were introduced for infringements.

*(1987)*

1 A strict limit was placed on donations for ordinary party purposes, this being 10 million pesetas per annum ($80,000) in the case of any individual/company donation; meanwhile anonymous donations when aggregated were limited to a maximum equivalent to just 5 per cent per annum of the total amount earmarked in the national budget for party subsidies. Parties receiving donations in excess of the legal limits would normally be fined twice the sum of the donation. Together, these measures represented a marked shift in the direction of a state-funded system, and they were accompanied by an increase in ordinary party subsidies of 150 per cent.

2 The powers of the Tribunal de Cuentas were increased, but it could only investigate possible irregularities on the basis of accounts presented by the parties themselves.

As in the case of the original legislation, the reforms were supported by a broad parliamentary consensus among parties that were desperate for financial assistance. The only dissenting voice was that of the Centro Democrático y Social (CDS), a relatively new party created by Adolfo Suárez during the UCD's disintegration in the early 1980s, which in 1982–84 had just two seats in the Congress of Deputies. The CDS expressed the interest of the small parties in having state subsidies shared out on the basis of votes won, rather than seats.[33] Among the larger parties, the only disagreement, essentially between the PSOE and AP, was over whether donations should be disclosed or remain secret. AP advocated secrecy in the 1985 law, claiming consistency with the principle of secret ballots and arguing that transparency would reduce the potential number of donors; the PSOE called for openness on the grounds that the public had a right to know where a party's financial backing came from, and that transparency was needed if the new limitations on donations were to be enforced. With their absolute majority in Parliament, the Socialists prevailed, but this was a disagreement that did not go away. During the 1990s the principle of encouraging private undisclosed donations would be pushed with even greater determination by AP's successor, the Partido Popular (PP), as a succession of scandals based on illicit financing of the parties discredited the reformed state-funded system.

Notwithstanding the increased state contribution to party finances, there were still compelling reasons for parties to engage in 'parallel financing activities': the problem of accumulated debt,[34] the fact that even now state subsidies would not cover current expenditure in full, persisting low levels of donations[35] and the still considerable ease with which the auditing arrangements could be circumvented. Moreover, there is evidence of public opinion being unfavourable to the state's funding of parties and to the possibility of the state assuming the parties' accumulated debts in order to establish a clean slate.[36] This has been seen as the major reason why even in 1987, when state funding was increased, the parties held back from using public money to completely resolve their difficulties. Instead they opted to take only half-measures openly and to supplement them with additional illicit measures, such as taking commissions from companies in return for public sector contracts and receiving payments from companies for the preparation of non-existent reports.[37] Finally, in the 1990s, when illicit financing scandals hit both the PSOE and the PP and threatened to completely discredit party politics in general, different approaches were considered: measures to reduce the costs of election campaigns and to encourage donations.

The party financial scandals of the early 1990s, together with the Grupos Antiterroristas de Liberación (GAL) scandal, in which prominent PSOE office-holders were associated with death squad activities against the terrorist organization ETA (Euskadi ta Askatasuna, or Basque Homeland and Liberty), brought discredit to the parties in general, thus having repercussions that went far beyond the individuals personally implicated

in them. The scandals brought to the fore considerable public questioning of state funding of parties. Commentators on
both sides of the political spectrum pointed to the paradoxical
situation that had arisen, in which parties that were highly
dependent on public money none the less had become highly
autonomous of the demands of society and had ended up appear-
ing as self-serving lobbies;[38] or put another way, the funding
arrangements that had been adopted seemed to have brought
into being a party state, in no way envisaged in the Spanish
Constitution. Parties had fallen in the public's esteem because
they were judged by the press and the intelligentsia in terms of
traditional liberal notions of democracy. In the eyes of many
Spaniards, the parties were supposed to represent the citizens,
act as vehicles of participation in government and serve as a
means of controlling the executive. Yet financially they needed
to be 'subsidised by the same apparatus that they [were] supposed to control [vigilar]' and this involved them in a contradiction: 'They are the expressions of the citizenry, but they have
to be maintained by the state. This creates a vicious circle
which inevitably leads to the creation of an oligarchy linked
by common interests to the state.'[39]

Charges of corruption surrounded the electoral decline of the
PSOE in the 1990s, although remarkably the Socialists were
still able to deny the PP an absolute majority in the general
election of March 1996 thanks to persisting popular distrust of
the centre-right party as part of a historical reaction against
Francoism. With both major parties concerned to avoid further
scandals, anxious that they might have systemic consequences
and not merely harm the guilty party that had been exposed
most recently, further reforms were countenanced. The Socialists were now ready to join the PP in offering tax incentives to
Spaniards wishing to contribute to party finances, although
they held out for transparency and resisted anonymity with
regard to donations. This left Izquierda Unida (IU) rather isolated
as the only parliamentary force advocating a financing system
based fundamentally on public funds, and fearing that a lifting
of the controls on private contributions would leave parties
open to manipulation by major donors. IU deputies in Parliament, only half in jest, depicted a future in which members of
the Cortes would start wearing the logos of their sponsors, in
the manner of sports celebrities.[40]

The second round of reform, initiated by a bill submitted to
Congress in June 1996, should make the parties more reliant on

private financial contributions. With party funding remaining a cross-party issue, the most radical reform proposals were discarded at an early stage in the legislative process. Indeed, so long as political competition in Spain is dominated by a battle for the centre ground, the reform debate will be about public-private *balance* rather than an exclusive option for one or the other. More generally, just as party funding was only one factor among several that shaped the party system and the nature of Spanish politics in the immediate aftermath of the Franco era, it is unlikely that radical political change will come purely through a reform of the funding regime.

## Conclusion

It would be inappropriate to finish by considering whether the funding reforms of the 1990s would have avoided political problems had they been introduced at the start of the Spanish transition. For while one can identify some measures that might usefully have been adopted, such as limits on campaign budgets and a rationalization of the electoral calendar, the real problems and dilemmas encountered in Spain arose from the necessary attempt to bring a party system into being almost overnight, when after such a prolonged period of authoritarianism it was impossible to rely for this simply on a rebirth of civil society. In the circumstances, a degree of state financial support for parties was deemed a more democratic solution than dependence on external support, which doubtless would have been much more pronounced in a system lacking state support.[41] Meanwhile, public opinion counselled against a system that was entirely state funded.

Eventually the emergence of a party state and the succession of corruption scandals did create problems of public disillusionment with the parties, but these were not new to the experience of western democracy and thus far they have not led to mass abstentionism or support for anti-system parties (see Table 4.1). Most of Spain's parliamentary parties have resorted to illicit means of funding themselves, thus making it difficult for voters to punish errant parties through the ballot box without thereby helping another offender. None the less, three-quarters of the electorate continue to participate in general elections, not least owing to the strength of PSOE–PP rivalry during the 1990s. Tempered by the knowledge that corruption is hardly a new national phenomenon, public reactions to financial scandals have been characterized by resignation as well as condemnation.

Spain's funding system has been far from perfect, especially when judged against the ideal of achieving fair electoral competition. However, it did help to ensure the survival of a range of parties that has offered a significant degree of choice to the electorate. State funding was particularly valuable in this regard during the late 1970s when the Left stood to lose out if a private funding model had been adopted. Since then the Socialist Party has become much more sympathetic towards business interests, and of late it has not been opposed to the principle of enhancing the role of private contributions. The success of this reform will depend not only on the response of Spanish society but on the continuation of recent cross-party efforts to reduce the costs of electoral competition.

## Notes

1 R. Gillespie, F. Rodrigo and J. Story (eds.), *Democratic Spain: Reshaping External Relations in a Changing World* (London, Routledge, 1995).

2 P. Heywood, 'Sleaze in Spain', *Parliamentary Affairs*, 48 (1995), 726–37; Heywood, 'Continuity and change: analysing political corruption in modern Spain', in W. Little and E. Posada-Carbó (eds.), *Political Corruption in Europe and Latin America* (Houndmills, Macmillan, 1996).

3 Pilar del Castillo claims that Spain was 'the first democratic country which adopted public financing of parties before the emergence of a party system.' See P. del Castillo, 'Financing of Spanish political parties', in H. E. Alexander (ed.), *Comparative Political Finance in the 1980s* (Cambridge, Cambridge University Press, 1989), p. 194.

4 There are few signs in the literature on party financing in Spain of another country's system of party funding having been particularly influential. However, Blanco Valdés makes passing reference to similarities with the pre-1993 Italian system and del Castillo points to Italian influence in relation to the ban on Spanish parties receiving donations from the public administration. See R. L. Blanco Valdés, 'Consideraciones sobre la necesaria reforma del sistema español de financiación de los partidos políticos', *Cuadernos y Debates*, 47 (1994), 40; and P. del Castillo, 'Financing of Spanish political parties', p. 197.

5 P. del Castillo, 'Financiación de los partidos políticos: la reforma necesaria', in J. J. González Encinar (ed.), *Derecho de partidos* (Madrid, Espasa-Calpe, 1992), p. 156.

6 R. Gillespie, *The Spanish Socialist Party* (Oxford, Oxford University Press, 1989), p. 26.

7 *Ibid.*, p. 336.

8 Under decree-law 20/1977 of 2 March 1977, on the funding of electoral participation, the formula was: 1 million pesetas for each seat won in the Congress of Deputies and Senate; 45 pesetas for each vote gained by lists securing at least one seat in the congressional election; and 15 pesetas for each vote won by candidates securing election to the Senate. These amounts, which tended to downgrade the

importance of the Senate, remained in force for the elections of 1979 and 1983. Under the Political Parties Law of 4 December 1978, the annual allocation to the parties to subsidize their ordinary (non-electoral) expenditure was again based on a certain amount allocated on the basis of seats won and another amount given on the basis of votes won (although here only the votes for parties winning a minimum of 3 per cent of the votes in each electoral district were computed, thus penalizing the smaller parties). This allocation came out of the national budget and no limit was placed upon it: the total sum available would be determined each year by the budget itself. There were also provisions for 'ordinary' subsidies for parliamentary groups in the Cortes and in legislative assemblies at the regional level. In the Cortes, parties were entitled to form a group if they secured a minimum of fifteen deputies or ten senators; parties with fewer members in the Cortes had to join a 'Grupo Mixto' which shared a single group financial allocation. The latter was composed of a standard allocation to each group plus a variable amount based on the size of the group. This subsidy came out of the parliamentary budgets and the total volume was fixed by the committee (mesa) in charge of the running of each chamber.

9  Initially, parties were free to receive individual or private company donations from Spanish sources, but could not receive foreign donations under the Law of Political Associations of 1976. The latter restriction was weakened by the Political Parties Law of 1978 which allowed for foreign contributions to ordinary party finances but retained the ban on electoral contributions from abroad.

10  Del Castillo, 'Financing of Spanish political parties', p. 181.

11  R. Cotarelo, 'Los partidos políticos', in Cotarelo (ed.), Transición política y consolidación democrática. España (1975–1986) (Madrid, Centro de Investigaciones Sociológicas, 1986), p. 306.

12  P. del Castillo, La financiación de partidos y candidatos en las democracias occidentales (Madrid, Centro de Investigaciones Sociológicas/Siglo XXI de España, 1985), pp. 210–13.

13  The PSOE's 48 per cent of the votes brought it 202 seats in the 350-member Congress of Deputies. This entitled the Socialists to have 80 per cent of their official electoral costs reimbursed (note 12 above, p. 225). However, the party's real electoral expenditure was much higher than the level officially declared: over 2.3 billion pesetas as opposed to the declared 1.3 billion, according to one estimate (del Castillo, 'Financing of Spanish political parties', p. 191). It should be noted in passing that the Spanish Left does not benefit from financial contributions from sympathetic trade unions.

14  El País, 14 June 1984.

15  After a series of highly successful election campaigns at national, regional and local level, the PSOE debt stood at 3.48 billion pesetas at the end of 1984 (del Castillo, 'Financing of Spanish political parties', p. 191). Between 1977 and 1987 AP accumulated a debt of 3 billion pesetas of which 1.2 billion pesetas was the result of the 1986 general election campaign. See M. Sánchez, Las tramas del dinero negro: del sumario Sanchis-Naseiro a la reforma de la ley electoral (Madrid, Tiempo, 1990), p. 100. According to official figures, state subsidies accounted for about 69 per cent of AP income in 1983 (del Castillo, La financiación de partidos, p. 220).

16  Del Castillo, La financiación de partidos, pp. 217–18.

17  Heywood, 'Continuity and change', p. 126.

18  See Gillespie, 'Factionalism, the left and the transition to democracy in Spain', in R. Gillespie, M. Waller and L. López Nieto (eds.), Factional Politics and Democratization (London, Cass, 1995).

19  There was apparently less international economic aid from the German foundations after 1979. See M. Pinto-Duschinsky, 'Foreign political aid: the German political foundations and their US counterparts', International Affairs, 67:1 (1991), 38, 55.

20 See del Castillo, 'Financiación de los partidos políticos', pp. 164–6, and J. Amodia, 'A victory against all the odds: the declining fortunes of the Spanish Socialist Party', in R. Gillespie (ed.), *Mediterranean Politics*, vol. 1 (London, Pinter, 1994), p. 178.

21 In the long term, the political influence of the bankers seemed to wane as (a) previous electoral performance became the crucial determinant of credit levels; (b) the volume of state subsidies to parties was increased in the 1980s, with arrangements being introduced also to pay a proportion of the electoral subsidy in advance; and (c) ideological preferences became less central to Spanish politics, with the PSOE moving to the right and finding new allies among the financial elite. During the 1980s, certain banks invested heavily in 'Operation Roca', the construction of a new centre-right force to challenge the PSOE, but this proved an electoral disaster. See J. M. Roca, 'Corrupción política: mecanismos democráticos imprescindibles', *Iniciativa Socialista*, 10 (1990), 13. However, recent evidence may point to the persistence of bank influence, or at least the potential for it to exist: the Tribunal de Cuentas, when analysing the party accounts for the years 1990–92, discovered that several parties (including the PP, PSOE and PCE) had benefited from the condoning of bank loans, a practice not envisaged in the Law on Financing of Political Parties of 1987. See *El País*, international edn, 6 January 1997.

22 J. Tusell Gómez, 'The Democratic Center and Christian Democracy in the elections of 1977 and 1979', in H. R. Penniman and E. M. Mujal-León (eds.), *Spain at the Polls, 1977, 1979, and 1982* (Durham, North Carolina, Duke University Press, 1985), p. 116.

23 As Tierno told PSP members in March 1978, 'If we continue, you must understand that it will be a long march through the desert . . . We owe many millions and we have no money. And they are not going to give us any. We are an annoyance, and annoyances are eliminated. They are going to eliminate us, and so we must choose . . . Join the PSOE, which is where you will be most sheltered, best protected, and with the best prospects.' Quoted in R. Gunther, G. Sani and G. Shabad, *Spain after Franco: The Making of a Competitive Party System* (Berkeley, CA, University of California Press), pp. 159–60.

24 R. López-Pintor, 'Francoist reformers in democratic Spain: the Popular Alliance and the Democratic Coalition', in Penniman and Mujal-León (eds.), *Spain at the Polls*, p. 197.

25 Gunther, Sani and Shabad, *Spain after Franco*, pp. 172–4.

26 Castillo, 'Financing of Spanish political parties', pp. 194–5.

27 *El Mundo*, 17 February 1996.

28 Gunther, Sani and Shabad, *Spain after Franco*, p. 131.

29 R. Gillespie and T. Gallagher, 'Democracy and authority in the socialist parties of southern Europe', in T. Gallagher and A. M. Williams (eds.), *Southern European Socialism* (Manchester, Manchester University Press, 1989).

30 R. Katz and P. Mair, 'Changing models of party organization and party democracy', *Party Politics*, 1:1 (1995), 17–21; M. Spourdalakis, 'PASOK's second chance', *Mediterranean Politics*, 1:3 (1996), 330–1.

31 A. Torres, *La financiación irregular del PSOE* (Barcelona, Ediciones de la Tempestad, 1993), p. 22.

32 Del Castillo, 'Financing of Spanish political parties', pp. 178–82; Castillo, 'Financiación de los partidos políticos', pp. 157–8; del Castillo, 'Objetivos para una reforma de la legislación sobre financiación de los partidos políticos', *Cuadernos y Debates*, 47 (1994), 98–100; E. Alvarez Conde, 'Algunas propuestas sobre la financiación de los partidos políticos', *ibid.*, pp. 24–5.

33 The idea of making votes rather than seats the fundamental criterion for financial subsidies was adopted in Portugal in 1974, with the basic allocation being decided by multiplying the number of votes won in the last election by a fraction of the national minimum wage. While this was more democratic than the Spanish

formula, it did not generate sufficient funding to avoid party malpractices. All the major parties defied a ban on foreign donations, which existed until the early 1990s. The Socialist Party apparently received substantial funding from Libya, the United States and European social democratic parties (including the SPD, Craxi's Italian Socialist Party and – on one occasion – the PSOE). Even the Portuguese Communist Party, which publicly opposed the granting of donations to parties, allegedly received $13.5 million, 100,000 French francs and 30 million escudos from the Communist Party of the Soviet Union (CPSU) between 1975 and 1990: the Russian government later attempted to recover these 'illegal currency exports'. On the funding of Portuguese parties, see T. C. Bruneau and A. Macleod, *Politics in Contemporary Portugal: Parties and the Consolidation of Democracy* (Boulder, Rienner, 1986), p. 30; Daniel Reis, 'Milhões de contos para financiar partidos', *Expresso* (Lisbon), 19 June 1993; *Expresso*, 6 February 1993; and *El Mundo* (Madrid), 28 January 1996, reporting the contents of the memoirs of the imprisoned former Soares lieutenant Rui Mateus, *Cuentos prohibidos: memorias de un PS desconocido*.

34 As the PSOE treasurer Francisco Fernández Marugán saw it (personal interview, Madrid, 28 May 1996), the problem of accumulated debt had grown up as a result of the absence of restrictions on party electoral budgets together with an inadequate volume of state subsidies prior to the mid-1980s; had controls been introduced earlier, the debt problem would never have been so great. Another problem for the parties was the time it took for the state to reimburse them for election expenses. In May 1996, they were still awaiting money in respect of municipal elections held a year earlier.

35 In 1995 the PSOE received a mere 19.5 million pesetas ($152,000) in anonymous donations, just 0.2 per cent of its 8,000 million peseta ($62.5 million) budget for the year – not enough even to cover the 60 million pesetas that it spent in that year on the legal defence of prominent members involved in judicial proceedings (*El País*, 30 June, 8 July 1996). In early 1997, the Socialist Party put its debt at over 8,000 million pesetas, while the other parties did not reveal their total debt (*ibid.*, international edn, 6 January 1997).

36 Del Castillo, 'Financing of Spanish political parties', p. 178; Torres, *La financiación irregular*, p. 19; Sánchez, *Las tramas*, p. 100.

37 J. L. Galiachot and C. Berbell, *Filesa: las tramas del dinero negro en la política* (Madrid, Temas de hoy, 1995).

38 Del Castillo, 'Objetivos para una reforma', p. 53.

39 Roca, 'Corrupción política', p. 15.

40 D. López Garrido, 'La financiación de los partidos políticos: diez propuestas de reforma', *Cuadernos y Debates*, 47 (1994), 71; *El País*, 29 June 1996.

41 It is not possible to gauge the real extent of external financial backing for the Spanish parties. Clearly it was a further factor favouring the concentration of the party system into a reduced number of political options, recognizable in European terms.

# 5

# Chile's new democracy: political funding and economic transformation

CARLOS HUNEEUS

In Chile, the issue of party funding and electoral campaigns has been prominent because of an increasing awareness that parties need public financing and that the contributions made by business to parties and candidates require regulation. The soaring costs of electoral campaigns were clearly visible in the congressional elections of 1993, and also in the municipal elections of 27 October 1996, when many candidates spent large amounts of money, something unprecedented in Chile's competitive politics. This display of financial resources was apparent not only in the campaigns of would-be senators and deputies belonging to the right wing opposition parties, Renovación Nacional (RN) and Unión Demócrata Independiente (UDI), but also among certain candidates from the major parties in the Concertación: Christian Democrat (PDC), Socialist (PS) and Partido por la Democracia (PPD). The issue, therefore, is not one that affects only right wing candidates; it is one that extends to centre and left wing party candidates. It is becoming clear that only candidates with a personal fortune, or with the support of business, can hope to find their way into Congress or local government.

Although Chile has a long-standing party system, there is no legal framework to support the parties in financial terms. As in most countries of Latin America, party funding is not discussed but none the less parties enjoy support through contributions from business people and professionals. Political conditions today are not conducive to setting up a legal framework either to regulate the terms under which political parties may obtain funds or to furnish them with public funding. First, the right wing parties have no difficulty in obtaining funds from corporations, hence they systematically oppose any legislation designed to provide public funding for political parties. As a result, the Concertación por la Democracia, the governing coalition, is prevented from getting such a law approved, given that it has no majority in the Senate because of the system of 'designated senators' instituted by General Pinochet and the government authorities prior to their relinquishing power in 1990. Second, Chileans have a poor opinion of all parties, especially in Congress, and this is reflected in low satisfaction regarding their performance and low levels of confidence in their efforts. This last trait is part of a general attitude of contempt for politics, a vast change from the attitude prevailing in 1988–89 when the regime passed from authoritarianism to democracy, and when there was widespread interest in, and respect for, politics. Ultimately, this is one of the consequences of seventeen years of authoritarian rule, characterized by the discrediting of politics and politicians.

Several Latin American countries are concerned about party funding because the exponential rise in electoral campaign costs can lead to two problems: the predominance of patrimonial relations between politics, business and individuals, and the risk that drug money may find its way into campaign financing. The cases of Italy and Colombia respectively are well known. The political crisis that arose in Italy as a result of relations established between political power and business, and which led to the crisis of the Christian Democrats and the Socialist Party, had profound effects on centre and left wing parties in Chile, which had kept up close relations with their Italian counterparts during the Pinochet dictatorship. Italy welcomed hundreds of Chilean exiles throughout the military regime, and gave decisive support to the democratic opposition in its struggle to recover democracy, including financial support.

The threat of drug traffic is kept alive by the accusations that money from drug trafficking helped to fund the electoral campaign of Ernesto Samper, the President of Colombia. Accusations have been levied even by some of Samper's closest collaborators, some of whom are currently in prison. The United States took sides in this situation and withdrew Samper's visa. In Chile, fear of the influence of drug traffic is rooted in the notion that the prevailing economic freedom significantly expedites the inflow and outflow of money – existing controls being insufficient to provide checks on the money's origin. Until recently, any Chilean or foreigner could change any amount of American dollars at money exchanges without identification being required – an ideal setting for money laundering. The military government, concerned only with suppressing the opposition and achieving economic development at any price, overlooked the dangers of drug trafficking and were weak in the struggle against it. On coming to office in 1990, the democratic administration had to clean up the high command of the civilian police because many officers were found to have links with drug dealers. This operation left the service without a large number of its higher ranking officers.[1]

This chapter examines party funding in the context of a new democracy established in the wake of prolonged military rule that had been characterized by harsh coercion and the personal domination of General Augusto Pinochet who, alone among the 'new Authoritarianisms'[2] in Latin America in the 1970s and 1980s, remained as head of state from the beginning to the end of the authoritarian administration (1973–90). This regime brought about significant economic transformations that have caused considerable economic growth, but have also produced major distortions in social and power relations – changes that altered the bases of Chile's long-standing democratic tradition, where political parties were an extremely important institutional element.

If it is true that the main challenge to the consolidation of the new democracies is to improve the quality of politics, the following is one of the forms that such a challenge takes.[3] The lack of mechanisms to regulate relationships between representatives elected by the people and donors in the business community may create conditions that undermine both politics and economic growth itself. The need for public funding to help reduce economic dependence on donors and for a regulatory framework to make known the support that business and private individuals give to parties and candidates, is greater when democracy is becoming consolidated in the course of economic change. In Chile this change is characterized by twelve years of constant growth averaging 7 per cent per annum, combined with the privatization of public services. As Schmitter has pointed out, when economic reforms are put in place, there is more danger that the connections between money and politics might lead to the trading of influence and, subsequently, the rise of corruption.[4]

It is a well-known fact that public funding for parties and electoral campaigns fails to resolve all the tensions and difficulties arising between money and politics, nor does public financing cover all the costs of electoral campaigning, and candidates must continue to seek financial support.[5] However, even partial support can help to decrease dependence, and prevent such dependence becoming total when government support is missing and when there is no regulatory framework to govern private contributions to candidates and parties.

The absence of a regulatory framework governing relations between money and politics and the lack of public funding for parties and electoral campaigns pose two central problems to the new democracy in Chile. The first problem is the damage done to the equality that ought to prevail in political activity, since the parties that enjoy better relations with business and wealth have an advantage over others. That all votes should be equal is one of the foundations of political representation.[6] This assumes a minimum of equal conditions among candidates. Of course, money does not always mean success for the wealthy – presidential candidate Nixon defeated Rockefeller for the Republican nomination in the United States in 1960 – but, without a doubt, it is an extremely important resource when it comes to choosing candidates to stand for election. Many refrain from entering politics because they lack personal means or are not prepared to become dependent on their supporters. The demand for equality is even stronger in a political system where the administration is left of centre and composed of parties that fought against a military regime, and who had denounced privatizations that had been carried out on highly advantageous terms for those who acquired the companies – many of whom were, or had been, government officials.

The second problem is the autonomy that any institutionalization process requires to develop fully.[7] Parties and members of Congress must enjoy sufficient autonomy to make their decisions. Max Weber had this in mind when he defined the professional politician as one having sufficient means to allow them to be independent and in a position to live *for* politics and not *off* politics. The *Honoratioren*, as described by him in the Germany of 1919, was a successful professional or small-scale business person with sufficient economic resources to act *vis-à-vis* interest groups and big business.[8]

As in many countries, the issue of campaign and party funding has not been systematically analysed in Chile, and information available is scarce.[9] Politicians are not particularly interested in discussing the matter, although certain business people make no secret of their support. Available information is minimal. For instance, figures in balance-sheets that parties have to submit to the Dirección del Registro Electoral (Electoral Register) are not close to actual incomes; membership fees are stressed, although everyone is aware that these fees fail to account for all party income, and that part of the total comes from business and private contributions. The latter are not mentioned in the balance-sheet because this is not required by law.

The issue is highly significant for the young Chilean democracy, which came into being on on 11 March 1990 following the harsh dictatorship of General Augusto Pinochet Ugarte which had begun on 11 September 1973, when a military coup had ended the long-standing democratic tradition of the country. Political institutions are well established, but not yet sufficiently solid and autonomous to ensure that relationships of dependency are not established between those in political power and the business community. Vigorous economic growth since the 1980s has led to an asymmetry between a strong business community composed of large companies with a presence elsewhere in the continent and an institutionally weak government; this makes it difficult for government to act independently of corporate pressures – for example, in respect of large scale investment projects with high environmental costs.

This asymmetry between a weak government and a strong and concentrated private economy is the result of the economic transformation pushed through by the military following the neo-liberal ideology of the so-called 'Chicago boys'.[10] This translated into policies designed to reduce drastically the size of the state with a wave of privatizations that transferred immense economic resources to the private sector, but it failed to set up the institutional conditions for the state to perform the necessary regulatory functions for upholding the dynamism of the economy and protecting consumers.[11] The strengthening of the private sector was further favoured by the authoritarian political context, which weakened the trade union movement; both coercion and a new labour law which, among many advantages given to employers, allowed various unions to be organized within the same company, reduced drastically the unions' ability to stand up to management successfully. A weakened union movement has prevented the unions from following a practice found in many European countries – that is, supporting the work of the parties most closely linked to them (mainly the left wing and Christian Democrat parties).[12]

The Chilean party system is composed of six parties. On one side are the four components of the government coalition: the Christian Democrat Party (PDC), the largest party with 28 per cent of the vote and which held the presidency with Eduardo Frei Montalva (1964–70); the Socialist Party (12 per cent) (PS); the Partido por la Democracia (PPD) (12 per cent); and the Radical Party (PR) (4 per cent). On the other side are the opposition parties: Renovación Nacional (RN) and Unión Demócrata Independiente (UDI). In the 1993 election of Deputies, RN won 16 per cent and UDI 12 per cent of the votes.[13] The government parties form a coalition known as the 'Concertación por la Democracia' (Democratic Concertation), which defeated General Pinochet in the referendum held on 5 October 1988 triggering the regime change to democracy; it won the presidential election of 1989, when Patricio Aylwin (PDC) was elected president, and later the election of 1993, when Eduardo Frei Ruiz-Tagle, son of the former president, was elected.

RN unites a large number of personalities who had belonged to the older right wing parties and politicians who had abstained from cooperating with the Pinochet regime. UDI was founded by Pinochet supporters belonging to the Movimiento Gremial (trade association movement), which until the military coup had had substantial influence within the student movement and independent right wing sectors coalescing around former president, Jorge Alessandri (1958–64).[14] While RN seeks to take up a position right of centre and keeps its distance from Pinochet, UDI is clearly placed to the right and defends the military regime.

The parties operate in an electoral system in which the President must be elected by an absolute majority of the votes, and a second round of elections is held if no candidate attains an absolute majority in the first round.[15] The parliamentary electoral system has broken with the tradition of proportional representation that had prevailed until 1973, and a two-member system has been introduced, whereby each electoral district has two seats. The Senate composition is mixed: there are nine designated senators, and thirty-eight senators elected for an eight-year term in nineteen districts;[16] the Chamber of Deputies has 120 members elected in sixty districts. Electoral alliances are allowed, and each list of candidates can carry only two names. Each voter must vote for one candidate in the Senate and one in the Chamber of Deputies. If one party list obtains twice the number of votes of the second-placed list, both its candidates are elected; otherwise, the candidates on these two lists obtaining the most votes are the ones elected.

In practical terms, the two-member system reflects and consolidates the two blocks that had formed around the 'yes' and 'no' votes of the referendum held in 1988, which in turn reflected the profound polarization produced by the military regime, especially since 1983, when the 'opening-up' policy and the protests and manifestations of opposition began.[17]

The electoral system obliged the parties to form alliances for the parliamentary elections. This forced the four parties making up the Concertación to present not more than two candidates per district in the form of *alliances by omission*, in other words, two sub-alliances – that is, one composed of the PDC and PR, and one made up of the PS and PPD, with one candidate for each sub-alliance. For the opposition, the alliance becomes somewhat simpler as there are only two parties, each with one candidate. The Concertación doubles the votes of the opposition in only a few districts; in all the others its candidates face a difficult task: each must strive to obtain more votes than the other person on his or her list, thus facing *internal* competition, while also mobilizing supporters against the right wing, the opposition, which provides *external* competition.

This electoral system has repercussions for party funding since, although it is true that it causes a reduction in office-seekers, the candidates for each alliance being so few, it is also true that the electoral struggle is a dramatic one. Unlike multi-member districts, where there is more likelihood of success, here each candidate either wins or loses the only possible seat for the alliance. As a result, campaigning is intensive and requires vast amounts of funds.

### Sources of party funding

The sole official information available on party funding is the balance-sheet that each party must submit to the Dirección de

**Table 5.1** Balances for 1995 as stated by the parties (Ch$)

| Party | Total income | Membership fees | % |
|---|---|---|---|
| Renovación Nacional | 71,307,219 | 60,786,188 | 85.2 |
| Democracia Cristiana | 159,615,637 | 102,519,407 | 64.2 |
| Partido por la Democracia | 77,316,536 | 68,650,000 | 88.5 |
| Partido Radical | | | |
| Social-Demócrata | 33,881,853 | 30,620,000 | 90.3 |
| Unión Demócrata | | | |
| Independiente | 68,339,304 | 67,042,000 | 98.1 |
| Partido Socialista de Chile | 77,113,231 | 75,577,110 | 98.0 |
| Unión de Centro Centro | | | |
| Progresista | 12,979,000 | 12,979,000 | 100.0 |
| **Total** | **500,652,780** | **418,173,705** | **83.5** |

*Source: Diario Oficial* 1996 (selection of issues).
*Note*: Ch$415 = US$1.

Servicio Electoral, which is published in the *Diario Oficial* or Official Gazette. As noted already, this reveals only part of the total funds available to parties, showing income amounting to Ch$500,652,780 or US$1.3 million for the year (see Table 5.1). It is none the less interesting to note the differences among parties and the significance that each attaches to membership fees. Unión de Centro Centro Progresista (UCCP), which is known to be funded by its founder, the wealthy businessman Francisco Javier Errázuriz, reports that 100 per cent of its income comes from membership fees. Democracia Cristiana (DC), the party with the most numerous membership, shows the lowest percentage of membership contributions (64 per cent).

Party funding comes from various sources, one source being contributions from members of Congress, through the monthly allowance they receive from Congress to pay for support staff (secretaries and activists) and office rental. In practical terms, both the offices and the staff working in them, as well as collaborators of the Congress member, are helping to carry out party activities. The allowance is paid by the Congress directly to the persons hired and to the owners of the premises rented, with each member of Congress (that is, all 45 senators and 120 deputies) receiving a monthly allowance totalling Ch$2,800,000 (Ch$415 = US$1; therefore, US$6,746).[18] In other words, excluding the allowances of the nine 'designated' senators who do not belong to a party, and so have no electoral or political activities to fulfil in an electoral district, elected politicians have a total of about US$13 million available to them each year.

Certain parties, like the PDC for example, collect a monthly contribution from the salary that each member of Congress receives, and this goes to swell the party treasury. Interestingly enough, this contribution is required from members of Congress but not from ministers, under-secretaries, or other high government officials. This is a paradox, for the prevailing political system is a markedly presidentialist one, the constitutional role of the Congress being notably diminished, and top government officials might be expected to be the first to come to the aid of the party, although it must be admitted that they earn much less than members of Congress.

For training leaders and activists, as well as for drawing up documents and surveys for party leaders and members of Congress, the parties can apply for support from private research institutes, which have their own funds provided by local companies or public agencies, and from projects financed by international organizations.[19] These institutes are independent of parties and they conduct extensive research and produce publications, which account for a large proportion of their expenditures. Their work, however, helps the parties. Since the parties in government can rely on information supplied by the administration for the purposes of legislation and public debate, these research centres have found their resources curtailed and have lost much of the importance they enjoyed during the Pinochet regime, when they provided the groundwork for drawing up the alternative programme, and from which many of the ministers, under-secretaries and other high government officials were recruited.[20]

The opposition parties have established an important research centre known as Libertad y Desarrollo (Liberty and Development), which supports both parties and their representatives in Congress. The institute is substantially funded by local companies and has sufficient funds to keep a dozen researchers on its permanent staff, together with a wide range of experts hired for specific studies. Its president is Carlos Cáceres, former Minister of Finance and later Minister of the Interior under General Pinochet, who is closely connected with the business community, since he is chairman or director of several companies. The executive secretary of Libertad y Desarrollo is Cristián Larroulet, at one time head of the office of former Finance

Minister Hernán Büchi. The latter is also a member of the board. Libertad y Desarrollo firmly opposes public party funding.[21]

Some members of the Congress are able to finance their political activity with their own means. The businessman Francisco Javier Errázuriz, presidential candidate in 1989, who obtained 14 per cent of the votes after a highly populistic campaign, is an example of this. As was mentioned above, he founded his own party, UCCP, and funded it through his various business ventures. The same applies to Senator Sebastián Piñera, who belongs to the liberal wing of RN and who is able to contribute to the funding of the party out of his personal fortune.[22] Such financial support has been instrumental in helping the liberal sector of RN, which seeks to detach itself from the authoritarian past, to resist pressure from more conservative business people who strive to hold RN to a policy line in keeping with the military regime.

Recently, following several years of opposition from right wing parties, the Chamber of Deputies approved a budget to support institute funding from 1997. The sum is a modest one totalling Ch$260 million (US$600,000), 15 per cent of which goes to the officers of the Chamber and 25 per cent to the parties; the balance may be drawn on by deputies, who may join forces to make better use of the funds. The modest amount received by the parties is in proportion to the percentage of the vote won by each of them and it is used to pay for specific projects. Even this low level of public support is the result of a prolonged effort by the parties of the Concertación, which until recently came up against resistance from the opposition parties.

Finally, for campaign purposes, the parties may benefit from free time on television during the last few days before an election, a point that is discussed further below.

## Party funding before military rule and during the transition

One of the features of the party system prevailing in Chile until 1973 was a high degree of organization and penetration throughout the country, in the student and union movements, and in slum areas. All of the parties could count on a large number of members and supporters, and they were able to recruit sufficient volunteer activists for electoral campaigns, who worked full time in the final stage of the campaign. One of

the main sources of volunteer workers was the student movement, known in Chile for its strong interest in politics and
for providing a large proportion of the Chilean political class.
Undergraduate activists played a major role in the DC electoral campaigns that swiftly made it the largest party in the
country, taking it to the presidency in 1964. At that time, the
PDC, through its student branch, had won the leadership of
all the student federations in the country and so could rely on
vast numbers of activists to help it in its electoral campaign.
In the 1970 presidential election, the students enrolled in the
'Movimiento Gremialista' at Universidad Católica (Catholic
University), gave significant support to Jorge Alessandri, the
right wing candidate, while left wing students at Universidad
de Chile and Universidad Técnica del Estado supported the
candidate for the 'Unidad Popular', Salvador Allende.

The parties were funded mainly with contributions from
members, especially professionals and business people, who
formed a minority sector at the time, since the national economy was based largely on copper production, which was in
the hands of US companies and the Chilean state. Campaign
costs, on the other hand, were not high, particularly since,
before the late 1950s, competitive politics was restricted to
those registered to vote, a small number when compared with
those eligible to vote. Until then, the Chilean electorate was a
limited one; citizenship required registration in the Electoral
Registers, and this was not compulsory. Under the electoral
reform of 1962, participation in official formalities was made
dependent on electoral registration, and this caused a considerable expansion in the number of registered voters.[23]

Modern electoral campaign techniques requiring vast
amounts of funds and involving large numbers of activists only
came into being in the 1960s. The presidential election of 1964
was the first of these types of campaign. The DC, led by Eduardo
Frei, was the first party to develop and apply modern campaign
techniques and to exhibit a well-developed programme, thanks
to the efforts of hundreds of professionals and student leaders
which, in turn, attracted large number of activists and voters.
The Left, led by a Socialist, Salvador Allende, campaigned similarly though not so vigorously as the DC. The Right had
organized a modern campaign in 1958, when the independent
candidate Jorge Alessandri, an engineer and businessman, was
elected to the presidency. However, it failed to maintain the

Conservative and Liberal Parties (its support base), and sub-sequently lost electoral strength to its competitor, the modern, well-organized, DC party. The Radicals remained outside this party modernization process in the 1960s, and that eventually caused their fall, and they became a minority party.

The high degree of polarization that arose in the 1960s per-meated the state bureaucracy to the extent that many civil ser-vants worked full time for the campaigns, particularly for the presidential election in 1970 and the congressional election in 1973. They also frequently used government vehicles for their campaign work. Those campaign costs were borne directly by the government, at a time when the government bureaucracy was not isolated from the polarization of the society.

Advertising was paid for only on radio and in the daily papers. There was no paid advertising on television, as there is in Venezuela.[24] Television channels were allowed to hold debates that could be attended by all candidates on equal terms, and were regulated by the Council of University Rectors. Law 17,377, enacted in 1970, established that only universities and the government could own television stations, leaving no room for the private sector. The National Television Channel was set up at the time, together with channels operated by three universities: Universidad de Chile, Universidad Católica and Universidad Católica de Valparaíso. The most successful of the three has been the channel owned by the Universidad Católica (Channel 13).

As this law has remained in effect through the referendum of 1988 and into the new democracy, some attention must be devoted to it. It established that television channels 'must devote at least one hour per day, free of charge, to debates or programmes prepared by the representatives of parties present-ing candidates' (Article 33). The time has to be distributed to parties in proportion to the number of votes obtained by each in the last parliamentary election; independent candidates are allotted the same amount of time as the party obtaining the lowest number of votes at that election. The time is allocated by the National Television Council. 'The duration of each space shall be not less than five minutes nor more than fifteen' (Article 33 para. 4). The law further provides that 'in order to improve the political culture of the nation, the television channel shall devote not less than 30 minutes a week to slots where different parties and political movements represented in the Congress can discuss national problems on the screen'. Paragraph 2 established that 'other than the [foregoing] slots, the television channels are forbidden to engage in political propaganda.'

Since the regime was convinced of its inevitable victory in the referendum called to confirm Pinochet as president, and was aware that such a victory must be credible to public opinion, at home and abroad, it opened television to opposition propaganda for the referendum.[25] Under law 18,700 of 1986, television channels are bound to devote thirty minutes of their transmission time free of charge to electoral propaganda in elections for president, senators and deputies, or in referendums, and this must be allotted equally to all candidates. In the case of congressional elections, the time is allotted to parties rather than to candidates, in proportion to the number of votes obtained at the latest election; any party not having taken part in that election is allowed the same time as the party with the lowest number of votes. When parties form an alliance, as they have done in practice, the time for each is added together. There is time allowed for 'independent' candidates, which is equal to the time allotted to the party with the lowest number of votes, shared equally by all independent candidates.[26]

In the event that presidential and congressional elections are held simultaneously, as happened in 1989 and 1993 (but will not happen in 1999, since the presidential term of office has been extended from four to six years), television channels must devote forty minutes a day to political propaganda, distributed equally between the presidential and congressional candidates. As already noted, television time is allocated by a public body, the National Television Council, and its members are appointed by the Senate from individuals proposed by the President from a number of persons suggested by the Concertación and opposition parties.

Propaganda on the radio is highly significant because of the very large number of radio stations operating across the country, their vast audience and their high degree of credibility. Many of them were free from political control during the military regime and offered the most reliable source of information, in contrast with the university and government television channels which understood their informative role as one of propaganda for the regime. There is also paid commercial advertising in the printed media, but there are few daily papers in circulation, the largest being *El Mercurio* and *La Tercera*, and thus the importance of newspapers as compared with radio and the 'TV space' is minor.

## Political campaigning in the new democracy

The new democracy after Pinochet's regime has seen a radical change in election campaigns compared with those that took place in the democracy that collapsed in 1973. Whereas previously parties and volunteer activists were the core of the campaigns, today the paid activists and marketing techniques are even more important than canvassing. There are two reasons for this. The first is the influence of a phenomenon that has emerged in the developed nations just as much as it has in the more advanced societies of the Third World: the weakening of social, cultural and political organizations, reflected in the plummeting numbers of members of political parties, unions, churches and so on. Individuals stay away from voluntary associations and show little interest in participating actively in politics, although they may vote. The other reason is the type of democratic transition that took place in Chile. A non-competitive election, held on 5 October 1988, triggered the transition with the opposition defeating Pinochet with 54 per cent of the votes when he sought re-election for an eight-year term as president. There was intense political activity then because the goal was democracy, and this activity continued during the presidential and congressional elections of 1989, but came to an end shortly thereafter. The initial phase of great interest and active participation in politics ceased when the novelty wore off and the new authorities were faced with the 'ordinary' problems of any democracy, such as solving economic and social issues. Under such conditions, interest in politics declines and indifference takes over, together with an increased critical attitude towards politics and politicians.[27]

In the late 1990s, unlike both before the coup and also 1988 and 1989, there is little interest in participating in electoral campaigns. Candidates must make a huge effort to win votes and they find it increasingly difficult to attract the cooperation of activists prepared to work without pay – there being fewer and fewer people ready to do so. Indeed, the congressional election campaign of 1993 and the municipal campaign in 1996 were based mainly on the work of paid activists who went out nightly to stick up posters and paint slogans on walls and buildings, painstakingly distributing pamphlets door-to-door, and helping in the preparations for the final campaign rallies.

This new trend has a twofold effect on electoral campaigns. In the first place, campaign costs spiral upwards; what used to be done free of charge by party members and supporters must now be done by paid personnel, a fact which has a great impact on total campaign costs. (In Chile, contributions to candidates commonly take the form of such practical resources as paper, paint, timber, free loans of vehicles or their rental for a token fee, as well as cash to pay for other campaign expenses.) For example, one winning candidate in the 1993 congressional elections for a district in Santiago spent between 55 and 60 per cent of all the money collected in paying for activists.[28] If an estimate of the non-monetary resources contributed is included, it may be concluded that payments to activists, which included a daily wage plus food, accounted for fully one-third of the total campaign cost. The costs of campaigning may rise depending on how intense the competition is, and the degree of antagonism or belligerence of the opponents – when competition is intense it may be necessary to go out every night to replace the posters that the paid activists of other candidates have destroyed, and so on.

Second, and this is the most sensitive issue from the standpoint of the political system, the hiring of paid personnel has occasioned a profound change in the meaning of electoral campaigns and the role of parties: for some, the job to be done means only gainful employment, and it is no longer done in the pursuit of ideals and interests embodied in political objectives. The 'quality' of politics declines, which is precisely the criticism that has been made of it; a campaign becomes just another service job, comparable to handing out fliers touting consumer products in a company's advertising efforts. The downward spiral of lack of interest in politics intensifies. As a result, the parties are becoming increasingly 'Americanized', to the extent of adopting the method of holding 'primaries', as the Concertación did in 1993, while greater importance is attached to images in the media than to the traditional work of the parties through the development of a significant bureaucratic apparatus.

Electoral campaign funding falls primarily on the candidate, who must make a personal effort to collect the money needed.

The party that he or she represents provides advertising on walls in the form of posters promoting all that party's candidates, but supplies no money for individual candidates to conduct the campaign. When senators and deputies are to be elected in the same district, and if the candidates are on good terms, they may work together in collecting resources and conducting the campaign; if the reverse is true, however, and this often happens even among members of the same party, with the candidate for senator regarding the candidate for deputy as a potential future rival, each proceeds on his or her own.

Business contributions are fundamental to campaign funding. Some candidates and some parties are supported by many business people; others by only a few. No major entrepreneur if approached by a candidate who is probably going to win is likely to refuse to cooperate, especially if the candidate belongs to the government coalition. In the framework of a market economy with a history of traumatic conflicts, the leaders of centre and left wing parties have a favourable disposition towards business people; somewhat surprisingly, some Socialist and PPD candidates seem even more 'attractive' to business people than DC candidates, who are viewed as being more prone to 'statism'.[29] As the Senate is the higher chamber, business people are even more likely to cooperate with senators than with deputies.

Chile is no exception in experiencing a problematic relationship between conservative parties and business, as far as party and electoral campaign funding is concerned.[30] The complex relationship between the autonomy that a party wants and the economic interests of business leads to tensions and conflicts that do nothing to aid stability. In Chile the influence exerted by a major sector of business and the political right wing, which is opposed to the existence of parties and thus stands in the way of their development, should be noted. The presence of autonomous parties hinders the defence of business interests, hence before 1973 and also after Pinochet's regime a major portion of the right wing has worked against the advancement of parties and has emphasized the role of certain personalities.

The man who symbolized this policy was former president Jorge Alessandri, who was a businessman and part-owner of one of the largest corporations in the country, while also being a leading personality of the two main interest groups of Chilean business, the Sociedad de Fomento Fabril (SFF, the Industrial

Development Association) and the Confederación de la Producción y del Comercio (the Production and Trade Federation).
Despite being the candidate of the Conservative and Liberal
Parties in the presidential election of 1958, which he won by a
narrow margin over the left wing candidate, Socialist Salvador
Allende, Alessandri dispensed with party support, formed a
cabinet with independent ministers, and did not refrain from
publicly criticizing the parties, even those that had elected
him to office. It was thus a conservative administration that
speeded up the weakening of the right wing parties, the latter
lacking human and financial resources to face the DC and the
Left, which were to win the presidential elections in 1964 and
1970 respectively. In 1970, when Alessandri was the right wing
candidate again, tension was also apparent between the leaders
of the Partido Nacional and Alessandri supporters responsible
for directing the campaign.

'Alessandrismo' found political expression in the post-
military regime period in a number of political leaders who
carry decisive weight in the two business associations mentioned above and who are clearly closer to UDI than to RN.
Though changes have taken place in the leadership of SFF and
the Confederación, even the most recent incumbents are closely
linked to UDI, the party founded by Jaime Guzmán, who was
the main Alessandri supporter from the late 1960s and the
principal ideologue of Pinochet. The business community tend
to look more favourably on UDI owing to this continuity with
'Alessandrismo' and because the party clearly defends the
regime of General Pinochet. That is the reason why UDI has
no difficulty in collecting funds, while the reverse is true of
RN, which is backed by a minority portion of the business
community.

Aside from the normal problems associated with obtaining
business contributions for the right wing parties, the latter enjoy
a clear advantage over government parties because they have
ample funds at their disposal. Accordingly, they oppose public
party and electoral campaign funding, utilizing a number of
different arguments, such as that the government needs to
emphasize social expenditure rather than supporting the parties, that public contributions set up dependencies in relation
to the government – as though private contributions did not
do the same in respect of business – and that campaign funding will only raise the level of campaign costs.[31]

The different approaches of the two right wing parties to the business community is one of the reasons why the government drew up a draft law on campaign funding, which laid down minimum disclosure conditions on individual and business contributions. UDI has declared its opposition to the draft, while RN supports it in principle; it remains to be seen whether the more conservative faction of RN in the Senate will eventually support the government proposal.

## Government proposals to regulate electoral campaign finance

President Eduardo Frei's government drafted legislation to restrict electoral campaign expenses and help to fund them. The proposal established a modest contribution to electoral campaigns totalling not more than US$10 million, to be distributed after the election in proportion to the number of votes received. One-third of the amount would be handed over directly to the party, with the other two-thirds going to the candidates – this was to prevent possible discrimination if the party leaders had sole charge of the distribution.[32] The proposal made no distinction between party and independent candidates, in order to provide support for the latter, something the Right often resorts to. The draft law established rules for the management of funds and regulated the way that contributions might be made to parties and candidates, limiting contributions to not more than 5 per cent of the maximum electoral expenses allowed under the proposed law. Any large contributions below the established limit had to be made by means of a document stating the name of the donor so as to prevent corrupt operations. A limit is also set on contributions by a single individual or company. Such private contributions are made directly to candidates rather than parties, for the same reason given on the subject of public contributions to campaigns.[33] The object of the draft law, as the then Minister who prepared the draft said at the time, was not only to restrict expenses but also to improve disclosure of the funds allotted to electoral campaigns.

The initiative found no support among the opposition. UDI rejected it outright, arguing that it was 'immoral' to bring this question up when there were immense needs in other areas – that is, health, education and housing, and concluding that in this way all Chileans would be paying for electoral expenses.[34]

As has been seen before, UDI is on good terms with major business ventures and is thus assured of receiving the necessary private contributions and can do without government support. The director of Instituto Libertad y Desarrollo argued along similar lines and suggested a 'tax democracy' that would leave individuals and businesses free to support the candidates or the parties of their choice on a tax-deductible basis.[35] José Antonio Guzmán, chairman of Confederación de la Producción y el Comercio, also proposed the establishment of tax deductions for contributions to electoral campaigns, arguing that they should be like those applicable to contributions to culture, education and sports.[36]

RN is divided on the issue, as it is on other major political problems. Party chairman Andrés Allamand is in favour of establishing some form of public funding and spending limits on electoral campaigns, and he justifies his position by arguing that both elements are essential to ensure the solidity of democratic politics. Politicians should be able to try and remain independent from the influence of big business. The more conservative sector, led by Senator Sergio Romero, rejected the proposal with arguments similar to those given by UDI. Allamand again declared himself in favour of public funding for electoral campaigns following the municipal election held in 1996, when the huge costs and vast amounts of funds available to UDI were once again obvious.[37] The superior level of party funding compared with RN was clear during this election in a major district of Santiago, Providencia, where the UDI candidate, a former military officer who was a close collaborator of Pinochet and who had obtained only 5 per cent of the votes in a southern district in the congressional election of 1993, won an easy victory over the RN and Concertación candidates.

## Conclusion

Party funding is a significant issue in Chilean politics today, since the political system is faced with the twofold task of 'deepening' the new democracy while promoting economic growth, a task that implies making substantial changes in the economic institutions established by the military regime. Both aims require the existence of political parties with sufficient autonomy to make their own decisions. Recent elections in the new Chilean democracy show that candidates have huge financial resources at their disposal, supplied by companies that are in a position to create conditions that restrict the parties' decision-making capability. A limit must be put on campaign expenditure and a legal framework must be set up that requires the disclosure of donations received by parties and candidates. In this context, public party funding is a step in the direction of setting minimum conditions to ensure party autonomy *vis-à-vis* economic interests.

To date, no progress has been made in obtaining legislation in favour of funding political parties because a sector of the opposition refuses to approve it, given that it has ample funds available from businesses, especially those that developed under the wing of the military regime or with its support. The political will of the parties in the government coalition is also lacking, for many members of Congress have donors who support them. The government is caught between two not entirely contradictory positions in its pursuit of approval for a law designed to set a limit to campaign costs, regulate the contributions of corporations and individuals, and provide public funding for candidates and parties.

It can be argued, therefore, that an agreement with the opposition is unlikely to be reached before the congressional election of 1997, and is even less likely to be reached before the presidential election of 1999. The absence of such legislation will increase the dependence of parties, members of Congress and mayors on big business. This will weaken the consolidation of democracy and have serious implications for the future of democracy and economic development. However, an institutional framework for parties and the conduct of election campaigns will eventually be established because a mature democracy and a dynamic economy require it, and those are both goals that Chile hopes to achieve.

## Notes

This chapter emanates from a research project on economic transformation in Chile, funded by the Volkswagen Foundation, Germany, which the author thanks for its support. All opinions are the author's sole responsibility and he acknowledges the help of Ricardo Gamboa, research assistant on the project.

1 A firm policy against drug consumption and traffic proposed by the new administration suffered a severe blow when Francisco Javier Cuadra, a former minister

under the military regime and a close collaborator of Pinochet, denounced drug consumption among certain members of Congress, without, however, submitting any proof, thereby drawing a cloud of suspicion over one of the branches of government. This turned public debate away from the problem of drug traffic towards the image of Congress and politicians.

2 D. Collier (ed.), *The New Authoritarianism in Latin America* (Princeton, Princeton University Press, 1979).

3 G. Sartori, 'Rethinking democracy: Bad Polity and Bad Politics', *International Social Sciences Journal*, 129 (1991), 437–50.

4 P. C. Schmitter, 'Dangers and dilemmas of democracy', *Journal of Democracy*, 5 (1994), 57–74.

5 C. Landfried, *Parteifinanzen und politische Macht. Eine vergleichende Studie zur Bundesrepublik Deutschland, zu Italien und den USA* (Baden-Baden, Nomos, 1994).

6 D. Nohlen, *Wahlsysteme der Welt* (Munich, Piper, 1978).

7 S. P. Huntington, *Political Order in Changing Societies* (New Haven, Yale University Press, 1968).

8 M. Weber, 'Politik als Beruf', in Weber, *Gesammelte Politische Schriften* (Tübingen, J. C. B. Mohr (Paul Siebek), 1971), pp. 561–86 (from a 1919 lecture, first published in *GPS*, 1921).

9 The literature on party funding in Latin America is scant. One of the few articles, though it is highly theoretical, is C. Anglade, 'Party finance models and the classification of Latin American parties', in A. J. Heidenheimer (ed.), *Comparative Political Finance* (Lexington, D. C. Heath, 1970).

10 P. Silva, 'Technocrats and politics in Chile: from the Chicago Boys to the CIEPLAN Monks', *Journal of Latin American Studies*, 23 (1992), 385–419.

11 O. Muñoz and C. Celedón, 'Chile en transición: estrategia económica y política', in J. A. Morales and G. McMahon (eds.), *La política económica en la transición a la democracia* (Santiago, CIEPLAN, 1993); D. Hachette and R. Lüders, *La privatización en Chile* (Santiago, Centro Internacional para el Desarrollo Económico, CINDE, 1992).

12 K. von Beyme, *Gewerkschaften und Arbeitsbeziehungen in Kapitalistischen Ländern* (Munich, Piper, 1977).

13 On the parties, see T. R. Scully, 'La reconstitución de la política de partidos en Chile', in S. Mainwaring and T. R. Scully (eds.), *La construcción de instituciones democráticas. Sistemas de partidos en América Latina* (Santiago, CIEPLAN, 1995).

14 Jorge Alessandri was also the right wing candidate in 1970, when he was narrowly defeated by Allende.

15 D. Nohlen, *Sistemas electorales y partidos políticos* (Mexico City, Fondo de Cultura Económica, 1994), pp. 241–2.

16 In the 1989 election, half of the Senate was elected for a four-year term.

17 This process has been discussed from the standpoint of the change in political regimes in C. Huneeus, 'La política de *apertura* y sus implicancias para la inauguración de la democracia en Chile', *Revista de Ciencia Política*, VII (1985), 25–84, and 'La inauguración de la democracia en Chile. ¿*Reforma* en el procedimiento y *ruptura* en el contenido?', *Revista de Ciencia Política*, 8 (1986), 22–87.

18 It should be noted that each deputy receives Ch$1,678,000 monthly for secretarial expenses, travel and accommodation; in addition, each receives Ch$329,469 for rental of office space in his or her district or in Santiago, plus Ch$645,213 for advisers. The last two items are paid directly by the Treasury of the Chamber of Deputies to cover the relevant contracts and invoices, without the money passing through the hands of the deputy. Senators receive a similar amount.

19 In the case of the PDC, funding comes from the Instituto Chileno de Estudios Humanísticos (ICHEH – Chilean Institute for Humanistic Studies) which is supported by the Konrad Adenauer Foundation in Germany, and which, in turn, is linked to the Christian Democrat Party (CDU) in that country. Socialists have

the study centre AVANCE. RN has Instituto Libertad. The Centro de Estudios Públicos (Centre for Policy Studies), CEP, which is not linked to any opposition party, groups liberal right wing intellectuals who follow the ideas of von Hayek and it receives funding from business and support from the Hans Seidel Foundation, in Germany, which is linked to the Bavarian-based Christian Social Union (CSU).

20 For information about these centres in the mid-1980s, see M. T. Lladser, *Centros Privados de Investigación en Ciencias Sociales en Chile* (Santiago, Academia de Humanismo Cristiano, FLACSO, 1986).

21 See C. Larroulet and P. Villagrán, 'Competencia, mercado político y financiamiento público', *Libertad y Desarrollo*, 1996, 18–21; 'Financiamiento de los partidos políticos y campañas electorales', *Serie Opinión Pública*, 43 (1996).

22 In the 1993 presidential campaign, his brother José Piñera, who during the Pinochet regime was Minister of Labour and later Minister of Mining, stood as an independent candidate, supporting his campaign largely through his own private means.

23 In the presidential election of 1958, only 20 per cent of the population was registered to vote; in 1964, the corresponding figure was 35 per cent.

24 Article 6 of law 16,094 of 6 January 1965, which amended the Law on Elections of 1962.

25 The referendum is discussed in C. Huneeus, 'La derrota del general Pinochet', *Opciones*, 15 (1989), 155–80.

26 In practice, 'independent' candidates receive support from UDI or RN, so that the term is formal rather than real. This is a legacy of the authoritarian proposal of reducing the significance of parties and letting 'independents' act on an equal footing with party candidates.

27 This sharp fall in interest in politics is a recurring trend in new democracies – for example, in post-Franco Spain, where the phenomenon was known as *desencanto*, or disappointment.

28 Information disclosed in personal interviews with the author. This member of Congress estimated the total cost of the campaign at Ch$80 million, or close to US$200,000. Some districts were even more costly – for example, Las Condes (Santiago), where each of the two right wing deputies who were elected in 1993 both spent more than US$1,000,000.

29 See the interview given by Enrique Correa, Socialist and former minister under Aylwin, *El Mercurio*, 1 December 1996, Section B. Correa states that 'there are two ways [to view the market] ... one is to take the market as a fact of life, an unpleasant one, but a fact that must be accepted. And the other is to see the market as a lever for growth. I feel identified to the second approach.' Earlier, during his term as president, Patricio Aylwin had said that the market was 'cruel', thus supporting the first approach.

30 See A. Rommele, *Unternehmenspenden in der Parteien- und Wahlkampffinanzierung. Die USA, Kanada, die Bundesrepublik Deutschland und Grossbritanien im internationalen Vergleich* (Baden-Baden, Nomos, 1996).

31 C. Larroulet and P. Villagrán, 'Financiamiento público de la política', *La Epoca*, 10 July 1996, p. 10. A similar argument is found in an article by the assistant director of Instituto Libertad y Desarrollo, Luis Larraín, 'Financiamiento público de campañas electorales', *El Diario*, 24 January 1994.

32 *La Nación*, 8 May 1996.

33 *La Epoca*, 12 May 1996.

34 Opinions of party Vice Chairman, Domingo Arteaga, *La Nación*, 8 May 1996.

35 Larroulet and Villagrán, 'Financiamento publico de la politica'.

36 *La Epoca*, 4 December 1996.

37 *La Segunda*, 4 December 1996.

# 6

# Funding parties and elections in Brazil

MARIA D'ALVA GIL KINZO

In the era of electronic mass media communication and highly specialized political marketing, election campaigns, in any part of the democratic world, have become very expensive enterprises. Brazil and its still young democracy are no exception.[1] Large sums of money are needed for a candidate to be elected to one of the country's 65,000 public offices. In spite of major differences between Brazil and the United States, it has been estimated that Fernando Collor de Mello's campaign in 1989 (the first elected president since 1964) cost as much as President Bill Clinton's for his first election in 1992: about $120 million. But, similarities between the two cases do not go beyond this point. Moreover, while President Clinton is in his second presidential term, Collor de Mello did not manage to complete his third year in office. Accused of corruption (related mainly to his campaign financing network), he was ousted from power, in 1992, by a constitutional impeachment.

In the 1994 election, the current president – Fernando Henrique Cardoso – did not spend such a large amount of money as in the previous election. Also, new regulations to control campaign financing and expenditure were issued as a result of Collor de Mello's case. Parties were to be bound to provide a detailed report to the Electoral Tribunal on the sums spent and the source of private contributions to their candidates, meaning, at least, that the official information about campaign funding was to be known and subject to press scrutiny.

None the less, the figures involved in any election in Brazil, particularly in presidential contests, are still astronomical, especially compared to democracies with much higher per capita income. For example, contributions both from individuals and private firms to Cardoso's election campaign in 1994 amounted to 32.3 million dollars.[2] Considering that these are only the officially declared figures and that the cost of an election campaign is estimated to be triple that which is reported to the Electoral Tribunal,[3] it is understandable that funding elections in Brazil is a real problem and that proposals for changing legislation are items on the country's political reform agenda.

The aim of this chapter is twofold: first, to explain the main factors that have contributed to making election campaigns in Brazil very expensive; second, to give an account of both the funding methods used and also the changes to the legislation on campaign financing as an attempt to improve fairness in electoral competition and to control corruption.

### The institutional background

Three assertions summarize the reasons for funding elections and parties in Brazil being so costly:

1 elections take place in a vast territory and with large constituencies;
2 elections are centred on candidates rather than on parties;
3 political parties are fragile organizations and have very limited funding sources.

In a country of such vast territory and with a large electorate like Brazil – with its 8.5 million square kilometres of territory and an electorate of about 95 million[4] – election campaigns, particularly at the national level, are bound to have high costs. Further, they are noticeably costly in a political system such as Brazil's where particular features of the electoral and party system add further difficulties to participating in political contests.

#### The electoral system and the parties in Brazil

Comprised of a federation of twenty-six states and the federal district, Brazil has different constituencies depending on the type of election. A nationwide constituency is the electoral basis within which direct election for president of the Republic is held, by a system of run-off ballot between the two leading candidates in the case of neither of them receiving an absolute majority in the first ballot. The same system is used for the election of both state governors and mayors of capital and other major cities. The size of their constituencies is, obviously, related to the size of the state or the city. It should be noted that in a system of two-round elections used in the context of highly fragmented party systems (as is the case in Brazil), to reach a majority in the first round is very difficult; consequently, a second-round election is more likely to occur, making for even higher campaign costs.

State constituencies are also the basis for the legislative elections at both federal and state levels. Here two systems are used. Senators are elected by the plurality system while members of the Federal Chamber (as well as of the State Assemblies) are elected by proportional representation (PR).[5] But the PR system used in Brazil has a particular feature affecting electoral competition and, consequently, funding arrangements: the open list. This means that the parties' list of candidates is not previously ordered; rather, it is the number of votes individually obtained by each candidate of a given party that determines his or her position on the party list and the chance of getting elected. Thus, candidates work to encourage voters to choose a particular candidate even though the law also allows voting just for a party label. The result is that competition takes place largely between individual candidates (even from the same parties), thus relegating party organizations to a less significant position in the election campaign of their representatives. In fact, as regards campaign funding, parties have a minor role in financing candidates' campaign in elections with this method of PR. Candidates are left alone to self-finance or to look for other channels of funding in order to compete in an election held in large areas, such as in states whose district magnitudes, in most of the cases, are very high.[6] Moreover, the number of candidates running in an election by a PR system with an open list is enormous, particularly in fragmented party systems, as every party is allowed to contest the election with a number of candidates (the party list) 50 per cent larger than the number of seats available in a given state. For example, in the election for São Paulo state's seventy representatives at the Federal Chamber, the number of competitors frequently surpasses a thousand. The participation of a large number of candidates not only makes electoral competition in general more intense, but also makes the use of radio and television broadcasting ineffective or simply impossible. Thus, in order to reach voters, candidates have to resort to other campaign methods, such as public meetings and visits (which involve long distance travelling over the state), distribution of large amounts of campaign material (that is, T-shirts, hats, pamphlets and so on), and of course patronage. The result of all this activity is a substantial increase in total campaign spending.

In sum, apart from having a presidential system under which the election for the head of government tends to be personalized, that is, focused on the candidates rather than on the parties,[7] Brazil has a PR system which tends to contribute to personalized competition. This is a major factor in the weakness of party politics in Brazil. In this respect, at least three problems can be pointed out. First, Brazil's party system is *unstable*. More than eighteen years have elapsed since the 1979 party reform law ending the compulsory two-party system created by the military and Brazil's party system is in flux. Even very recent data show the continuing fluidity in the party system.[8] The period covering the current legislature (inaugurated in 1994) is sufficient to give an idea of the variation both in the number of representatives from each party and the overall party composition in the two Houses of Congress as a consequence of party mobility. Table 6.1 presents the situation at three points in time; data from other years would give the same changeable picture. As can be seen in the table, the Brazilian Democratic Movement (PMDB), the Democratic Labour Party (PDT) and the Brazilian Labour Party (PTB) lost members in the House of Deputies, while the Liberal Front Party (PFL) and the Brazilian Social Democratic Party (PSDB) increased their numbers. The data for January 1996 (for the Chamber of Deputies) indicates that the correlation of forces has changed: a new party – the Brazilian Progressive Party (PPB) which resulted from the merging of the Renewing Progressive Party (PPR) with the Popular Party (PP) – replaced the PSDB as the third largest party in the House of Deputies.

Much of the mutability of the party picture has to do with the PR system of open lists. In fact, because votes are cast for individual candidates, electoral competition is not based on parties, consequently, party organization is almost unnecessary; this de-couples the relationship between party and representatives and, therefore, discourages party discipline. Because, in most of the cases, the party's contribution to their electoral success is virtually limited to the provision of a party label, deputies feel free to act as individual political agents, moving from one party to another as often as they wish.

**Table 6.1** Composition of Congress, 1995–96

| Political parties | Chamber of Deputies Number of seats | | | Senate Number of seats | | |
|---|---|---|---|---|---|---|
| | Feb. 1995 | Jan. 1996 | Oct. 1996 | Feb. 1995 | Sept. 1995 | Oct. 1996 |
| Brazilian Democratic Movement – PMDB (centre) | 107 | 96 | 97 | 22 | 23 | 24 |
| Liberal Front Party – PFL (centre-right) | 89 | 95 | 100 | 18 | 21 | 22 |
| Brazilian Social Democratic Party-PSDB (centre-left) | 62 | 80 | 84 | 11 | 12 | 12 |
| Brazilian Progressive Party – PPB (right) | 52 | 88 | 91 | 6 | 5 | 5 |
| Workers' Party – PT (left) | 49 | 49 | 50 | 5 | 5 | 5 |
| Popular Party – PP (centre-right) | 36 | –* | – | 5 | 3 | –* |
| Democratic Labour Party – PDT (centre-left) | 34 | 26 | 25 | 6 | 3 | 3 |
| Brazilian Labour Party – PTB (centre-right) | 31 | 29 | 25 | 5 | 4 | 4 |
| Brazilian Socialist Party – PSB (centre-left) | 15 | 14 | 12 | 1 | 1 | 2 |
| Liberal Party – PL (centre-right) | 13 | 10 | 8 | 1 | – | – |
| Brazilian Communist Party – PCdoB (left) | 10 | 10 | 10 | – | – | – |
| National Mobilisation Party – PMN | 4 | 2 | 2 | – | – | – |
| Social Democratic Party – PSD (centre-right) | 3 | 3 | 3 | – | – | – |
| Social Christian Party – PSC (centre-right) | 3 | 1 | 1 | – | – | – |
| Social Popular Party – PPS (ex-CP) | 2 | 2 | 2 | 1 | 1 | 1 |
| National Renovating Party – PRN (centre-right) | 1 | – | – | – | – | – |
| Green Party – PV | 1 | 1 | 1 | – | – | – |
| Popular Representation Party – PRP | 1 | – | – | – | – | – |
| Social Liberal Party – PSL | – | 2 | 2 | – | – | – |
| None | – | 5 | – | – | 3 | 2 |
| **Total** | **513** | **513** | **513** | **81** | **81** | **81** |

*Source:* Tribunal Superior Eleitoral.
*Note:* * In late September 1995 this party was merged will the PPR forming the PPB.

Second, the party system is *highly fragmented*. No fewer than eight out of the eighteen parties with seats in the House of Deputies can be classified as relevant parties, according to Laakso & Taagepera's index of party fragmentation.[9] Moreover, none of them holds more than 20 per cent of the seats, so that no majority can be achieved without a coalition of at least three parties. Party fragmentation has very little to do with the characteristics of Brazil's social structure. Although Brazilian society is socially, racially, ethnically, religiously and regionally diverse, its party system does not reflect those cleavages. For instance, there are at least four parties in the right (and centre-right): PPB, PFL, PP and PTB. However, none of them could be differentiated by special links with a group in society – be it sectoral, regional or religious. The same could be said for the other side of the ideological spectrum. There are three parties that would claim to be centre-left (PDT, PSB, PSDB), and three others that are on the left (PT, PCdoB, PPS). This is not to mention the PMDB (the largest party) whose internal diversity accommodates most of the political spectrum. As the party system does not reproduce cleavages in society, the parties are more fragile as channels of representation. Social interests can therefore be voiced by members of several parties which form groupings that, sometimes, operate in a more effective way than the parties. A typical example is the 'bancada ruralista' (the parliamentary group defending rural interests). It has more than 130 deputies and thirty senators. Its members come from no less than twelve parties with representation in the House of Deputies (and six parties in the Senate). Nineteen per cent of the group come from centre-left parties, 19 per cent from the centre and 62 per cent from the right and centre-right parties.[10] As the parties are not clearly identified with specific interest groups, it is not surprising that business firms make donations for the election campaigns of candidates from all parties from the left to the right. Party fragmentation derives not only from the system of PR, but also from a very permissive party and election legislation that, apart from facilitating the creation of new parties, offers no incentives for party loyalty.[11] On the contrary, it facilitates mobility and undermines party discipline. Moreover, by allowing party alliances for any kind of electoral contest, which means that the most diversified electoral alliances can be formed (even in local elections), it facilitates the survival of parties that have no significant electoral support on their own.[12]

Third, the party system is *fragile*. A party system that is in constant flux cannot be strong. Neither can a situation of high fragmentation, such as Brazil's. Instability and high fragmentation are certainly not features of an institutionalized party system, or, using Sartori's terminology, a structurally consolidated system.[13] Institutionalization implies some stability or, at least, continuity over time. It is, therefore, unlikely that a party system could be structurally consolidated if its main components do not last over time. Institutionalization has also to do with the definition of 'spaces of action', namely a given institution has a specific function which gives it a role and an identity in relation to the system as a whole. On the other hand, a party system, both in theory and in practice, is not only associated with the idea of divisions (or parts), but also with that of connection (grouping together). In this sense, a party system in which the degree of division is such that connections, if they exist, are so unstructured that the parts almost coincide with individual units, is meaningless. Thus, as a sub-system, a situation of high party fragmentation is almost as irrelevant as that of a one- or no-party system.

These problems associated with the Brazilian party system have made parties ineffective both for political negotiations in Congress and for structuring electoral contests.[14] This does not mean that parties have no function in elections. Formally they are the main actors since it is through parties that candidates run for an elected office. Thus candidates are chosen in party conventions, and have their electoral publicity stamped by a party or party coalition. They are officially elected through a party ticket, and have to inform the party about their campaign expenditures (which will be gathered in the party financial report to be sent to the Electoral Tribunal). But, in reality, Brazilian parties are not the central channel through which election campaigns are organized and managed. Even in elections for executive offices, when there is only one candidate for each party or alliance, the campaign is organized by a special team of supporters chosen by the candidate him/herself. It is the candidate's team (electoral campaign committee) that is responsible for both setting the campaign strategy and infrastructure as well as searching for financial support. Particularly in financial matters, parties have no central role, as private contributions are made mainly to candidates rather than to parties. In spite of the fact that it is the parties that are responsible for producing the campaign spending report to be sent to the Electoral Tribunal, they have very little control over their candidates' campaign spending. In fact, the election law does not favour the party in this matter, as it allows donations both to parties and to candidates. As the actors in the competition are the candidates, usually the donations go to them rather than to their parties.

Given the fact that parties in Brazil are fragile organizations and have a limited role in the organization of electoral campaigns, the question, then, is how are the Brazilian parties funded? It should be clear from the discussion so far that in Brazil party funding and campaign funding, though related, are different things. Thus in order to understand how politics is financed one needs to explain the two different types of funding.

## Party and campaign funding

As political organizations, parties are relatively poor in Brazil. Most parties are a mix of cadre and catch-all parties in the sense that they have weak and loose organizational structures operating in the context of a mass electorate.[15] Therefore, they have very few means of self-financing, such as contributions by membership fees and interest groups. The exception to this general rule is the PT (the Workers' Party) which is an ideological and disciplined mass party supported by organized sectors of the working class. But even in this case, the difficulties are enormous for keeping the party organizational structure in operation with its own resources.

For maintaining their organizational structure, Brazilian parties have two official financial sources:

1 *Contributions from party members holding elected offices*
For example, in most party statutes a percentage of the parliamentarians' salary is specified as their party contribution. But in most cases either this rule is not followed or the contribution is very small (around 1 per cent of the salary). The exception is the PT which not only made this contribution compulsory, but substantially increased the percentage (for example, federal legislators have to give 24 per cent of their salary to the party).

2 *A quota of the Party Fund (that is, the Special Fund for Finance Assistance to Political Parties) is allocated annually by the state*
This comes from: (a) fines collected from electoral penalties (including those due to voters' unjustified absence for an obligatory vote) and (b) a share of the federal budget which was recently introduced (the total of which must not be lower that the sum of the number of electors multiplied by R$0.35 (or the equivalent of this in August 1995).[16] One per cent of this Fund is shared equally among all the parties having the Electoral Tribunal licence; the remaining 99 per cent is distributed among the parties that have seats in the Federal Chamber, in proportion to the number of votes they had in the previous election for that House. Although very small in the past, the sum allocated, especially to the main parties, has recently been quite substantial. For instance, in 1996 the annual quota assigned to the PMDB – which has the largest number of representatives – was about $7 million. This sum, however, is designed to cover not only the administrative costs of the party's national office but also the running costs of twenty-seven regional branches and thousands of municipal branches. Another good example is that of the PT. According to its treasurer, the party's total income in 1996 was about $7.2 million.[17] Forty per cent of this total was spent on the party leaders' travelling expenses and on publication costs. The salary of the forty-one party central staff members was paid for by the party's national budget. This meant that other funding methods had to be used to cover at least the costs of the remaining party staff.

Apart from the two funding sources mentioned above, parties in Brazil have, by law, free access to television broadcasting.[18] As paid advertisements on radio and television are prohibited, all parties that have seats in Congress are granted per semester: (a) forty minutes of television prime time to be used for party broadcasting (half of it to be used for national party programmes and half for state programmes, to be broadcast simultaneously by all channels); and (b) another forty minutes to be used by the parties in thirty- to sixty-second advertisements during the normal TV programmes. Parties that have no representation or very few seats in the Federal Chamber, but who have the Electoral Tribunal licence, are granted two to five minutes per semester for national TV broadcasting. As is mentioned later, special time is allotted for an election campaign.

Clearly, the party's income resulting from the sources referred to above is insufficient to maintain an organizational network in operation in a country that not only has a very large area but whose parties are bound, by law, to have a nationwide organization.[19] The consequences of this situation are threefold. First, parties can hardly keep their organizations effectively in operation over the year, limiting their activities, particularly in the local branches, to holding formal proceedings for renewal of party leadership and nomination of candidates for elections. Although television broadcasting is free, the cost of producing a party programme using professional producers and political consultants to make it more attractive is quite high, and thus is difficult to maintain in non-election years.[20]

Second, parties end up being unofficially subsidized by the state. This refers not only to the customary distribution of patronage which depends on the parties' position *vis-à-vis* the government but also to other kinds of indirect public contributions. That is, contributions that are related to congressional positions and the benefits associated with holding such elected offices. The most striking example is the fact that most of the parties have no place of their own for housing their central headquarters but, instead, make use of office space at the Congress (or State Assemblies and local councils) allocated to them. The PFL (Liberal Front Party) – the second largest party – has its national headquarters in the Senate's main office building where it occupies an entire floor. The same type of free accommodation for party headquarters is enjoyed by other main parties. This means that not only do they have free office space, but they also have the complementary facilities that go with it – telephone, electricity and even administrative staff – all paid for from the legislative budgets.

With regard to party personnel, a revealing example was disclosed in early 1997 by the press, and this led to a heated debate on the question of party funding. In fact, it was an embarrassing case because it involved the general secretary of the PT, a party which, apart from having a strong ideological orientation is known for using public morality as one of its main banners. The problem was the disclosure by the press that the PT general secretary had been one of the so-called 'ghost civil servants' for more than three years. Although he had been employed as a medical doctor in the municipal public health service, he was actually working full time for the PT's central office. This kind of arrangement was possible even for opposition parties such as the PT because of the fringe benefits enjoyed by parliamentarians at all levels of government. For instance, every elected municipal councillor in São Paulo is entitled not only to make seventeen personal appointments, but also to have three municipal civil servants informally borrowed from the municipal executive to work for her or him (this latter case is called commissioned personnel). The PT general secretary was a 'commissioned person'. But the most startling fact was that, officially, he was not at the service of any of PT's municipal councillors; rather he was serving officially the municipal council president, who is a representative of the PPB – the right wing party in control of the São Paulo's city council and local administration. This example shows clearly how staff resources, which are designed to provide legislators with specialized assistance, are used for other purposes, such as to cover the costs of party machines.

The third consequence of the poor state of party funding in Brazil is that parties become very dependent on private contributions, as far as election campaigns are concerned, and, consequently, on economically powerful interests. And this leads to the second aspect of financing politics in Brazil: election campaign funding.

As already mentioned, election campaigns in Brazil are expensive and candidate-orientated. Millions are spent by candidates in the election for any kind of office. However, actual costs are difficult to assess since official figures are always understated. The activities that most contribute to increased costs are those involved in the production of radio and television commercials (accounting for about 50 per cent of total expenditure). Although radio and television campaign coverage is free, the production of commercials runs to several millions of dollars.[21] If one adds public opinion research and the work of political advisers, items that have become essential for a successful campaign in the media, the costs are even higher. And this is the case not only in the presidential election campaigns but also in the campaigns for state governors, senators and mayors of large cities. The exceptions are those campaigns for legislative offices (based on the PR system), where radio and television broadcasting is hardly used because of the excessive number of candidates.

Before discussing the methods of financing the high cost of Brazilian election campaigning, it is worth giving an account of the legislation on this issue. The first point to note is that, since democratization began, almost every election in Brazil has been preceded by a revision of the legislation, particularly with regard to funding methods. Thus, instead of thoroughly revising the Electoral Code (which dates back to 1965), legislators have been adjusting regulations for specific elections to take place the following year. This frequent change of rules is obviously an indication of the lack of consolidated democratic institutions in Brazil. But it is also an indication that attempts have been made to control the influence of both powerful interests and corruption, an issue that has become of greater concern after the political scandal that led to President Collor de Mello's impeachment.[22] The disclosure by a Parliamentary Inquiry Commission of the illicit means by which Collor de Mello's campaign treasurer collected enormous sums of money made imperative the need to establish mechanisms to stamp out electoral corruption.[23]

Thus measures were aimed at adding transparency to the funding process and increasing the control over private contributions. In 1993 new funding rules were passed by the Congress to regulate the national elections of the following year. The objective of these rules was both to strengthen the supervision of the Electoral Tribunal and to formalize the practice of private donations for electoral campaigns. They established that candidates or parties could receive contributions not only from individuals (who were allowed to donate a sum of not more than 10 per cent of their income in the previous year) but also from private firms (whose maximum contribution is equal to 1 per cent of their operational revenue in the previous election). An Electoral Voucher, printed by the Treasury, was also introduced. Like a paper currency, this voucher of different values (which could be used for tax reduction) was given by the parties and/or candidates to donors in exchange for their contributions. With this mechanism, private donations were legalized and donors could be identified. The regulations issued in 1993 implied that prior to the election period parties were required to send to the Electoral Tribunal an estimation of their candidates' campaign costs as well as the number of electoral vouchers they would need for fund raising. This meant that parties were obliged to publicize a more detailed report on their campaign expenditure including the names of donors. The introduction of the electoral voucher, however, was not very successful, since there were candidates who were using it to launder illegal money, and this was disclosed by the press. As a result, in 1995 the legislation was changed again for the following election (1996). The electoral voucher was replaced by a receipt specially made to serve as proof of private contributions received by the candidates' campaign. The changes in the legislation on election financing introduced in 1993 and in 1995 legalizing the practice of private contributions have, none the less, retained a serious distortion that is harmful to working-class-based parties. This is the prohibition on a party or candidate to receive donations from trade unions or other associations. Thus while donations from business firms have become a legal practice, those from unions are still prohibited.[24]

Apart from the official private contributions, campaign costs can be covered by the amount each party receives from the public Party Fund, which in election years are more substantial as the law allows a larger share in the national budget for this purpose (double that of a non-election year). Also guaranteed by law is a daily ninety minutes' free radio and television broadcasting that parties share during the two months preceding an election. One-fifth of that daily broadcasting time is equally divided between all parties that are contesting the election, while the remaining four-fifths is shared proportionately by the parties' representation in the Federal Chamber. For obvious reasons, radio and television companies strongly oppose these provisions, which are regarded as authoritarian, particularly because they require simultaneous broadcasting. None the less, this is an established rule that guarantees at least some radio and television exposure for candidates from all parties.[25] Clearly, other exposure depends on the broadcasting companies' position *vis-à-vis* the candidates in the election. In this regard, Brazil has interesting examples of television companies' help in the promotion of candidates. The support provided by the powerful Globo television network to Collor de Mello's presidential campaign is the most revealing example. Actually, much of the political ascension of Collor de Mello – an unknown politician, a governor of a small state in the north-east region – can be explained by his successful media performance, due not only to his own merits as a communicator but also to the generous news coverage provided by Globo television.

Finally, as concerns campaign financing, governments' indirect funding should not be forgotten – that is, those unofficial contributions (prohibited by law) that governments at national, state or local level (depending on the election) extend to parties and electoral alliances they favour. The methods adopted for such support range from the use of personnel employed by government agencies to work in the election campaign to the allocation of larger amounts of national or state budget to specific social policies and regions in time to influence the election result in its favour. Allegations of this kind of practice are frequently reported by the press during the period of electoral campaigns. For example, the newspaper *Jornal da Tarde* reported in 1994 that central government transfers to the municipalities in August of that year – a period that coincided with the peak of the electoral campaign – were five times larger than the monthly average in the preceding semester. The information disclosed by this report also shows the government's clear priority to invest in social areas during election periods: most of the transfers sent to the cities and towns had come from the Ministries of Education, Health, Social Welfare and Regional Integration.[26]

In spite of the various problems in financing elections in Brazil, it should be noted that the present legislation represents an improvement in the regulation of party and election financing. The fact that it is possible to identify the main private donors and, therefore, to make public the sources of financial support for those who are elected is an important improvement. This does not mean, however, that covert funding methods are under control. For example, some business corporations still prefer not to have their names associated with specific candidates so as to avoid future allegations of involvement with illicit transactions with politicians. Others, even when using legal means, prefer not to show their great generosity to a candidate's campaign, thus understating the sum of their contribution. As an official from the Electoral Tribunal explains: 'there are costs that will never be checked. How could it be possible to know that a businessman donated five thousand dollars if he preferred to have a receipt of only two thousand?'[27] As mentioned before two-thirds of the campaign costs are covered by non-official transactions (the so-called 'caixa 2')[28] about which very little is known, other than the fact that very large sums of cash in dollars are involved.

**Table 6.2** Private donations for the 1994 presidential campaign

|  | F. H. Cardoso | Lula da Silva | Eneas | O. Quercia |
|---|---|---|---|---|
| Votes (%) | 54.3 | 27.0 | 7.4 | 4.4 |
| Donations (total in |  |  |  |  |
| $ million) | 32.3 | 4.0 | 0.1 | 9.3 |
| Individuals (%) | 3.0 | 38.1 | 87.0* | n.d. |
| Firms (%) | 93.2 | 41.2 | n.d. | n.d. |

*Sources*: Electoral Tribunal data published in the newspapers *Folha de São Paulo* (08/10/95) and *Estado de São Paulo* (25 February 1995).
*Note*: * According to this candidate's report, the money came from his own pocket.

However, because donors if they use official channels are identifiable in the party reports sent to the Electoral Tribunal, the present legislation makes it possible to have access to some information about campaign financing. At least it is possible to know that the main method of funding campaigns in Brazil is through private firms – especially those in the civil construction and banking sectors. As shown by Tables 6.2 and 6.3 which present official data for the 1994 presidential and gubernatorial elections respectively, private firms were responsible for most of the campaign costs. In the presidential election (Table 6.2), 93 per cent of private contributions to the eventual winner came from business donations, especially from banks and the civil construction sector. The staggering role played by business in financing campaigns is not limited to parties on the right and centre of the political spectrum; it also makes extensive contributions to left wing parties and candidates. Thus, even in the case of Lula – the Workers' Party presidential candidate – private firms' contributions amounted to 41 per cent of this party's total expenditure. The same picture is evident in the elections for state governors (Table 6.3): for example, private firms were the main source of funding not only for the centre-rightist PFL candidates (about 99 per cent of donations) but also for both the leftist PT and PDT candidates (accounting for 99 per cent of donations for the winner in the state of Espirito Santo and 94 per cent for the winner in the state of Paraná). In fact, as a means to secure good relations with future governments of any colour, firms (particularly those in the civil construction sector that depend on

**Table 6.3** Private donations for the 1994 gubernatorial campaign in thirteen states

| State | The winner's party | Cost per vote (in $) | Total donations ($) | Firms (%) | Individuals (%) |
|---|---|---|---|---|---|
| Minas Gerais | PSDB | 2.51 | 10,980,100 | 97.3 | 2.7 |
| São Paulo | PSDB | 1.14 | 9,935,900 | 97.1 | 2.9 |
| Pará | PSDB | 1.00 | 878,000 | 93.7 | 6.3 |
| R. Grande Sul | PMDB | 1.01 | 2,726,300 | 97.9 | 2.1 |
| S. Catarina | PMDB | 0.92 | 1,198,000 | 88.6 | 11.4 |
| Rondonia | PMDB | 6.32 | 1,570,300 | 99.0 | 1.0 |
| Paraiba | PMDB | 0.37 | 299,100 | 74.1 | 25.9 |
| Piaui | PMDB | 0.49 | 306,800 | 88.4 | 11.6 |
| Bahia | PFL | 2.79 | 6,250,300 | 99.9 | 0.1 |
| Maranhão | PFL | 3.60 | 2,713,500 | 99.1 | 0.9 |
| Acre | PPB | 11.83 | 1,088,900 | 96.1 | 3.9 |
| Paraná | PDT | 1.78 | 3,685,000 | 94.2 | 5.8 |
| Espirito Santo | PT | 1.24 | 643,700 | 99.0 | 1.0 |

*Source*: Electoral Tribunal and *Folha de São Paulo*, 8 October 1995.

**Table 6.4** Official private donations for the main candidates for mayor of São Paulo city, 1996 election

|  | Celso Pitta | L. Erundina | Jose Serra | F. Rossi |
|---|---|---|---|---|
| Vote (in million) | 3.2 | 1.9 | 0.8 | 0.4 |
| Total donations (in $ million) | 6.4 | 1.9 | 8.0 | 1.6 |

*Source*: Electoral Tribunal and *Folha de São Paulo*, 21 November 1996.

public construction projects) tend to diversify their support, contributing to the campaign of all contenders that have some chance of success. In connection with this, candidates' positions in the opinion polls during the period of the electoral campaign are very important.

It is worth noting, however, that in spite of the importance of business firms' contributions to candidates' campaigns, this is not a guarantee for electoral success. As shown in the Table 6.2, the candidate that received the second largest sum of money from private contributions ($9.3 million) got only 4 per cent of the vote, while Lula who received $4 million came in second in the presidential race. The same can be said in the case of the 1996 municipal election (Table 6.4). The candidate that spent the large sum of money ($8 million) – José Serra (from the PSDB) – came third in the municipal election, that is, behind Luiza Erundina (PT) who came second, in spite of having spent four times less in her campaign. But the information about the three different elections presented in the tables can also suggest that to be first in the electoral race does require the spending of a substantial sum of money. And it should not be forgotten that the figures shown have the limitation of being based just on the official reports sent in by the candidates to the Electoral Tribunal.

## Conclusion

The debate about the need for improvement in the legislation that regulates party and election funding has been going on for some time. The main issue raised concerns the increase in the influence of powerful economic forces that private donation represents, a problem that became more evident after this method of funding was regulated by law. The proposals for change are mainly in the direction of increasing state funding, which is seen as the only means of preventing candidates, when elected, from being manipulated by major donors, of securing fair competition and, therefore, of improving democracy. An attempt in this direction has already been made by the Senate. In October 1996, its Constitution and Justice Committee approved a bill establishing restrictions to private donations while substantially increasing state funding for elections. This reform initiative was badly received, however. The critics alleged that taxpayers' money should be used for more urgent public needs, suggesting that the reform in electoral financing should be concerned instead with ways of reducing the cost of electoral campaigns as well as increasing the Electoral Tribunal's capacity to control private donations. A final decision on the Senate's bill was not reached, and it is unlikely that the issue will be solved in the near future. The main problem is how to solve the dilemma of having to impose strict limits for private funding in countries like Brazil, where elections are very expensive and state funding is either limited (in the face of scarce resources and giving social policies the priority they deserve) or is not acceptable to public opinion as a way of financing campaigns and parties.

## Notes

I want to thank Ben Schneider and Alan Ware for their suggestive comments on an earlier version of this essay. I would also like to thank Simone Rodrigues da Silva who helped me in the research of newspaper material.

1 After a twenty-one-year period of military-authoritarian regime, Brazil has been under civilian rule since 1985. This twelve years of democratic experience, whose development was not without difficulties, was important enough to make people believe that this time democracy is permanent. This does not mean to say that it has already achieved strong roots. If one looks at the unsettled or provisional state of some components of Brazil's institutional structure, it is difficult to affirm that the system is consolidated. Perhaps as a consequence of the gradual and controlled character of the transition from military-authoritarianism to civilian rule – which would make compromise between the old and new political forces an imperative, and mark the Brazilian experience as a negotiated transition rather than a democratic one – this country has had difficulty in establishing an institutional framework on a more stable basis. In fact, the first step towards liberalization of the political system started when the military government introduced the party reform of 1979, which means that eighteen years have passed since Brazil started a process of political reform and this has not yet been concluded. The

most typical example is the constitutional framework. Established in 1988, it has been under constant revision since then. The same can be said as regards election legislation: almost every election has been preceded by the issuing of specific rules to regulate the process. This has been the case particularly as regards campaign funding. This implies that rules are still in the process of change.

2 The candidate from the PT (the Workers' Party) – Luis Ignácio Lula da Silva – who came second in the presidential race, spent about $4 million.

3 See an interview by the newspaper *Folha de São Paulo* of a campaign treasurer who agreed to talk under the cloak of anonymity. *Folha de São Paulo*, 8 October 1995.

4 After illiterates were enfranchised in 1985, all citizens have had the right to vote: 16 is the minimum age for enfranchisement, and voting is compulsory for electors aged between 18 and 70 years.

5 A senator's term is eight years, but there are elections every four years: alternatively for one-third and for two-thirds of the Senate. Seats in the lower house and in state assemblies are contested every four years The PR system is also used in elections for municipal councillors.

6 Districts' magnitude, which is defined by the number of seats each state is entitled to according to its population, varies considerably in Brazil: from eight to seventy. Fourteen states are entitled to have less than ten seats each, while six states have more than thirty seats. The states of São Paulo (seventy seats), Minas Gerais (fifty-three seats) and Rio de Janeiro (forty-six) have the largest representation in the Federal Chamber.

7 On this see especially L. Epstein, 'Political parties: organisation', in D. Butler *et al.* (eds.), *Democracy at the Polls – A Comparative Study of Competitive National Elections* (Washington, DC, American Enterprise Institute for Public Policy Research, 1981).

8 On the Brazilian party system see M. Kinzo, 'Consolidation of democracy: governability and political parties', in Kinzo (ed.), *Brazil: Challenges of the 1990s* (London, British Academic Press, 1993), and S. Mainwaring, 'Brazil: weak parties, feckless democracy', in S. Mainwaring and T. Scully (eds.), *Building Democratic Institutions – Party Systems in Latin America* (Stanford, Stanford University Press, 1995).

9 On such indices, see R. Taagepera and M. Shugart, *Seats and Votes – The Effects and Determinants of Electoral Systems* (New Haven, Yale University Press, 1989).

10 It is not by chance that when the group's leaders decide to mobilize their members their power is effectively shown. This was the case in April 1995 when the rural parliamentary block was able to defeat the president's veto on the elimination of indexation of bank loans to the sector.

11 In 1986, as a result of that year's election, the number of relevant parties was 2.8 in the Chamber of Deputies. Prior to the 1990 election, this number jumped to 7.2. After that election there were six relevant parties in the Chamber of Deputies. In the period prior to the 1994 elections, the number of relevant parties increased again to 8.6. This index had a slight decrease (8.1) after the 1994 election. This shows that fragmentation occurs mainly in the period between elections – a consequence of both party legislation that facilitates the creation of a political party and the PR system that allows party fragmentation to reproduce itself. On the index of relevant parties, see Taagepera and Shugart, *Seats and Votes*.

12 For example, in the 1996 municipal elections in the state of São Paulo, not less than 84 per cent of the mayors elected had made an alliance with other parties to contest the election; moreover, 31 per cent of them were elected by an alliance made of more than four parties. See M. Kinzo, 'Reforma política descaracterizada', *Estado de São Paulo*, 22 November 1996.

13 See G. Sartori, *Parties and Party Systems – A Framework for Analysis* (Cambridge, Cambridge University Press, 1976).

14 As Mulé points out in her chapter in this volume on the western European cases, party organizations were created for raising funds for election campaigns. In Brazil, in contrast, party organizations were created, in most cases, for complying with the rules established by the election law that require candidates to contest an election only if he or she is affiliated to a political party. Regarding political negotiation, party leaders have had difficulty making backbenchers follow the party line. The negotiation of every term of a proposal is a hard task and all sorts of political resources end up being used and justified as a political imperative.

15 On cadre party see M. Duverger, *Political Parties – Their Organisation and Activity in the Modern State* (London, Methuen, 1955). On catch-all parties see O. Kirchheimer, 'The transformation of the Western European party systems', in J. LaPalombara and M. Weiner (eds.), Political *Parties and Political Development* (Princeton, Princeton University Press, 1966).

16 According to the new party law, established in 1995, this Fund can also be enlarged by donations made by individuals and corporations (juridical persons) who will benefit from tax reduction for this purpose.

17 See the newspaper *Estado de São Paulo*, 4 January 1997.

18 Parties are also granted tax exemption in property, income and services.

19 This is a constitutional requirement that has been in force since 1945. And according to the recently issued party law, a party needs to be organized in at least one-third of the Brazilian states, and have the support of at least 0.5 per cent of the voters distributed over one-third of the states, with 0.1 per cent in each of them.

20 According to a PMDB member, this party broadcast made in 1995 was made possible thanks to a PMDB senator who financed the entire production of the television programme. See M. Kinzo and S. Silva, *PMDB – Partido do Movimento Democrático Brasileiro* (São Paulo, Fundação Konrad-Adenauer, 1996).

21 According to estimations reported by the magazine *Revista Veja*, the cost of this item in the 1996 election campaign for mayor in São Paulo city was about $6 million. See *Revista Veja*, 11 September 1996. An undervalued amount estimated by the same magazine in the 1994 presidential election was about $9.6 million. See *Revista Veja*, 7 September 1994.

22 The impeachment of President Collor in 1992 on charges of corruption was an unprecedented event marked not only by an impressive popular mobilization, but also by the respect shown for the untested constitutional mechanisms needed to remove the head of state and, consequently, by the recognition of the role played by Congress in a representative democracy.

23 As Fleischer points out, political corruption has always been a common practice in Brazil. But Collor de Mello's group not only created new and more effective methods but also went too far. First, the fund raising for his presidential campaign (in 1989) was coordinated and controlled by his treasurer who apparently classified the type and amount of contributions so as to fix the type of reward to be granted to the donors when the new government was inaugurated. Second, after Collor's inauguration (March 1990), PC Farias – the campaign treasurer – continued his fund-raising activities on a different basis: demanding a 40 per cent commission in return for public sector contracts in the Collor de Mello administration. See D. Fleischer, 'Financiamento das campanhas eleitorais', in *12 de Outubro – Revista de Ciência Política*, Fundação Pedroso Horta, Ano 1, no. 2, June 1994.

24 According to the legislation, parties are not allowed to receive contributions, direct or indirect, from trade unions or any other kind of professional associations. Neither are they allowed to receive donations of any kind from government agencies and state firms, nor from any foreign institution or government. This does not mean that the prohibitions are complied with, as the control capacity of the Electoral Tribunal is low. For example, allegations that the Central Union of Workers (which is linked to the PT) has given funds for this party's electoral

campaign are frequently made in the press, but they have never been proved or led to indictments.

25 Paradoxically, the prohibition on paid advertisements on radio and television was established in Brazil in the early 1960s, that is, during the time of the military regime. In fact one of the peculiarities of the Brazilian military regime is that it did not outlaw party politics and did not prevent elections (even though they were held under restricted circumstances and for only less central positions). The electoral code that regulates current election is still the one issued in 1971, the year when paid advertisements on radio and television were prohibited.

26 See newspaper *Jornal da Tarde*, 26 and 30 August 1994 and *Correio Brasiliense*, 27 August 1994.

27 *Revista Veja*, 11 September 1996.

28 'Caixa 2' is the extra-money gained in a transaction in which payment of a service is over-valued so as to provide resources for an extra-budget to be used for purposes other than the one involved in that contract.

# 7

# Party funding in post-communist east-central Europe

PAUL G. LEWIS

A number of major questions arise in the context of studying party funding in contemporary east-central Europe.[1] One concerns the general issue (common to virtually all democracies) of how to get – or just maintain – a political party on the road as a going concern, when the whole concept of a mass party seems to be passing from the scene and the idea of a membership-funded organization is largely a thing of the past.

A second, more fundamental, challenge concerns resistance throughout the region to the idea of a party-based democracy and continuing reluctance among the public as a whole to embrace the idea that party building (and the need to sustain the accompanying costs) is necessarily a good thing. Democratization in east-central Europe was achieved on the one side (and primarily) by elite initiatives and, on the other, by various social movements and different kinds of civic fora, both of which were also often antithetic to the idea of established parties. A general hesistancy with regard to the idea of party overall has thus conditioned the approach taken to the issue of party funding. A third question – again one specific to the region – arises from the legacy of the former communist regime and directs attention, in at least some cases, to the contested inheritance of the resources and property of former communist establishment parties. This has had a major influence on the general view taken of party finances overall.

## Party accounts: the balance-sheet

Information on party funding is patchy and often of dubious accuracy. Nevertheless, for new democracies east-central European party records in this sensitive area are quite helpful. Early

**Table 7.1** Czechoslovakia: party income in 1991 (million crowns)

|                  | CPBM | CM       | CPP | CSP | FP  |
| ---------------- | ---- | -------- | --- | --- | --- |
| Membership dues  | 41   | 0.062    | 2.5 | 0.8 | 0.2 |
| State subsidy    | 9.5  | 14       | 8.5 | 1   | 1.5 |
| Donations        | 49   | 1        | 2   | 9   | –   |
| Party activities | 12.5 | 3        | 3   | 5   | 1.5 |
| Other            | –    | –        | –   | 0.2 | 0.3 |
| **Total**        | **112** | **18 (sic)** | **16** | **16** | **3.5** |

*Source*: V. Mlynář, 'Jak bohaté jsou naše strany', *Respekt* 1992/48, p. 4.
*Notes*: The parties are:
CPBM: Communist Party of Bohemia and Moravia
CM: Civic Movement
CPP: Czechoslovak Peoples' Party
CSP: Czechoslovak Socialist Party
FP: Farmers' Party.
$1 = 31 crowns (mid-1991).

indications of the emerging situation can be derived from Czechoslovak reports (Table 7.1). Well-documented records are also to be found in Hungary, and Table 7.2 presents a summary breakdown of the income of the six parliamentary parties there for 1995. The table provides a general snapshot, although the picture for that year was coloured by the large amount of income derived by the Hungarian Socialist Party (HSP), Fidesz and, particularly, the Hungarian Democratic Forum (HDF) from the sale of special assets – largely property. Nevertheless, a general picture emerges of parties subject to a major degree of financial differentiation and funded to a large extent by the state (as had emerged in some cases in Czechoslovakia during 1991). Significantly though (also following Czechoslovak experience), while the Socialist Party received most state funds, it also received far more than the other parties in the form of membership contributions.

Detailed accounts of only one party elsewhere in the region have been obtained, and they relate to the Polish Labour Union (Table 7.3). The role of state refunds for campaign expenditure is here very clearly evident in a context where parties are not generally funded by the state. State support thus turns out to be a fundamental variable in all countries. But attitudes towards the role of the state more generally have also been highly influential in the region.

**Table 7.2** Hungary: party income in 1995 (million forints)

|  | HDF | HSP | Fidesz | AFD | ISP | CDPP |
|---|---|---|---|---|---|---|
| Membership dues | 9.7 | 19.5 | 0.7 | 3.1 | 4.7 | 4.9 |
| State subsidy | 135.0 | 302.7 | 97.7 | 198.1 | 112.0 | 97.9 |
| Donations | 9.9 | 43.1 | 0.8 | 9.4 | 6.3 | 1.4 |
| Electoral gains | 0.2 | – | – | – | – | – |
| Further income | 854.4[a] | 230.3 | 443.3[b] | 7.6 | 4.6 | 20.0 |
| **Total[c]** | **1,009** | **596** | **543** | **218** | **128** | **124** |

*Source*: *Magyar Közlöny* 1996/34, Budapest.
*Notes*: The parties are:
HDF: Hungarian Democratic Forum
HSP: Hungarian Socialist Party
Fidesz: Alliance of Young Democrats
AFD: Alliance of Free Democrats
ISP: Independent Smallholders' Party
CDPP: Christian Democratic People's Party.
$1 = 122 forints (mid-1995).
[a] Includes single item for 824.5 forints described as 'sale of assets', known to be its headquarters building.
[b] HSP and Fidesz sources also not specified, but in fact also concerned sale of property
[c] Figures are to the nearest whole number.

**Table 7.3** Poland: Labour Union income, 1993–95 (thousand new złoty)

|  | 1993 | 1994 | 1995 |
|---|---|---|---|
| From members and deputies | 5.8 | 35.9 | 52.6 |
| Candidates' contributions/ |  |  |  |
|    state campaign refund | 59.9 | 623.5 | – |
| Donations | 13.4 | 1.7 | 12.2 |
| Bank interest | – | 87.2 | 115.6 |
| **Total** | **79.1** | **748.3** | **180.4** |

*Source*: Official party accounts.
*Note*: $1 = 1.6 new złoty (beginning 1993) and 2.4 new złoty (end 1995).

## Party funding and the state

The communist state was, of course, perceived to be the major agent of political repression and obstacle to democracy in eastern Europe, and particular care was often taken in drafting

legislation to separate new parties from the sources of administrative and economic power that had been a central part of
the political establishment under the former regime. There was
a strong awareness of the way in which communist parties
had been enmeshed with the state apparatus and the extensive
(indeed, virtually unlimited) control they had exercised over
its resources. The amended Hungarian constitution thus decreed
that 'Parties shall not exercise public power directly'. In similar spirit, the law of July 1990 in Poland banned all party
activity from the workplace (cells of the former communist
party had been located in the place of work rather than that
of residence). The extent to which the new parties should be
empowered to involve themselves in economic activity was
also much debated.

But precisely how political forces were to be sustained
during the early phases of democratic transition and how they
survived at all during the initial stage is not at all clear. It was
certainly the case that western foundations and foreign agencies
played a significant role in the process, although the precise
extent of their contribution remains uncertain.[2] This, however,
was a transitional arrangement in any case and something of
a grey area that could hardly provide a framework for party
activity in a more institutionalized post-communist context.
Polish legislation, for example, explicitly forbade financial support from abroad. It was, however, a proscription 'laughably
easy' to get round.[3] State funding – in various guises – in fact
soon became the major support of party life throughout east-
central Europe.

In some ways this trend seems to follow empirical tendencies
recently established in western democracies,[4] as well as reflect-
ing models of contemporary party development like the cartel
party.[5] There are, on the other hand, reasons to doubt whether
such models do shed much light on post-communist developments.[6] Ruud Koole may well be right that the 'ever closer
symbiosis between parties and the state' may have a different
impact and divergent meanings in different situations.[7] The
history of communist dictatorship in particular is likely to
have had a specific influence on party development in those
countries affected.

It is necessary, too, to draw from the outset a clear distinction between the different forms of state subvention at issue.
These include:

1  the state funding of parties *per se*,
2  the reimbursement of election expenses,
3  the provision of salaries, resources and payment of expenses to parliamentary deputies,
4  diverse forms of support for parliamentary groups.

Despite the general importance of state resources for party development in east-central Europe, the precise pattern of state subvention varies considerably. In Poland there is no direct support from the state and analysts can pronounce unambiguously that 'political parties in Poland are not financed by the state budget',[8] although there are certainly other ways in which state funds flow into party coffers.

In Hungary state funds played a large part from the outset and their role in party development soon grew more prominent. The proportion of state financing in party budgets was generally already high in the case of Hungarian parliamentary parties in 1990, ranging from 93 per cent for the Independent Smallholders' Party and 88 per cent for the Christian Democratic People's Party, falling as low as 24 per cent only for the Hungarian Socialist Party, which derived far more than the others from membership fees.[9] The overall balance in the sources of party finance did not change much in subsequent years, with receipts from membership fees actually falling in most cases up to 1994. The flow of state funds, on the other hand, continued to rise by – in the case of the Democratic Forum – a minimum of 46 per cent to as much – for the Socialist Party – as 225 per cent (see also Table 7.2).[10] This reflected the striking success of the Socialists in the 1994 elections, and thus had the result of reducing the role of membership funding even in the HSP.[11]

The electoral victory of the Hungarian Socialists made a considerable difference. For apart from the reimbursement of election campaign expenses, 25 per cent of an annual state allocation is divided equally among the parties represented in Parliament, and the rest divided among all parties on the basis of the proportion of the vote gained in the first round of elections.[12]

A similar system operates in the Czech Republic, under which all parties represented in Parliament receive 0.5 million crowns per year for each seat they have won and those that receive at least 3 per cent of the total vote (that is including parties which do not reach the 5 per cent threshold to enter Parliament) receive 100 thousand crowns for each 0.1 per cent of the total vote gained. So, the role of direct state funding was also significant here. Preliminary calculations suggest, for example, that membership fees contributed 9 per cent of the income of the ruling Civic Democratic Party (CDP) in 1994 contrasting with the 40 per cent drawn from state funds. State transfers to the party were, as in Hungary, rising rapidly – by 7 per cent between 1993 and 1994, but by 62 per cent between 1994 and 1996.[13]

## State reimbursement of election campaign expenses

The direct funding of political parties is not the only way in which the state has underwritten the organizations' expenses. Another important source of support has been the reimbursement of election campaign costs, contributions that were critical not just to helping the parties survive the most expensive activity they were ever likely to be engaged in but also, in most cases, to providing some sort of secure financial base for subsequent party activity. Parties find themselves operating under very different conditions in this respect. The amount spent on the 1993 election campaign in Poland varied considerably across the parties, smaller parties like the Labour Union and Confederation for Independent Poland spending up to less than a sixth of that laid out by a big spender like the Democratic Union.[14]

Differences during the 1996 Czech elections were even greater, with small spenders like the Communist Party (6 million crowns) and Pensioners' Movement (1.5 million crowns) being quite dwarfed by the costs of 140 million crowns incurred by the CDP. State reimbursement, however, more than covered even this level of expenditure by the CDP, and in most cases presented all electorally successful parties with a handsome surplus – the exception here being the Civic Democratic Alliance (CDA). As the CDA entered the campaign with major debts (more than any party but the Social Democrats) this left it even more financially exposed. With its small initial outlay it was in fact the Communist Party that made the largest profit at 56 million crowns.[15] State reimbursement for campaign expenses was in all cases more than twice the sum received by the parties as the direct annual subvention they received from the state.

It is in Poland, however, that the reimbursement of campaign expenses has particular importance due to the general absence of direct state funding for party activity. Unlike the other countries, too, only parties with parliamentary representation receive anything at all which, with the application of a 5 per cent threshold and the use of the d'Hondt system for determining the final apportionment of seats, means that electoral victors are distinctively favoured in terms of both parliamentary representation and financial support.[16]

The victorious Union of the Democratic Left thus recouped nearly twice its electoral outlay, and the Peasant Party – with which it has been in governmental coalition since 1993 – did nearly as well. The Democratic Union (which according to official records spent the most of all parties) did far less well and received only 58 per cent of its outlay, while the Non-Party Bloc for the Support of Reform (the ill-conceived creation of President Wałęsa) got back only 18 per cent. Other significant political forces (mostly on the right wing) did even less well and received nothing at all. More recently, parliamentary legislation proposed that state funds should be spread more widely and that parties that received 2.5 per cent of the vote – even if they did not reach the threshold for entry into parliament – should also be reimbursed.[17]

In sharp distinction to existing Polish practice, the 1989 electoral law in Hungary provided for each party to have its campaign financed in proportion to the number of candidates presented. By early 1997, however, there was already some resistance to underwriting the profligate activities of some candidates, and so proposals emerged to set limits on personal and institutional contributions to campaign funds.[18] In the Czech Republic, while there was a 5 per cent threshold for parliamentary representation, that for the reimbursement of campaign expenses was set at 3 per cent which provided at least some support (in addition to that provided for party activity overall) for the smaller organizations. On this basis, ninety crowns were awarded for each vote cast for the party, giving the Civic Democratic Party $5.8 million and the Civic Democratic Party (the smallest in the 1996 parliament) $1.3 million.

This was considerably more generous than the equivalent provision in Poland. Twenty per cent of the overall electoral budget was allocated there for campaign refunds, which provided 145 million złoty (defined as the equivalent of $7,650) for each deputy elected to the two chambers in 1993.[19] This amounted to a sum of around $1.4 million for the Union of the Democratic Left (dominated by the Social Democracy of the Polish Republic), but only $119 thousand for the Reform Bloc (the smallest party represented in the main legislative chamber).

But such amounts could still play a highly significant part in the budgets of the smaller Polish parties, whose outgoings might be quite modest and where other forms of revenue are very limited. Precise judgements on the make-up of the account sheets of individual Polish parties are nevertheless very difficult to make, as such information (with one notable exception) is closely guarded. One leading Polish analyst acknowledges that, despite legal exhortations, 'the principle of openness does not apply to party finances'.[20] Such transparency was clearly built into the 1990 legislation, but public practice soon showed that it was a complete dead letter.[21]

The balance-sheet of one Polish party has been open to examination, however. Thus it emerges that the reimbursement of 623.5 thousand new złoty that came the way of the Labour Union after the 1993 election represented 83 per cent of the party's entire income in 1994 (see Table 7.3). When debts were paid off the remainder went into the bank, where the resulting interest contributed 64 per cent of the party's (much reduced) income in 1995. This was by far the largest item in party revenue, and represented more than twice the amount contributed both by members' fees and deputies' payments (it would not, of course, be identified as a form of state funding in the accounts, but it is clearly the case that the state is where it came from). Some two hundred thousand złoty of this sum remained in November 1996, and the Union was the only party to admit that it had some funds ready to fight the election due to be held in 1997.[22]

Czech and Hungarian arrangements, apart from providing for regular state funding for a reasonably wide range of parties, were also relatively generous in their system of campaign expenditure reimbursement. But while there were some proposals to set limits on campaign contributions in Hungary, related discussions in Poland were beginning to accept the need for more regular state funding of party activity and support for some of the most important non-parliamentary parties. After a period of some divergence, then, official views on party funding in east-central Europe seemed to be showing some signs of convergence. Direct party funding and the reimbursement of campaign expenses were, however, by no means the only means by which parties could draw on state funds.

### Deputies' salaries and expenses

The salaries and expenses of parliamentary deputies are, of course, quite a different thing from the funding of political parties. But the two are closely linked not only through the fact that deputies often tend to represent their party in the legislature more effectively than they do their constituents (particularly when elected on a party list), but also because some deputies regularly pass on part of their salary to the central party office (the Confederation for Independent Poland was known to be particularly insistent on this practice). In the absence of regular state funding for party activity in Poland, this was one major way in which most leading parties planned to finance their 1997 election campaign.

The salaries quoted in the different sources show some variation, and additional payments for the performance of particular functions and allowances to support specific activities complicate the picture still further. One survey identifies a basic salary for the Polish deputy of $434 per month plus minimum allowances of up to a further $1717; Hungarian deputies were reported to receive a basic $519 plus a further minimum of $130 for expenses.[23] Ágh refers to Hungarian salaries being frozen at the 'very low level' of around $600.[24] Whatever the precise level, it certainly appears that Hungarian expenses and parliamentary allowances were considerably lower than those provided in Poland where, as Table 7.4 suggests, generous funding in this area helped compensate for the absence of direct state funding for party activity.

The allowances and expenses referred to above are minimum amounts and it is clear that a large part of the parliamentary budget in both Poland and Hungary is used to help deputies perform their parliamentary duties both at national and constituency level. Parliamentary directives insist that such monies should not be used to finance party activity, but there is really no way in which any firm distinction can be enforced or even made in effective terms, and there have certainly been strong suspicions of backdoor state financing in Poland where it does not formally exist.[25] The issue of deputies' salaries and their allowances thus shades inevitably and highly ambiguously both into the question of party funding in general and into that of the financing of parliamentary clubs and of the party as parliamentary actor in broader terms. Many of the features noted above, then, are seen differently from another perspective.

## Funding party clubs

The various forms of support – generally from parliamentary budgets and thus from state coffers – given to the different kinds of political, mostly party-based clubs, and further augmented by some of the allowances given to deputies and senators to support their parliamentary activity, can be seen as a form of marginal funding. However, one Polish analyst has taken a different view. Stanisław Gebethner has argued that deputies' allowances are, either in whole or part, used for the needs of a parliamentary club or circle – and thus for purposes specific to a party or other form of political grouping, this depending on the character of the party and its form of behaviour. This was indeed an established procedure, although there was no doubt that it was 'quite illegal' (as another commentator states).[26] The costs of maintaining constituency offices, although at the disposition of the individual deputy, are also directly linked with party membership. Payment of such costs should therefore be seen as a form of *party* funding in its most important and fundamental sphere of activity (according to Gebethner).[27]

On this basis Gebethner calculates the total amount allocated in 1995 to support the activities of parliamentary clubs, circles and their members as well as the sum of deputies' allowances and expenses for running constituency offices. He excludes only the lump sum (*ryczałt*) described as being paid to those who have given up all paid employment to devote themselves to full-time parliamentary work.[28] Even from this perspective, however, the perks enjoyed by Polish deputies in the form of free public transport (by land or air) and the free use of hotel accommodation in Warsaw are left out of the calculation.

Table 7.4 thus presents an estimate of the subsidies provided for all parties represented in the Sejm following such a calculation. Tables 7.5 and 7.6 present the amounts reported for Hungary[29] and the Czech Republic[30] in terms of the levels of

**Table 7.4** Poland: state funding of parliamentary clubs and circles, 1995

| Club or circle | Amount in złoty (million) | Dollar equivalent (million) |
| --- | --- | --- |
| Union of Democratic Left | 9.792 | 3.980 |
| Peasant Party | 7.920 | 3.220 |
| Freedom Union | 3.744 | 1.522 |
| Labour Union | 1.872 | 0.761 |
| Confederation for Independent Poland | 0.768 | 0.312 |
| Non-Party Reform Bloc | 0.720 | 0.293 |

*Source*: After Gebethner (*see* note 16).

**Table 7.5** Hungary: state assistance for parties, 1994/95

| Party | Amount in forints (million) | Dollar equivalent (million) |
| --- | --- | --- |
| Alliance of Free Democrats | 236.070/198.100 | 2.186/1.501 |
| Hungarian Socialist Party | 232.879/302.700 | 2.156/2.293 |
| Hungarian Democratic Forum | 208.769/135.000 | 1.933/1.022 |
| Independent Smallholders' | 132.613/112.000 | 1.228/0.848 |
| Fidesz | 114.737/ 97.716 | 1.062/0.740 |
| Christian Democratic People's Party | 102.767/ 97.900 | 0.951/0.742 |

*Source*: Ágh (*see* note 29).

**Table 7.6** Czech Republic: state funding for parties, 1996

| Party | Amount in crowns (million) | Dollar equivalent (million) |
| --- | --- | --- |
| Civic Democratic Party | 63.7 | 2.275 |
| Social Democratic Party | 56.5 | 2.018 |
| Communist Party | 21.4 | 0.764 |
| Christian Democratic Union | 17.1 | 0.611 |
| Association for the Republic | 17.1 | 0.611 |
| Civic Democratic Alliance | 13.2 | 0.471 |

*Source*: 'Volby '96' (*see* note 13).

state funding for the major parties in those countries, although such totals would in practice be significantly raised by the payment of further subsidies and expenses. Note generally, though, that the better-supported Polish parties get more from this source than parties in other countries do from direct state subsidies *per se*. A mixed picture, therefore, emerges in the Polish context. In terms of the international context and formal dollar equivalents, the Polish deputy earns considerably less than western equivalents, although pay is set at a higher level than in Hungary and Slovakia. In relation to national per capita GDP, though, the Polish deputy is paid more generously than any other, even if this still leaves him or her way behind international leaders in terms of purchasing power like the United States, France and Germany.[31]

Even when diverted to support the party organization, however, this finance is a form of funding that only sporadically trickles down to maintain local party activity, and financial constraints are generally seen as the dominant problem at this level. Membership fees emerge as the major source of Polish local party income, on occasion supplemented by grants from local enterprises or local government agencies. A big difference to party activity is made if a local deputy has an office in the locality which, although clearly illegal if used for general party purposes, can quite definitely be decisive for the success of party activity in a given locality.[32] In terms of party organization and the level of financial and material support received, then, local activity in Poland emerges as highly differentiated. But it was equally clear from one study that branches of the post-communist coalition in power since 1993 were strongly advantaged in this situation and that parties in the post-Solidarity camp and others on the right were considerably less favoured.[33]

Such arrangements can be placed in the context of broader considerations of party development. The Polish pattern of funding seems clearly to flow in the direction of strengthening the 'party in public office' to the emphatic detriment of much serious development of the 'party on the ground', although the party on the ground is in a considerably better situation if its national leadership is also strongly represented in Parliament.[34] With different funding regimes there are signs that the outcome might also vary, in particular that the 'party in central office' also benefits from the particular arrangements that have developed in the Czech Republic.[35] In either case, though, it is the party at national level rather than the local organization that benefits.

Against this background new proposals were made by the Polish Labour Union about party legislation and the regulation of party finances. One suggestion concerned the provision of state funds to all parties receiving 2 per cent or more of the total vote.[36] The view of the parliamentary commission working on the issue seemed to be firming up in favour of state funding for all parties that secured more than 2 or 2.5 per cent of the popular vote, and for disbursements to be made annually rather than immediately after the election.[37]

## Disputations of the communist inheritance

The regime change in east-central Europe was distinctive in that it broadly took the form of a negotiated revolution without a violent or even sharp rupture with the old order. This raised specific questions of continuity in both personal and institutional terms, particularly as they related to the dominant organization of the old regime. For the communist parties that had ruled in east-central Europe pre-1989 were not only dominant political forces and the central pillar of the ruling dictatorship, but had also been major economic powers in their own right. The questions of what properly belonged to the communist party and what to the state, and the extent to which the reformed or reconstituted communist parties should continue to enjoy former assets was recognized as posing major political, constitutional and legal problems at an early stage. They emerged as a highly sensitive area in the process of democratic transition.

The legacy from the communist period certainly played a major part in the survival and resurgence of communist and post-communist forces in the early 1990s, if only in terms of organizational capacity, membership loyalty and established patterns of participation. There was a widely held suspicion, however, that the economic settlement had not just left the communist and successor parties with legitimate financial advantages but that the parties had, in some cases, both benefited unduly from the form the settlement had taken and failed to abide by the legal decisions taken.

Considerable care was taken during the reconstitution of the communist parties in Hungary and Poland to place the new, post-communist parties in as advantageous a financial position as possible. In contrast, the speed of communist collapse in Czechoslovakia took things out of their hands and all major assets were confiscated before the party could take its own measures.[38] Nevertheless, the early procedures appeared to run reasonably smoothly, despite widespread doubts in Poland not just about the fate of 'Moscow gold' but also about continuing control of the post-communists over former assets. These doubts could hardly fail to grow after, first, the electoral victory of the new Polish Social Democrats in 1993 (amplified politically by the way in which parliamentary seats were distributed and economically by the enhanced funding of those dominant in the legislature) and, second, by the defeat of President Lech Wałęsa by a post-communist candidate in 1995. This carried a range of legal and constitutional implications, as well as those of a more directly political character.

Even in the Czech Republic, though, public concern about the financial probity of leading parties and growing reluctance to tolerate the rough and ready procedures that had been taken in the early post-communist years seemed to underline the difficulties increasingly faced by the ruling Civic Democratic Party.[39] Questions were raised about the CDP in terms of payment for dinners with its leader, the prime minister, and the doubtful source of some donations: one supposedly from someone already deceased and another from a Hungarian benefactor who denied the transfer. Potentially more serious were allegations about an attempt by the Civic Democratic Alliance to reschedule its debt on advantageous terms with one of the rather numerous Czech banks that went bust. The accusations of abuse of office by one of the party's members were, however, denied and the affair appeared not to have any lasting consequences.[40]

The Hungarian parliament, too, showed increasing interest during October 1996 about the disposal of property allocated to Fidesz and the Democratic Forum and the possibility of speculative use having been made of it in 1992. Even in the Czech Republic some questions had been raised about the occupation of property by the former communists and Social Democrats, and the old satellite parties certainly benefited from the use made of the property they had inherited. But the Hungarian allegations made something more of an impact as they implied collusion between formal political opponents. A major political crisis also developed in Hungary when it emerged that $5.1 million had passed from the privatization agency into the hands of a private consultant – and were probably intended to be used for party election purposes.[41] The transfer, it appeared, was designed to establish a fund for the 1998 elections to be used by both members of the ruling left wing coalition.[42] Despite official denials, a minister and heads of the state privatization agency were dismissed.

Such conflicts and doubts in Hungary and the Czech Republic formed part of broader processes of political and parliamentary conflict, as well as shifting currents of public opinion. In Poland attention focused more sharply on the economic status of the Social Democracy and its contested legal relationship with the property of the powerful communist ancestor. Questions about the ownership of former communist property were more of a central political issue in Poland, and it was in this context that the main questions about the financial viability of some of the leading parties were posed. While the extent of illegal activity is indeed difficult to ascertain, it is certainly clear that the post-communist party consistently flouted both the spirit and the letter of the decisions taken in 1990 about the expropriation of the former assets.[43]

Although, like many other Polish parties, the Social Democracy was reported to have some debts – a total of 500 million złoty (about $28 thousand)[44] – the party was generally perceived during the period preceding the 1993 election to be quite well off.[45] Apart from inherited property, which remained the subject of some legal dispute, the Social Democracy party was also reported to have inherited 148 milliard złoty from hard currency accounts.[46] At the same time careful observers noted that the murky financial condition of the parties whose status and activities were central to the operation and successful development of the new democracy called for urgent attention. Unless some effective framework for the regulation of party finances was devised it was likely, in the view of one writer, to be a matter of a relatively short time before a scandal on the scale of those recently seen in Italy or Japan erupted.[47]

While various procedures continued in matters concerning the fate of the assets of the former communist party, though, there was relatively little public or political concern shown for the subject. Moreover, the gains made by the victorious Social Democracy from the state purse after the election and the generous provisions for leading parliamentary forces clearly relieved that party of any major worries about previous debts or its current financial situation. New issues came to the fore, however, after the presidential election of November 1995.

The fate of the law on the return of the former Workers' Party property, which was finally passed in November 1990, had already been closely linked with changes in the office of president. Jaruzelski had queried some parts of the original legislation and it had fallen to Wałęsa to put it into force. Following the victory of the Democratic Left in 1993, further amendments to the law were passed by the Sejm after which it then had to submit to the presidential veto. For a period of eighteen months this veto suspended legislation, and it was only after the election of a post-communist president that the amended law came into force.[48] Meanwhile, legal procedures to recover former communist assets had been making slow progress, the main problem then being that the Social Democracy was unwilling or unable to abide by court decisions.[49]

By early 1996 the party was pleading bankruptcy, having lost a number of cases brought by those charged with applying accepted portions of the 1990 legislation on the transfer of the former communist party's property.[50] The government plenipotentiary in Gdańsk, Marek Biernacki, had won seven court cases and established that the Social Democracy was in debt to the State Treasury to the tune of 300 thousand złoty ($118.6 thousand). In these cases (as in others) the party confirmed its inability to pay but continued to practice its normal political (and, indeed, social) activities. Against this background, the plenipotentiary made approaches to the Constitutional Tribunal in the attempt to change the party's statute to enable it to be liquidated in the case of proven bankruptcy. In August he lodged a legal demand for the party's accounts to be opened. The party's leadership eventually acknowledged the extent of its debt, but continued to affirm its inability to pay.

The initiatives of the Gdańsk plenipotentiary were equally blocked by the Justice Minister, and there was still little progress made. In November 1996, however, the efforts of the persistent plenipotentiary were repaid by his powers being removed (the day after a further judgment against the Social Democracy by the Constitutional Tribunal) by the newly installed Social

Democrat provincial governor. Not surprisingly, this provoked an immediate response from the parliamentary opposition, one of whose representatives charged that the Social Democrats were using the power of the state for party interests.[51]

For some time the party had refused to reveal publicly the extent of its debts. They were, however, reported in November 1996 to stand at around 22 million złoty ($8 million). At the same time the sum of 2.4 million złoty was liable for return following the legal judgments in Gdańsk. In the case of a property in Kraków the return of an amount of more than 2 million złoty (at least $962 thousand) was involved. The building had, in fact, been sold for the equivalent of $1 million as far back as 1990.[52] Matters moved inexorably forward in terms of legal procedure, and in February 1997 the Warsaw Regional Court ordered the Social Democracy to disclose its assets.[53]

## Conclusion

Considerable diversity in terms of post-communist development is therefore already evident from the limited information on party funding available in connection with the countries at issue. Poland appears to stand out in terms of its lack of direct funding for political parties and the growing salience of the communist party property issue. While matters concerning such property rights were generally settled at an early stage in Hungary and the Czech Republic (although by no means irrevocably, as later developments were to show), there is growing evidence of the importance of a 'sleaze factor' in these countries as well, albeit in somewhat different areas. Such an atmosphere is hardly conducive to the further development of a civic culture, but it is difficult to conclude that east-central Europe has suffered unduly in this respect. While there is growing evidence that public financing has not been as effective in curbing corruption in established democracies as some had hoped,[54] the recent experience of east-central Europe does not cast any distinct light on the issue.

There is, indeed, no clear evidence that the presence or otherwise of direct state funding has had a significant effect on political developments in the different countries of east-central Europe in any unambiguous sense. The question of whether state funding freezes the existing pattern of parliamentary representation and blocks new entrants must remain open at the present time. Financial conditions were most severe in Poland and there have certainly been suggestions at local level that incumbent power-holders are unduly favoured.

Nevertheless, this did not prevent the formation of the Non-Party Bloc for the Support of Reform in 1993 and its subsequent representation in parliament (admittedly under the aegis of President Wałęsa). The failure of all mainstream right wing forces was equally striking, but this was hardly primarily (and possibly not even significantly) linked with funding conditions. The 5 per cent electoral threshold and tendency to internal conflict and fragmentation on the Polish right were certainly no less significant. Similarly, while state funding in east-central Europe might encourage various forms of elitism (either parliamentary or that based on the party leadership), it is likely to be the case that a generous (and, in all probability, very weakly controlled) system of parliamentary allowances strengthens this tendency even more.

The differences between the three east-central European countries studied may not be as great as variations in the funding regimes might suggest. They certainly stand in considerable contrast to Russia as a further case of post-communist development where, as Vladimir Gel'man suggests elsewhere in this volume, a more explicitly privately-funded form of party development has been chosen. From this perspective the east-central Europe/Russia contrast seems to shadow that of the different forms of political finance seen in the United States and western Europe, with the apparent emergence of a generic, broadly public funded form of party activity in Europe and a tendency to favour private finance in both the (former or actual) superpowers. It does not seem to stretch the correspondence too far to suggest that the distinctive political cultures of North America as 'campaign and candidate oriented'[55] are also reflected in contemporary Russia – at least in this particular sense.

The party systems of east-central Europe have therefore developed rapidly and acquired apparent stability in relatively few years. The nature of the parties that have emerged, their relation with the post-communist state and the kind of democracy they promise to support will, however, remain the object of interest for some period of time. Further study of the way they are funded will be a central part of this investigation.

# Notes

1 Several people have helped in providing information and guidance in this relatively unexplored area. Among them the author would particularly like to acknowledge the assistance of A. Ágh, Z. Enyedi, S. Gebethner, R. Gortat, P. Kopecký, T. Kostelecký, M. van den Muyzenberg and G. Wightman.

2 G. Pridham, 'Transnational party links and transition to democracy: Eastern Europe in comparative perspective', in P. G. Lewis (ed.), *Party Structure and Organization in East-Central Europe* (Cheltenham, Edward Elgar, 1996), pp. 201–3.

3 M. Chmaj and M. Żmigrodzki, *Status prawny partii politycznych w Polsce* (Toruń, Wydawnictwo Adam Marszałek, 1995), p. 61.

4 H. E. Alexander (ed.), *Comparative Political Finance in the 1980s* (Cambridge, Cambridge University Press, 1988), pp. 12–13; J. Mendilow, 'Public party funding and party transformation in multi-party systems', *Comparative Political Studies*, 25 (1992), 90.

5 R. S. Katz and P. Mair, 'Changing models of party organization and party democracy: the emergence of the cartel party', *Party Politics*, 1 (1995), 15–16.

6 Lewis, *Party Structure*, pp. 13–14.

7 'Cadre, catch-all or cartel? A comment on the notion of the cartel party', *Party Politics*, 2 (1996), 520.

8 S. Gebethner and R. Gortat, 'Pan-European cooperation between political parties: the Polish case', paper delivered to a conference on *European Dialogues* in Brussels (1995), p. 3.

9 A. Ágh, 'Partial consolidation of the east-central European parties', in *Party Politics*, 1 (1995), 511.

10 The accounts for three parties in 1995 were strongly coloured by a large inflow of 'unspecified income', mostly the one-off sale of property. Where such flows were not evident, like the AFD, the state subsidy continued to provide as much as 91 per cent of party income. While this was, indeed, a strikingly high figure, state funding to the tune of 83 per cent or more has also been noted in the case of some German and Italian parties. See K.-H. Nassmacher, 'Structure and impact of public subsidies to political parties in Europe', in Alexander, *Comparative Political Finance*, pp. 252–4. Overall, half the annual budget for national party organizations in Austria, Germany, Italy and Sweden came from state funds. See K.-H. Nassmacher, 'Comparing party and campaign finance in western democracies', in A. B. Gunlicks (ed.), *Campaign and Party Finance in North America and Western Europe* (Boulder, CO, Westview, 1993), p. 256.

11 A. Ágh, 'The end of the beginning: the partial consolidation of east central European parties and party systems', *Budapest Papers on Democratic Transition*, 156 (1996), pp. 26–8.

12 A. van der Meer-Krok-Paszkowska and M. van den Muyzenberg, 'Orientation to the state? Parliamentary parties in Hungary and Poland and their relations with party in central office', paper delivered to a conference on *The New Democratic Parliaments* in Ljubljana (1996), p. 6.

13 1996 figures on the basis of recent elections from supplement 'Volby '96' to *MF DNES*, 11 June 1996.

14 For details see P. G. Lewis and R. Gortat, 'Models of party development and questions of state dependence in Poland', *Party Politics*, 1 (1995), 606.

15 *OMRI Daily Digest*, 2 January 1997.

16 S. Gebethner, 'Problemy finansowania partii politycznych a system wyborczy w Polsce w latach 90', in F. Ryszka (chief ed.), *Historia – Idee – Polityka* (Warsaw, Scholar, 1995), p. 431.

17 'Pieniądze dla małych partii', *Rzeczpospolita*, 6 March 1997.

18 *OMRI Daily Digest*, 13 February 1997.

19 Meer-Krok-Paszkowska and van der Muyzenberg, '*Orientation*'.

20 Gebethner, 'Problemy', p. 425.
21 P. Winczorek in *Rzeczpospolita*, 21–22 August 1993.
22 'Stan kas partyjnych', *Rzeczpospolita*, 21 November 1996.
23 A. van der Meer-Krok-Paszkowska and M. van den Muyzenberg, 'The position of parties in the Polish and Hungarian parliaments', paper delivered to a conference on *Transformation Processes in Eastern Europe* in The Hague (1996), Appendix: Table 1.
24 Ágh, 'Partial consolidation', 504.
25 Meer-Krok-Paszkowska and Muyzenberg, 'The position of parties', p. 8.
26 K. Groblewski in *Rzeczpospolita*, 1 February 1995.
27 Gebethner, 'Problemy', p. 433.
28 Although the *ryczałt* is generally described elsewhere as a form of basic expenses.
29 Ágh, 'End of the beginning', pp. 26–8, *Magyar Közlöny* 1996/34.
30 'Volby '96', p. 26.
31 'Zarobki parlamentarzystów w różnych krajach', *Rzeczpospolita*, 7 February 1997.
32 K. Siellawa-Kolbowska, 'Partie polityczne w terenie', conference paper, Warsaw (1996), pp. 11–12.
33 K. Pankowski, 'Polityka i partie polityczne w oczach działaczy partyjnych szczebla lokalnego', conference paper, Warsaw (1996), pp. 6–7.
34 P. Mair, 'Party organizations: from civil society to the state', in R. S. Katz and P. Mair (eds.), *How Parties Organize* (London, Sage, 1994), pp. 3–4.
35 P. Kopecký, 'Parties in the Czech parliament', in Lewis, *Party Structure*, 1996, p. 75.
36 'Jawność finansów partii, posłow i urzędników', *Rzeczpospolita*, 22 February 1996. Fuller details of the parliamentary proposals were contained in 'Partie dotowane z budżetu', *Rzeczpospolita*, 28 February 1996; and 'Między zasadami a wolnością', *Rzeczpospolita*, 1 March 1996. A further account of the parliamentary discussion appeared in 'Partyjne pieniądze', *Słowo Ludu*, 15 March 1996, a special report also appeared as 'Raport Polityki', *Polityka*, 30 March 1996.
37 'Państwo powinno dotować partie', *Rzeczpospolita*, 9 January 1997; 'Pieniądze dla małych partii', *Rzeczpospolita*, 6 March 1997.
38 S. L. Wolchik, *Czechoslovakia in Transition* (London, Pinter, 1991), pp. 85–6.
39 *The Prague Post*, 26 June 1996.
40 *Lidové noviny*, 21 December 1994.
41 Z. Szilagyi, 'Privatization scandal threatens coalition's future', *Transition*, 2 (1996), pp. 46–7.
42 *OMRI Daily Digest*, 11 February 1997.
43 Gebethner, 'Problemy', pp. 429–30. Unlike the assets of the PUWP, those of former Peasant Party were not nationalized and remained under the control of the successor PSL. Its relations with the Agricultural Bank have nevertheless been the object of investigation for some years, and a recent judgment of the Administrative Court has confirmed that its claim to the party headquarters is not valid. 'Siedziba PSL własnością gminy', *Rzeczpospolita*, 28 November 1996.
44 M. Janicki in *Polityka*, 6 February 1993.
45 K. Olszewski in *Rzeczpospolita*, 28 July 1993.
46 *Wprost*, 24 March 1996.
47 P. Winczorek in *Rzeczpospolita*, 21–22 August 1993.
48 'Los partyjnej własności', *Rzeczpospolita*, 7 November 1996. See also *Rzeczpospolita*, 9–10 March 1996.
49 A judgment of the Supreme Court further confirmed the legal liability of the party in early 1996. See *Rzeczpospolita*, 26 April 1996, 21 May 1996.
50 There was considerable resentment throughout the party organization about the way it was being treated. See *Dziennik Zachodny*, 10 March 1996.
51 'Powołac Komisje Etyki Poselskiej', *Rzeczpospolita*, 14 March 1996; 'Dwugłos o długach SdRP', *Rzeczpospolita*, 8 November 1996.

52  Eryk Mistewicz in *Wprost*, 24 March 1996.
53  'SdRP ma ujawnić majątek', *Rzeczpospolita*, 21 February 1997.
54  H. E. Alexander and R. Shiratori (eds.), *Comparative Political Finance Among the Democracies* (Boulder, CO, Westview, 1994), p. 3.
55  Nassmacher, 'Comparing party and campaign finance', p. 262.

# 8

# The iceberg of Russian political finance

VLADIMIR GEL'MAN

On 19 June 1996, just three days after the first round of the Russian presidential elections and only two weeks before the run-off between Russian President Boris Yeltsin and his Communist rival Gennadii Zyuganov, the President's security service arrested two men at the exit gate of the Russian White House. Those arrested, Arkadii Yevstafiev (an assistant to Anatolii Chubais, one of the key figures in Yeltsin's election campaign) and Sergei Lisovskii (who was in showbusiness but who also played an important role in Yeltsin's campaign), were carrying a Xerox-paper box containing $538,000 in cash; the money was to be used as payments to pop stars involved in pro-Yeltsin propaganda. According to their account, Yevstafiev and Lisovskii had been handed the box by Boris Lavrov, a commercial bank officer, who, in turn, had received the money personally from the Russian Deputy Minister of Finance. Yevstafiev and Lisovskii were released the following morning. However, the consequences of their arrest were far more far-reaching than those of a normal criminal incident. On 20 June Yeltsin signed decrees for the resignations of Alexander Korzhakov (his Security Service chief), Mikhail Barsukov (the Director of the Federal Security Service) and Oleg Soskovets (a First Deputy Prime Minister); the former two were among Yelstin's closest allies.[1] Then, following his victory in the run-off election, Yeltsin assigned Chubais as his Chief of Staff.

But what of the $538,000 in the box? In his public speeches Chubais referred to a 'provocation' by Korzhakov, allegedly aimed at disrupting the run-off election, and Chubais denied that there had been any intention of using that money for campaign purposes. However, almost five months later a popular newspaper, *Moskovskii Komsomolets*, published what it claimed to be the transcript of a meeting in June between Chubais, Viktor Ilyushin, a senior presidential aide, and one more person, still unknown, in which ways to cover up the use of the money in the campaign were discussed. This alleged meeting took place after the arrest of Lisovskii and Yevstafiev; in what is alleged to be its transcript Ilyushin was quoted as saying that he had told President Yeltsin they could catch fifteen to twenty men leaving the President Hotel (Yeltsin's campaign headquarters) with sports bags full of cash.[2] Since both Chubais and Ilyushin deny that this conversation ever took place, it is hard to be sure that Ilyushin was the man at the alleged meeting. But whoever that man was, he was absolutely correct in the main point he made: men with such sports bags could be caught near all candidates' campaign headquarters – during campaigns almost every party and almost every candidate running for office in Russia used extra-legal (though not always illegal) payments of cash of, to put it mildly, either doubtful origin, or so-called 'black cash' (chernyi nal).[3]

Thus, the incident involving the cash in the Xerox-paper box was not an isolated incident in Russian political life. Even Communist rivals of Yeltsin's used similar methods in their campaigns; although one hard-line Communist, Viktor Ilyukhin, the Chairman of Duma Committee for Security, touched upon this topic in a press conference, that was his own private initiative. Before the run-off election all the media, except for *Obshchaya gazeta*, a moderate opposition newspaper, remained silent on the issue and almost all politicians followed suit.

What does this story suggest about Russian political finance and Russian politics more generally? Does money play the central role in campaigning and in day-to-day political affairs? What legal and political controls over political finance, if any, have been created so far, and how do they function? Last, but certainly not least, can the outcomes of elections and other aspects of Russian politics be bought? An attempt will be made in this chapter to answer these questions.

## The institutional framework and the resources of the political game

Anyone who tries to analyse Russian (or post-Soviet) politics, is faced first with the problem of understanding the relevant institutions. The constitutional framework might be thought to be based on western models, because it includes institutions such as a presidency and a Constitutional Court that are borrowed from the experience of democratic (or, in Russian slang, 'civilised') countries. However, the functioning of these institutions often has little in common with the western prototypes. For instance, the absence of censors does not yet mean there is complete freedom of speech; again, although there may be competitive elections, the regimes are not always truly democratic – the Lukashenka regime in Belarus being the clearest example of this. This general point can also be made with respect to specific aspects of electoral and party politics. For example, the electoral law in Russia would seem in principle to conform with several liberal principles, such as judicial defence of electoral rights or the banning of the use by civil servants of their official status for the purpose of campaigning. While these objectives were laudable, they did not work in practice because the penalties for violations provided for in the law were of a purely symbolic kind.

Because of this, applying to post-Soviet politics notions such as 'democratic consolidation'[4] or 'post-communist authoritarianism'[5] should be undertaken with caution. When anaysing the emerging political regime in Russia, models of a 'halfway house', like delegative democracy',[6] seem to be more helpful in trying to understand political affairs in Russia.[7] On the one hand, elections under the communist regime could be described as neither free nor fair. That is, there was neither free competition between parties and candidates, nor fair access to the means of campaigning, nor, indeed, equal legal guarantees for electoral contestants. On the other hand, the ideal of liberal democracy is free and fair elections: a fully competitive contest between parties and candidates for the voters' support, with equal opportunities for all contestants. If elections under communism and those in an ideal liberal democracy represent the two ends of a continuum, then the practices of post-Soviet transitional regimes are far from either end. Russian elections may be described as free but not fair. They are free with respect to the level of competition; after December 1993 no single influential party or candidate at the national level could be stopped from participating in elections. Consequently, moves by the Central Electoral Commission (CEC) aimed at barring two opposition parties – Yabloko and Derzhava – during the 1995 parliamentary elections were halted by a decision of the Supreme Court.[8] But not all of the post-communist electoral process in Russia may be recognized as fair, since the competitors do not enjoy equal access to resources.[9]

Similar points can be made when considering aspects of party organization. The Soviet Union was a one-party state, while the ideal of liberal democracy is that of a multi-party system with organized parties competing for public offices. But what is 'a party' in post-communist Russia? Could the forty-three so-called 'electoral associations' that competed in the 1995 parliamentary elections be regarded as parties? Certainly, some of them were real political organizations based on popular leadership (such as the Liberal Democrats led by Vladimir Zhirinovskii, or Yabloko led by Grigorii Yavlinskii); some had an ideological label (like, the free-market-liberal Democratic Choice of Russia (DCR), led by Yegor Gaidar, or the hard-line Communists Working Russia for the Soviet Union, led by Viktor Anpilov). However, when using some kind of organizational definition of a political party,[10] only the Communist Party of the Russian Federation (CPRF), which claims to be the heir of the banned Communist Party of the Soviet Union, could be taken for a party. With the exception of the CPRF, Russian parties are not yet 'fully-fledged parties' on the local and regional levels as far as organizational development is concerned.[11]

At the same time, decision-making processes in Russian politics (including decision-making within the parties) is based mostly on patron–client relationships.[12] This has no legal recognition, but it is important – an example being the so-called 'party of power' which includes officials of the executive branch of the government and their allies.[13] Since 1991 there have been several attempts in Russia to institutionalize this quasi-party but none have been fully successful. 'The party of power' phenomenon is based partly on the use of informal networks in the making of political-decisions. This defines their mobilization strategy which could be understood as administrative mobilization. Administrative mobilization, which is especially effective in small towns and rural areas, includes the use of state or municipal resources for the purposes of executive officials and their allies, but sometimes, especially in ethnic republics, it looks more like some kind of informal contract of mutual loyalty between the elite and civil society.[14]

As far as ideology is concerned, the Russian party system is highly developed and embraces a vast spectrum – from libertarians to hard-line Stalinists.[15] With respect to organization, however, the Russian party system is underdeveloped. Operating in a 'delegative democracy' regime, where the government is not accountable to the parliament – either at national or subnational levels – and without responsibility on the part of parties for the governmental agenda, it can be argued that the party system may be 'frozen' in its present form and may continue without much variation for many years.[16]

Sometimes the 'halfway house' state of party politics, as well as the political system as a whole, is understood as a temporary or 'unclear' stage of the transitional period. However, the argument being made here is that it may not necessarily be a phase of development of a standard model during a 'transition to democracy'.[17] Even at the micro level, such as in the case of political finance, much may remain unchanged. As the Russian political experience shows clearly, informal mechanisms of political practices have become embedded and they survive – at least in the form they have taken since 1993. An analysis of the structures of political parties, as well as electoral campaigning, does not reveal any tendency towards a transition to democracy, but, instead, there seems to be a stable form of politics with its own, written and unwritten, rules of the game, and with no tendency towards permanent change.

So what kind of strategies are deployed and resources used by parties and/or individual politicians in their competitive game, either during their day-to-day work or in seeking support during elections? There is no single model. Some, like the 'party of power', are using institutional resources. Others, like Zhirinovskii, for instance, are exploiting personal charisma. Still others, mainly communists, rely partly on their membership and partly on financial resources. However, as is shown below, the use of financial resources is usually ineffective unless it is combined with other resources which, in their turn, cannot be used effectively in the absence of money. If the former seems to be like eating salt without food, the latter is like eating food without salt.

1 *Power resources, direct and indirect.* The advantages of incumbency (or being backed by incumbents) seems to be the most valuable resource. Incumbents, or incumbent-backed

candidates, have the use of additional resources, from the support of the press (and free, indirect, 'advertising' in the media) to the use of civil servants in their own campaigns. The official support of a powerful official (from a governor to the President) is also very helpful in raising money for campaigning and the everyday needs of parties and politicians.

2 *Personality resources.* Some popular political figures rely on the sheer popularity of their names to start their campaigning without sufficient funds. For instance, the former Russian Vice-President, Alexander Rutskoi, who was born in Kursk, paid very little for the campaign he conducted there prior to the regional gubernatorial elections in October, 1996. Moreover, his campaign started just two days before the elections after Rutskoi had won a legal suit in the Supreme Court which allowed him to register as a candidate. Nevertheless, Rutskoi was supported by 78 per cent of voters. Some other charismatic leaders, quite popular in their constituencies, have also used personal popularity as the main resource in the political struggle.

Vladimir Zhirinovskii, the leader of the Liberal Democratic Party of Russia (LDPR), found another way to use personality resources. During the 1993 parliamentary elections he, as the party leader, used almost all the state-granted money to pay for air time when making more than twenty speeches on television. These speeches, aggressive but skilful, appealed to different social groups and were full of all kinds of promises (for instance, he promised a man to every woman).[18] However, the case of Zhirinovskii, who is such a good television campaigner, is somewhat exceptional in Russian politics.

3 *Cadres.* The myths of the 'gold of the Communist Party' must be ignored; Russian left wingers and their candidates (especially the CPRF) do not have 'big money' either for campaigning or for everyday needs. However, these parties are not poor either, and, especially before the 1996 presidential elections, they were busy establishing links with representatives of various sectors of Russian business.[19] But the main resource of the CPRF and its allies still lies in the significant number of local activists; they are well organized in local units based on old communist networks. (According to CPRF data, in January 1995 the number of party members was close to 500,000 which is more than the combined membership of all other Russian parties.) This resource provides

opportunities for campaigning in different regions of the country, especially in rural areas. As the CPRF representatives noted themselves, they are using cadre resources for large-scale 'door-to-door' campaigning which, it seems, is more effective for their purposes than expensive advertising on a huge scale.[20]

4 *Financial resources.* 'Big money' as a single resource works badly in Russian politics. The candidacies in elections in the period between 1993 and 1996 of so-called 'New Russians' and 'traditional' business people were common, but also a failure in most cases. Vladimir Bryntsalov, the owner of the largest Russian pharmaceutical company, found himself in last place behind eleven other candidates in the 1996 presidential election. Vladimir Groshev, the Chairman of the board of one of the larger Russian banks, 'Inkombank', failed in the 1995 parliamentary election in a single-member district in Ryazanskaya oblast, despite the fact that his expenditures came to more than $200,000 (according to unofficial sources). The attempts of some 'New Russians' to create their own parties or 'blocks' were also unsuccessful. In 1993 the Party of Economic Freedom, led by Konstantin Borovoi, a self-proclaimed 'party of big business', was unable even to collect the 100,000 voter signatures of voters needed by a party in registering for the election. In fact, the 'New Russian' style of campaigning – including huge billboards, massive and expensive TV advertising, and a 'shocking' manner of delivering speeches – played a role in this failure: most Russian voters with their low standard of living, facing delays in the payment of wages and so on, instinctively disliked candidates who evidently had 'big money' backing their campaigns.

However, financial resources are necessary for both campaigning and everyday party needs. Money, if used in addition to power, personality and cadre resources, can be effective in Russian politics. However, both the amounts and sources of the money used in politics remain somewhat mysterious.

## The iceberg of political finance: the above-water and under-water elements

The electoral practices of the late-Soviet period give us clear examples of unfair campaigning. All the electoral costs were state-financed. The later amendments of the Constitution provided for the creation of a special 'common' electoral fund for the making of donations by individuals and companies. These donations were supposed to be distributed equally among all candidates. The same principle supposedly also guided access for all candidates to the media and to other means of campaigning.[21] However, the system proved unworkable. No one was committed to the idea of equal resources, and in many respects it also proved technically impossible to implement; for instance, it was supposed to provide for an equal number of public speeches by all candidates, and that was just not possible. At the same time, the state-owned resources (television, newspapers, other means of public address, and so on) were used to the advantage of those candidates supported by the Communist Party and their allies.[22] Their opponents, newly emerging political associations, had to resort to the use of illegal means of campaigning, using resources provided by the emerging private businesses and even some of the state-owned companies.[23] Although electoral commissions had the right to revoke the registrations of candidates who violated electoral law, legal sanctions during campaigning periods were not actually used because, as a legal analyst noted, events were moving too quickly for that to happen.[24] In the post-communist period, there was only a partial change in the situation: private funding was permitted, and the widely-proclaimed equal-access principle was abolished. Still, workable legal sanctions were never devised, nor did the use of state-owned resources for the benefit of incumbents disappear.

While institutional design, including electoral law, in the post-communist east European countries, was the result of national bargaining,[25] neither Russia's electoral system nor its constitutional arrangements were the result of any kind of round-table agreement; the same was also true with the decision on a constitutional assembly. Initially, it was the choice of a relatively narrow circle of free-market-liberal-orientated politicians and lawyers led by Dr Viktor Sheinis, a deputy of the Supreme Soviet of the Russian Federation. In the spring of 1993 this group drafted an electoral law which then was discussed by Russian politicians and experts.[26] However, almost all their comments concentrated on the electoral formula or on matters other than those of party finances. Moreover, according to one scholar, even the opponents of the reforms came up with no critique of the initial proposal.[27] Almost the entire draft was included in the set of electoral rules approved by Yeltsin's decree after the disbanding of the parliament in September 1993.[28]

The core of the reform of political finance was based on the principle of special 'electoral funds' to be used for the purposes of campaigning. According to Sheinis (in an interview given to the author in August 1994), he had borrowed this idea from the experience of political action committees in the United States. However, while in the United States such committees served as special organizations for campaigning, the electoral funds, according to the Russian law, were just bank accounts opened for donations. The sources of financing in Russia would vary between equal opportunity public funding approved by electoral commissions, donations from individuals and organizations, and the spending of candidates' own money or money from party funds. Donations from foreign nations and organizations, international institutions, state or local government institutions, military units, religious or charitable organizations, and companies whose capital contained more than a certain proportion of foreign capital were prohibited. (The latest rules have limited the permitted share of foreign capital in a donating company to 30 per cent of the total capital.) The maximum permitted size of funds was limited, by being tied to the kind of election involved and linked to the current level of minimum wage. For example, during the 1995 elections the maximum amount a party (or 'electoral association' in Russian legal terms) could spend during any one campaign was 10.9 billion roubles (about $2.4 million) and spending by a candidate in a single-member district was limited to 437 million roubles ($95,000). Individuals could make donations of up to $188 to a single-member district candidate and $282 to an 'electoral association', while companies could donate as much as $1,880 and $18,800 respectively. By contrast, the public funding component of each party's funds came to just $25,500. So private funding was now the main source of campaign finances.

The regulations concerning the use of the media were based on a similar principle. The law provided for the right of each candidate or party to an equal number of speeches published free of charge. The electoral law and regulations issued by the Central Electoral Commission (CEC) applied only to the coverage provided by the so-called 'state' media, that is newspapers, television and radio stations either established, owned or sponsored by the state or municipal authorities, or financed from their budgets, or having some tax privileges.[29] This meant that the majority of TV and radio stations as well as some regional and local newspapers had to provide equal opportunities to all candidates and/or parties for pre-election campaigning. Indeed, candidates and parties did receive equally divided free newspaper space and air time. For instance, prior to the 1995 Duma elections each party was given thirty minutes of free air time on each of the nationwide television and radio stations. Additionally, they had the right to purchase more space or time, but the regulations required that the amount of purchased newspaper space or air time could not exceed the amount provided free. However, the cost of air time is high. During the presidential campaign in 1996 the price of a one-minute prime-time slot on the nationwide channels was $30,000. The distribution of air time and newspaper space (free or paid for) by state-owned or sponsored media was done by lot. As for non-state-owned media, the law remains silent as far as campaigning is concerned. The same is also true for editorial coverage of campaigns in state-owned media.

In making their initial proposals the reformers were informed by both their ideological preferences and their office-seeking interests. The ideological preferences were based on anti-state attitudes on the one hand, and on an overestimation of the virtues of entrepreneurship and private property, on the other. Their doctrine is based on the idea of a minimal state,[30] and the reformers rejected the idea of increasing the level of public financing for election campaigns and public financing of political parties in general. (The draft of the law on political parties, which included such a proposal, failed to pass in the parliament in 1994 and later was rewritten without any mention of public political financing. Eventually it passed in the lower chamber but was rejected by the upper chamber.) As Dr Sheinis said in an interview to the author in 1994: 'It is not quite so bad that some rich people buy votes and come to power. It is the state-owned redistribution that does the most harm to Russian democracy.'

Similar views are held by the leader of DCR, former Prime Minister Yegor Gaidar, who defined the social basis of his party as 'intelligentsia and entrepreneurs',[31] while one prominent DCR Duma deputy argued that the party' would become the medium of interests of large capital'. Alexey Ulyukaev, an ally of Gaidar's and the leader of the Moscow branch of the DCR, says that the branches of a party should be established as commercial structures for the sake of financial independence and the strengthening of the party's social basis.[32] In practice, this can lead to criminal activity by local DCR activists. For instance, for six months the DCR party structure was headed by Oleg Boiko, a businessman who owned a company that turned out to be a pyramid-type scam. (Despite the fact that Sheinis has long been a member of social-liberal Duma faction, Yabloko, his attitudes and political practices are closer to those of the DCR.)

However, one reason above all other for 'institutional design'[33] taking this particular form is the reformers' own interests in running for public office. While reformers are in favour of supporting private business, they are also involved in taking control of state-owned resources, including, in 1993, television. Democratic Russia (whose successor in the 1993 elections was the Russia's Choice block and, later still, the DCR) used both of these resources in their campaigning.[34] The rules crafted for Russia's Choice (as well as for other kinds of 'parties of power') facilitated various practices in relation to large-scale advertising (television clips, billboards, colour posters, direct mail, and so on) and 'grey' propaganda – that is, indirect advertising and comments on television and other state-owned media, and the use of official status and privileges for electioneering.[35]

Generally speaking, all electoral procedures were constructed on this sort of basis. For instance, the nomination of a candidate (or a party list) is controlled through the collection of voters' signatures necessary for the registration (a minimum of 1 per cent of all voters in a single-member district, or 100,000 signatures for a national list). Supposedly, to be able to register a party needs to demonstrate at least a minimal level of popular support for its candidates. In reality, two other ways of signature collection were developed. The first, or 'industrial', method involves coercion applied to signatories at state institutions, enterprises, army and police barracks, universities and so on. The second method was a simple purchasing of signatures (during the 1993 campaign a signature could be purchased for between 100 and 500 roubles ($0.05 to $0.25)).[36] As a result the system of political finance created by the more liberal reformers can be likened to an iceberg: there is the visible ('above-water') portion of it consisting of electoral funds used for the purchasing of air time on TV and radio. According to various sources this portion of political finance constitutes between 5 and 10 per cent of total expenditures in a campaign[37] and does not even come close to covering day-to-day party expenses. Anyone analysing the official data on campaign finances (that is, the amount donated by companies or individuals, the breakdown of party expenditures, and so on), provided by the financial department of the CEC (Vybory deputatov, 1996), will see only the 'above-water' portion of the iceberg. This data gives no indication at all as to the resources forming the 'under-water' part of it.

Some techniques used in the area of hidden political finance have been described by two Russian political journalists, Elena Dikun and Lev Sigal.[38] Ironically, their article was published the very day that the two Yeltsin campaigners were arrested while carrying $538,000 in the Xerox-paper box. A number of ways of raising and spending money have been identified by Dikun and Sigal, and by other investigators as well, and some of the techniques used in the 'hidden' component of Russian political funding are indicated below.

1 *Direct payments in 'black cash'.* This method is never used when paying for the means of propaganda (such as air time), but is used mainly to cover other costs such as the salaries of campaign employees, the services of observers at polling stations, security guards, current office expenses, payments during signature collections, and, most of all, payoffs for 'grey propaganda'; these are payments to journalists who show a party's candidates in a favourable light (or the opponents in an unfavourable light) and to popular actors, singers, sports personalities and other popular figures who support publicly the candidate or party in question.[39] Then again, there are lottery sales, charitable acts in the name of the candidate or party, among other techniques.

2 *Concealment of payments from 'black cash'.* With this method some services, such as the making of posters and television clips containing pre-electoral promises such as the lowering of prices, are nominally paid for out of electoral funds, but this is a facade because the payments are actually made using 'black cash'.

3 *Payments for state-controlled services bypassing official electoral funds.* Some banks and other companies either receive tax concessions or incur no penalties for tax underpayment

in exchange for covering expenses in the election campaign of an incumbent candidate. At the same time, such companies often make simultaneous donations to the campaigns of opposing candidates as a form of insurance in case of political change. This kind of game can be dangerous. After the 1996 presidential elections one large and well-known Russian bank, Tveruniversalbank, which had close ties with the Communists – the former Soviet Prime Minister Nikolai Ryzhkov headed its board of directors – went bankrupt. This was a punishment from the 'Party of Power' for its contributions to the 'wrong' candidate. There were also rumours about the imminent bankruptcy of another bank, Inkombank, which supported Alexander Lebed. However, Inkombank, the fifth largest bank in Russia, still remains in business.

4 *The selling of key positions in the parties.* During the 1995 parliamentary elections the seventh candidate on the LDPR party list was Mikhail Gutseriev, a businessman from the Ingush Republic (a Russian region on the Chechen border), who had, among others, sponsored 'invisible payments' to the party's campaign but who had never been a member of the party. After the elections, Gutseriev was nominated as a Deputy Chairman of the State Duma by the LDPR as a reward for his support. The same picture unfolds when looking at Yabloko, where, at the same elections, the number 8 position on the party list was held by Mikhail Yur'ev, an entrepreneur who also had never been known to be a member of the party. He had hardly any political experience at all but he too was nominated as a Deputy Chairman of Duma. The same practice has been observed in some regional and local elections (St Petersburg, Sverdlovskaya oblast).

However, the 1993 campaign clearly shows that the connection between the level of resources available and electoral successes is not always a straightforward one.[40] For example, even according to the official data, the most expensive campaign (that of Russia's Choice) cost the party 183 times as much as the total costs of the CPRF campaign, while the number of seats they obtained came only to 25 per cent of the total (forty as against the thirty-two won by the CPRF). Although there is only incomplete data on the financing of campaigns in sub-national elections, particular examples from that level of election show a similar picture.

Although almost every parliamentary faction condemned this system of political finance, the new electoral law (On Basic Guarantees of Electoral Rights of Citizens of the Russian Federation worked out in the Duma and passed in 1994) as well as the law relating to parliamentary elections passed in 1995 left the 1993 financial scheme intact, and it still remains largely unchanged. The new law simply limited the maximum permitted size of electoral funds and the amount of ('paid-for') time on television, and banned the use of 'black cash' as well as bribes to voters. However, the law failed to introduce any effective sanctions to deter these practices.

It is clear why the right wingers supported the status quo rules but the logic of the left wing in supporting it, to their own disadvantage, is still unclear. In all probability, the CPRF and its allies hoped for electoral success because of their massive membership, and in counting on door-to-door campaigning they paid little attention to the role of money. As is shown below, this approach has not been wholly successful, since traditional electioneering practices did not prove sufficient to produce successful outcomes in presidential elections.

## Can elections be bought?

A crucial question should now be asked – can elections in Russia be bought? The answer to this question must be somewhat Delphic: 'no and at the same time – yes'! On the one hand, buying votes directly has usually produced little success. The best-known case of this sort goes back to the 1995 parliamentary elections in the 209th (single-member) district in St Petersburg, when Lev Konstantinov, the head of the company, Khoper-Invest, paid 15,000 roubles ($3.3) plus free food to every pensioner who voted for him. Konstantinov was prosecuted, but in any case he had received just 2 per cent of the vote, finishing ninth out of the twenty-four candidates.[41] In certain rare cases, when financial resources are supplementing personal popularity, greater success than this is possible. An example of this occurred during by-elections to the State Duma in the 109th (single-member) district in the Moscow region in October 1994. Sergei Mavrodi, a businessman, and the head of a pyramid-type company, MMM, was accused of having not paid taxes; he needed to get elected as a deputy, before a decision was made to prosecute him, in order to take advantage of immunity from prosecution that holding office would grant him. Mavrodi posed as a victim of tax investigators, and he paid cash and dispensed gifts to voters, including promising a donation of $100,000 to local development projects, supplements to pensions for all elderly people in the district, and so on. He was elected.

Buying votes, irrespective of the form of payment – beer, tea, cigarettes, promises of money from pension funds or insurance companies, lottery tickets, charitable donations, or whatever – does not usually help candidates, and it may have very little effect on the way the votes are cast. In contrast, however, buying votes indirectly, through various forms of implicit advertising and administrative mobilizations of voters is more effective, and this proved especially true during 1996 elections.

The campaigns of 1995–96 showed that the legal guarantees of access to the media for candidates and parties were observed to some degree, at least at the national level. This was not always so at local levels though. There were cases of damage thereby being done to some candidates' campaigns. For instance, the advertisements of one of the candidates in Kalmykia were stopped when he became critical of the Kalmykian President. In Moscow and the Moscow Region certain local television companies, such as MTK and Podmoskov'e, refused to guaranteed free air time to candidates since there was no profit in it for them. This was important since, in general, television advertisements, both the free ones and those that are paid for, play an important role in campaigning.

The under-water component of the 'financial' iceberg, which is inaccessible to the law and to regulation, has given candidates ample opportunities to use indirect forms of campaigning and to employ resources such as air time and newspaper space, even on state-owned media. Non-political television and radio programmes were used for this. At the time of 1995 parliamentary elections Irina Khakamada, the leader of pre-electoral block Obshchee delo, appeared on the lottery show, Wonder Field, while before the elections in 1993 candidates from the pro-government block Russia's Choice showed up on television talking about tennis, theatre and similar topics. Then again, during 1995 elections ORT, the so-called Russian Public Television, but in fact very much a supporter of the current government, kept showing films made by popular movie maker

Nikita Mikhalkov who was second on the candidate list of the ruling party, Our Home – Russia (OHR).

In addition to pre-election advertisements in the 1995 and 1996 campaigns, ORT ran so-called 'social advertising clips'; these contained no electoral slogans but they were designed to create a psychological environment favourable to candidates of the ruling party.[42] Mikhalkov himself played the role of an aeronaut flying over Russia before returning home (which was meant to symbolize the electoral return of OHR). Officially this was not considered to be advertising but, clearly, it was understood that way by the viewers.

Since television news programmes are popular among voters, and therefore have strong effects on them, the candidates supported by the sponsors of television stations were shown in a favourable light, while their rivals were shown in an unfavourable light or were ignored. For instance, during the 1996 presidential election campaign three nationwide television channels ORT, RTR and NTV devoted 53 per cent of prime air time between 6 May and 3 July to coverage of Yeltsin while Zyuganov had only 18 per cent of the time, and the remaining candidates received a mere 11 per cent between them. More significantly, the positive references to Yelsin outnumbered the negative ones to President Yeltsin by 492 while the negative references to Zyuganov outnumbered by 313 the positive references to him. Clearly, television stations were used for manipulation media, to the advantage of pro-government candidates.[43]

Analysis of press coverage undertaken by the European Institute for the Media, in Dusseldorf, revealed a similar picture. News and comments in general were described as 'strident, harsh and one-sided'.[44] The same style of news coverage was noted during the elections for regional governors.

Yeltsin's team used illegal methods without hesitation and with total impunity. As an official on the presidential staff stated: 'We are not about to give the Communists equal time or conditions. They don't deserve it.'[45] But what were the origins of this kind of one-sided coverage? Of course, several journalists had strong anti-Communist (or pro-government) attitudes and had personal reasons to engage in unfair campaigning. Nikolai Svanidze, a Russian Television Company commentator admitted: 'There is a political fight on here that has no rules. And should Communists win the media will lose independence. There is no choice.'[46] On the other hand, the use of administrative mobilization, especially at regional and local levels, was strong. During the elections for the Governor of St Petersburg in May 1996 all the local newspapers, even those not owned or sponsored by the state, broadcast news and comments favouring the incumbent, Anatolii Sobchak. When some journalists from the newspaper *Nevskoe vremya* expressed their independent views, they were forced to resign. In return for its loyalty to Sobchak this newspaper had been given a prestigious office at a low rent, and its editor-in-chief had been given a fashionable apartment in the centre of St Petersburg.[47] Opposing candidates were not mentioned and were totally excluded from both television and newspapers' news coverage, leaving these candidates with only their own air time and space in the newspapers. Again, during the 1996 presidential campaign, mentioning the name of one candidate, Grigorii Yavlinskii, was prohibited by television officials and governors in some areas.

Yeltsin's campaign in 1996 had no monetary problems. Since the legally permitted, 'above-water', portion of the financial 'iceberg' consisted of just $3 million, the under-water portion was many times the size of this – possibly hundreds of times its size. (There are different evaluations of Yeltsin's 'under-water' component, ranging from $100 million to $500 million.) Covering the costs incurred in his campaign involved both state-controlled and other resources. One part of the state-owned resources used by the President in the campaign was the so-called 'executive vertical' which consisted of the whole hierarchy of civil servants, from the the top down. The effects of administrative mobilization could be illustrated by the case of Novosibirskaya oblast. Here, the Regional Governor Vitalii Mukha (a former regional Communist Party leader who had been dismissed by Yeltsin, but then returned to power after election) rejected the idea of his participation in Yeltsin's campaign, on the grounds that that would be in violation of the law. In fact, Yeltsin's results in the first round of the elections in that area were much worse than in the neighbouring Omskaya oblast, while the levels of support for the Communists were almost the same. The President and his government then used every opportunity to delay paying wages and pensions in Novosibirskaya. Then there is the case of Nikolai Fedorov, the popularly elected President of Chuvashiya Republic where Yeltsin was defeated, who wrote a letter to the President after the election asking him not to punish the people of Chuvashiya by withholding budget transfers from Moscow in retaliation for their 'wrong' voting.

The campaign resources that did not come from the state budget were donated by large capitalist interests, mainly banks and the oil and gas industry.[48] This money was used primarily to pay for the means of propaganda. Pop and rock stars gave shows in the Russian provinces, under the title 'Golosui, a to proigraesch' ('Choose or lose'), which was paid for in 'black cash', including the cash from the notorious Xerox-paper box mentioned earlier. During the campaign an anti-Communist newspaper, Ne dai Bog! ('God Forbid'), circulated 10,000,000 copies through direct mail. According to personal messages addressed to top-level Yeltsin campaigners, the salaries of these people during the campaign were about $3,000 to $4,000 per month, paid in 'black cash' (the minimum monthly wage at that time was about $20). The installation of certain top business-men at the highest levels of official hierarchy in the wake of the elections (Vladimir Potanin as the Deputy Prime Minister, Boris Berezovskii as the Deputy Secretary of Security Council), might also be interpreted as a kind of payment for their financial backing of the President in his campaign.

Four months after the elections, a Communist-backed news-paper, Sovetskaya Rossiya, published some records relating to the 'under-water' portion of the iceberg of Yeltsin's campaign finances.[49] According to these unofficial notes on the expenses incurred in Yeltsin's campaign, money had been paid for par-ties and public appearances at which public statements in support of Yeltsin had been made (for instance, the support of the Women of Russia movement had cost about $160,000). Payments were also made for the services of state-owned and 'independent' television and radio stations, information agen-cies, newspapers, and so on, which had presented the campaign from a 'correct' angle. Some actions on behalf of Yeltsin's cam-paign were paid for directly by business groups or business people who had been given substantial privileges by the Pres-ident. For example, there is the National Sports Fund, which up to 1996 had held customs privileges with respect to the importation of tobacco and alcohol.

As a result, the CPRF and Yeltsin's other opponents were defeated. The Communists, being well organized, were able to compete against the administrative mobilization and financial domination of their opponents, but ultimately they were unable to overcome the combination of the latter's extraordinary financial resources and the full force of the state machine.

## Conclusion

As the preceding observations show, the role of money in Russian political campaigning and day-to-day political affairs is relatively important, although not yet decisive. The anti-state attitudes and liberal reformers' interest in the support of business people resulted in the massive use of 'black cash' and other hidden resources – all of this happening in the absence of any effective degree of public control. These conditions created an environment of political corruption at all levels of Russian politics.

The iceberg-like system of political finance has, certainly, made many opponents. Scandals like the one involving the money in the Xerox-paper box erupt from time to time;[50] they resonate both in public opinion and among the political elite, but with no real consequences. In well-established democracies, such as Italy or Japan, scandals in the realm of political finance have forced some politicians to try to shift to 'clean hands' politics.[51] By contrast, in Russia's 'halfway house', not a single politician involved in corruption has ever left his or her post after being caught, although some of them may have been placed under investigation following their resignation from powerful positions. Situations like this sometimes look similar to the practices of the late-communist period when members of 'nomenklatura' could be prosecuted after leaving the Communist Party and powerful positions.

Since the Russian political elite has achieved an accord concerning the main policy-making issues, but not democracy,[52] this kind of 'elite settlement'[53] expresses the political society's own interests rather than the attitudes of their constituency. For instance, since 1994 there have been eight cases where prosecutors have applied to the deputies of both chambers of the Russian Parliament for permission to arrest Russian MPs, but only in one case (the above-mentioned Sergei Mavrodi) has the State Duma voted in favour of giving such permission. This makes the destruction of the iceberg unlikely to happen soon. On the one hand, the CEC declared in October 1996 that special legislation on political finance designed to end the 'financial iceberg' phenomenon was necessary, and that it was planning the drafting of a new law to this effect. However, having such a law approved by the Russian political elite – that is, by both chambers of the Parliament and the President – will be difficult.

Thinking in more general terms, the status of political finance depends entirely on the overall status of law and order in Russia. If extra-legal relationships continue to dominate over legality, it is unlikely that the system of political finance will function without violating the law. Certainly the key question is: how long can the 'halfway house' political regime in Russia last? If further steps are taken toward democratization and they become irreversible, then the political elite will be forced to shift towards a 'cleaner' set of rules of the game, and that should include political finance. But if the present sort of political regime becomes 'frozen' for the duration, then the 'iceberg' of political finance will not melt.

## Notes

1 A. Politkovskaya and E. Dikun, 'Natsional'naya tragediya na prokhodnoi pravitel'stva', *Obshchaya gazeta*, 25:8 (1996).
2 A. Khinstein, 'Golosui, a to . . .', *Moskovskii konsomolets*, 15 November 1996, p. 3.
3 E. Dikun and L. Sigal, 'Milliardy dlya dictatury elektorata', *Obshchaya gazeta*, 24:8 (1996); D. Skillen, 'Media coverage in the elections', in P. Lentini (ed.), *Elections and Political Order in Russia: The Implications of the 1993 Elections to the Federal Assembly* (Budapest, Central European University Press, 1995), pp. 97–123.
4 R. Orttung, *From Leningrad to St Petersburg: Democratization in a Russian City* (Basingstoke and London, Macmillan, 1995).
5 P. Roeder, 'Varieties of post-Soviet authoritarian regimes', *Post-Soviet Affairs*, 10:1 (1994), 61–101.
6 G. O'Donnell, 'Delegative democracy', *Journal of Democracy*, 5:1 (1994), 55–69.
7 S. Fish, 'The advent of multipartism in Russia, 1993–1995', *Post-Soviet Affairs*, 11:4 (1995), 340–83; V. Gel'man, 'Regional'nye rezhimy: zavershenie transformatsii?', *Svobodnaya mysl'*, 9 (1996), 13–22.
8 V. Gel'man, 'Vybory deputatov Gosudarstvennoi Dumy: pravila igry, zakonodatel'naya politika i pravoprimenitel'naya praktika', *Konstitutsionnoe pravo: vostochnoevropeiskoe obozrenie*, 1 (1996), 20–34.
9 P. Lentini, 'Overview of the campaign', in Lentini, *Elections and Political Order in Russia*; R. Sakwa, 'The Russian Elections of December 1993', *Europe-Asia Studies*, 47:2 (1995), 195–227; Skillen, 'Media coverage'; M. Urban, 'December 1993 as a replication of late-Soviet electoral practices', *Post-Soviet Affairs*, 10:2 (1994), 127–58.
10 J. LaPalombara and M. Weiner, 'The origins and developments of political parties', in La Palombara and Weiner (eds.), *Political Parties and Political Development* (Princeton, NJ, Princeton University Press, 1966), pp. 3–42.

11 S. Fish, *Democracy from Scratch: Opposition and Regime in the New Russian Revolution* (Princeton, NJ, Princeton University Press, 1995); Fish, 'The advent of multipartism'; V. Kolosov (ed.) *Rossiya na vyborakh: uroki i perspectivy* (Moscow, CPT, 1995).

12 M. Afanas'ev, *Pravyyashchie elity i gosudarstvennost' posttotalitaarnoi Rossii* (Moscow, Institut Prakticheskoi Psikhologii, 1996).

13 D. Badovskii, 'Tranformatsiya politicheskoi elity v Rossii: ot 'organizatsii professional'nykh revolutsionerov – k partii vlasti', *Polis* 6 (1994), 42–58; A. Ryabov, '"Partiya vlasti": popytka prevrashcheniya novoi rossiiskoi elity v veduschyu silu publichnoi politiki', in V. Kuvaldin *et al.* (eds), *Partiino-politicheskie elity i elektoral'nye processy v Rossii* (Moscow, CKSIiM, 1996), pp. 5–16.

14 Afanas'ev, *Pravyaschie elity*; Badovskii, 'Transformatsiya politicheskoi'; Gel'man, 'Regional'nye rezhimy'.

15 A. Salmin *et al.*, *Partiinaya systema v Rossii v 1989–1993 gg: opyt stanovleniya* (Moscow, Nachala Press, 1994); Fish, 'The advent of multipartism'.

16 A. Panebianco, *Political Parties: Organization and Power* (Cambridge, Cambridge University Press, 1988).

17 G. O'Donnell and P. Schmitter, *Transitions from Authoritarian Rule: Tentative Conclusions about Uncertain Democracies* (Baltimore and London, Johns Hopkins University Press, 1986); S. Huntington, *The Third Wave: Democratizaton in the Late Twentieth Century* (Norman and London, University of Oklahoma Press, 1991).

18 J. Hughes, 'The "Americanization" of Russian politics: Russia's first television election, December 1993', *Journal of Communist Studies and Transition Politics*, 10:2 (1994), 125–50; M. McFaul, 'Osmyslenie parlamentskikh vyborov 1993 g. v Rossi', *Polis*, 5 (1994), 124–36; Urban, 'December 1993'; Skillen, 'Media Coverage'.

19 A. Zudin, 'Biznes i politika v prezidentskoi kampanii 1996 goda', *Pro et Contra*, 1:1 (1996), 46–60.

20 Hughes, 'The "Americanization" of Russian politics'.

21 A. Postnikov, 'Finansirovanie vyborov', in V. Vasil'ev (ed.), *Izbiratel'naya reforma: opyt, problemy, perspectivy* (Moscow, Manuscript, 1993), pp. 95–8.

22 V. Kolosov *et al.*, *Vesna-89: Geografiya i anatomiya palamentskikh vyborov* (Moscow, Progress, 1990); Orttung, *From Leningrad to St Petersburg*.

23 Y. Brudny, 'The dynamics of "Democratic Russia", 1990–93', *Post-Soviet Affairs*, 9:2 (1993), 141–70.

24 Postnikov, 'Finansirovanie vyborov'.

25 A. Lijphart, 'Democratization and constitutional choice in Czecho-Slovakia, Hungary and Poland, 1989–91', *Journal of Theoretical Politics*, 4:2 (1992), 207–23; B. Geddes, 'Initiation of new democratic institutions in Eastern Europe and Latin America', in A. Lijphart and C. Waisman (eds.), *Institutional Design in New Democracies: Eastern Europe and Latin America* (Boulder, CO, Westview, 1996), pp. 15–41.

26. B. Strashun and V. Sheinis, 'Politicheskaya situatsiya v Rossii i novyi izbiratel-'nyi'zakon', *Polis*, 3 (1993), 65–9; D. Levchik, 'Osnovnye elementy elektoral'nogo prava i ikh primenenie v rossikom zakonodatel'stve 1992–1994', *Kentavr*, 5 (1994), 105–14; McFaul, 'Osmyslenie parlamentskikh vyborov'; Salmin *et al.*, *Partiinaya systema v Rossii*; Urban, 'December 1993'; A. Salmin, 'Vybory i izbiratel'nye sistemy: opyt Rossii v 1989–1993 godakh', *Sapere Aude*, 2 (1995), 8–27.

27 Levchik, 'Osnovnye elementy'.

28 'Polozhenie o vyborakh deputatov Gosudarstvennoi Dumy Federal'nogo Sobraniya Rossiikoi Federatsii v 1993 godu', *Bulleten Central'noi Izbiratel'noi komissii*, 1 (1993).

29 'Federal'nyi zakon "Ob osnovnykh garantiyakh izbiratel'nykh prav grazhdan Rossiikoi Federatsii"', *Rossiikaya gazeta*, 10 December 1994, 4–5; 'Federal'nyi zakon "O vyborakh deputatov Gosudarstvennoi Dumy Federal'nogo sobraniya Rossiikoi Federatsii"', *Rossiikaya gazeta*, 28 June 1995, 4–6.

30 Y. Gaidar, *Gosudarstvo i evolutsiya* (Moscow, Eurasia, 1995).
31 Y. Gaidar, 'Vystuplenie na uchreditl'nom s'ezde partii "Demokraticheskii vybor Rossii"', *Otkrytaya politika*, 2 (1994), 49–54.
32 A. Ulyukaev, *Liberalizm i politika perekhodnogo perioda* (Moscow, Eurasia, 1995).
33 Geddes, 'Initiation of new democratic institutions'.
34 Y. Brudny, 'The dynamics of "Democratic Russia"'.
35 Hughes, 'The "Americanization" of Russian politics'; Urban, 'December 1993'; Lentini, 'Overview of the campaign'.
36 Urban, 'December 1993'; Lentini, 'Overview of the campaign'; Gel'man, 'Vybory deputatov'; S. White *et al.*, *How Russia Votes* (Chatham, NJ, Chatham House, 1997).
37 Dikun and Sigal, 'Milliardy dlya dictatury'.
38 *Ibid.*
39 Dikun and Sigal, 'Milliardy dlya dictatury'; Kas'yanenko, 'Protokoly kremleviskikh mudretsov'.
40 Hughes, 'The "Americanization" of Russian politics'; McFaul, 'Osmyslenie parlamentskikh vyborov'; Urban, 'December 1993'; Skillen, 'Media coverage'.
41 Gel'man, 'Vyboroy deputatov'.
42 *Ibid.*
43 White *et al.*, *How Russia Votes.*
44 Quoted in White *et al.*, *How Russia Votes.*
45 *Ibid.*
46 *Ibid.*
47 T. Drabkina, 'Sankt-Peterburg v mae 1996 goda', *Politicheskii monitoring*, 5:1 (1996); B. Vishnevskii, 'Nevezenie na nevskikh beregakh', *Rossiiskaya Federatsiya*, 21 (1996), 18–20.
48 Zudin, 'Biznes i politika'.
49 Z. Kas'yanenko, 'Protokoly kremleviskikh mudretsov', *Sovetskaya Rossiiya*, 10 October 1996, p. 2.
50 Kas'yanenko, 'Protokoly kremleviskikh mudretsov'; Khinstein, 'Golosui, a to . . .'; Politkovskaya and Dikun, 'Natsional'naya tragediya'.
51 H. Alexander and R. Shiratori, 'Introduction', in H. Alexander and R. Shiratori (eds.), *Comparative Political Finance Among the Democracies* (Boulder, CO, Westview, 1994), pp.1–11.
52 A. Fadin, 'Obshchestvennoe soglasie v tselom dostignuto', *NG-scenarii*, 4 (1996), p. 1.
53 M. Burton *et al.*, 'Introduction: elite transformations and democratic regimes', in J. Higley and and R. Gunther (eds.), *Elites and Democratic Consolidation in Latin America and Southern Europe* (Cambridge, Cambridge University Press, 1992), pp. 1–37.

## 9

# Building democracy on the basis of capitalism: towards an east Asian model of party funding

PETER FERDINAND

Japan has the longest-established democracy in Asia. Its first parliament was founded in 1891 and political parties had already been established by then. Although it was supplanted by political and military extremists in the 1930s, democracy was re-established immediately after the Second World War on the command of the Allied administration. Since then it has prospered, as has the country. Even this shorter period of existence would make it the longest-lived democracy in continental Asia, pre-dating that of India by two years. How far, therefore, might its experience have lessons to offer to more recent democratizing regimes?

This chapter will focus upon the experience in funding parties of Japan, and also of Taiwan and South Korea. In the twentieth century both Taiwan and South Korea were only freed from Japanese colonial rule after the Second World War and since then for most of their existence they were ruled by military-backed authoritarian regimes. Coincidentally, however, both introduced or reintroduced democratization in 1987, since when both have made significant progress in consolidating democracy.

In addition to this regional and temporal proximity of democratization, there are three further factors which make the hypothesis of a similar model of, or at least approach to, democratization plausible.

The first is the fact that both Korea and Taiwan were colonized by Japan from 1895 until 1945. Since Japan was democratic for most of that time, there is a possibility that a common orientation towards political processes might have emerged. After all, the single-vote multi-member constituency system for the parliaments still extant in Taiwan and South Korea was inherited from Japan, where it was in force for the Diet until 1996.

The second is the process of economic modernization and later democratization which is common to all three of these states. They have managed to organize and sustain political life in traditional rural settings where traditional political culture was antipathetic to democratic values. And they developed the flexibility to do this at the same time as they reached out to more mobile sections of society who were abandoning the old-fashioned villages for industries in the new towns and cities.

The third common feature is the set of popular expectations in all three states about the social role and status of elected representatives, which is quite different from other parts of the world. This poses particular challenges for the funding of political parties and their regulation. Basically representatives are supposed to be linked to their constituents by a set of reciprocal obligations as if they were part of one family. The citizens' obligations are less onerous. They are expected to cast their votes. But the representatives are expected to help constituents with all kinds of assistance when dealing with authority. In many cases this may include intervention over the application of regulations or laws by officials which might damage the livelihood of constituents. For more active political supporters this could include gifts on important family occasions: births, weddings and deaths.

This increases enormously the cost of being a representative. A group of younger Liberal Democratic Party (LDP) Diet members in Japan calculated in 1987 that they would need to give anything between 20,000 and 70,000 yen for weddings in families which were members of their supporters' club, and 10,000 yen for condolence money at funerals. In one year these sums would mount up to around 18 million yen, that is around US$120,000. New-Year and mid-year gifts would add a further 6 million yen.[1] In none of the three states is it conceivable that a representative in the national legislature could make do simply on the parliamentary salary. Extra money has to be found, and although citizens may in general condemn 'illicit' money-gathering by politicians, their criticism has usually been modified by gratitude for the gifts which their families have received. In a sense this has made most of society complicitous in the raising of illegal political contributions. So from an early date the practice of condoning some forms of 'illegal' political fund raising became established, since all actors could see that it was impossible to make the rules work and yet satisfy all expectations. On the other hand, propriety would have been infringed by too open a hunt for money by politicians. Instead most of the funds would be solicited and obtained by 'middlemen', who could be sacrificed if some scandal emerged – although it rarely did.

Because the process of democratization has lasted far longer in Japan than in Taiwan or South Korea, this chapter will begin by outlining in separate sections the initial stages in each of these three states, before returning to consider more recent attempts at the reform of party funding in Japan. The basic argument is that the pro-business orientation of political debate in each of these three states created the conditions for political parties to attract substantial funding. More recently, however, the problems of 'money politics' have fuelled public debates over the need for greater state regulation of party funding and possibly for state support, so as to ensure greater accountability and greater equality of opportunity for parties.

## Japan: the early postwar years

Money has always been an important issue in Japanese democracy. It was money politics and the sense of corruption which discredited the pre-war Japanese parliamentary system and favoured the takeover by the military. This mood had been exploited by extreme nationalist parties and groupings, which closely associated themselves with the army. It was one of the chief factors in the assassination of Premier Inukai in 1932. The army then took advantage of this to suspend normal political activity.

With the Second World War over, the occupying powers, especially the United States, wanted to ensure that democracy was enshrined – if possible liberal democracy. Thus on the one hand there was official encouragement from the highest level for competitive party politics to be resurrected, and in the first elections in 1946, over 260 parties put up candidates.[2]

On the other hand the occupying forces came predominantly from the United States, where there was no habit of state subsidy for political parties. So it was not seriously contemplated for Japan either. Yet the necessary costs of running parties were still high, indeed they were proportionately higher then than subsequently because the economy had been ravaged by the war and there was little money to pay for anything. So individual party leaders began to search for business people who could make large contributions to their organizations. In the business climate which prevailed at that time, these were predominantly to be found among black-marketeers and those who wanted to evade official scrutiny, or to gain government licences to protect their markets. The profits from this type of business activity escalated rapidly as the Cold War, and especially the Korean War, began in earnest. Politicians relied upon local 'bosses' – landowners, enterprise owners and so on – to deliver votes for them. In turn these local 'bosses' used the authority of the politicians to further their business interests.[3] In addition the need of the Allies to ensure that communism was defeated also meant less searching analysis of the accounts of individual parties because, if nothing else, they stood for the free world.

Very rapidly then by the 1950s money had returned to play as prominent a role in national politics as it had in the 1930s, and so too did scandals. Official rules on campaigning laid down rules on how much individual candidates could spend for their campaigns. These have been periodically updated to take account of new kinds of infringements.[4] Parties, however, did not have a clear legal status in between elections and so the state was handicapped in its attempts to control their spending activities. Politicians and fund donors would set up harmless-sounding associations through which money could be channelled, but whose activities were very difficult for the state authorities to penetrate. Parties reported funds which they 'officially' received, but did not necessarily include funds channelled to individual politicians or groups of politicians. Candidates would set up secret deals with the rich through intermediaries. Only if it could be shown that the politician was personally aware of such dealings could legal action be taken against them.

Two major consequences followed from this. The first concerned the orientation of political debate. Although there was no official bias in favour of one type of political view or another, the need for significant sums of money gave advantage to those parties with a pro-business outlook. The spur to the realignment of parties which took place in 1955 and lasted until 1993 was the formation of the Japan Socialist Party (JSP). This was for a short period the largest party in the Diet and caused apprehension not merely in Japan but also in the United States over the direction of Japanese politics, when the Cold War was still at its height. All of this provided the glue which finally cemented the alliance of the previously separate and rival Liberal and Democratic Parties to provide a united pro-business party, the LDP. This became the largest party in the Diet and it managed to retain its dominant position for the next thirty-eight years largely because of its fund-raising ability. It was reported in 1974 that the LDP and its factions gained four-fifths of the total of 51.6 billion yen (US$170 million) in income reported by all the party headquarters to the Home Affairs ministry.[5] Until 1995 the employers' association, the Keidanren, actively collected money on the LDP's behalf. Though this was by no means the only source of funds at the disposal of the LDP, it was by far the largest. For a long time there was no official limit on contributions which could be given to a party, and the LDP was qualitatively different from the other parties in the share of its declared income which came from donations rather than membership dues. Still in 1991 58 per cent of its income came from corporate donations, while only 28 per cent came from membership dues, and no other party could match that.[6]

The second consequence concerned the structure of the LDP's organization. Since money became such a key issue, the party was not solely responsible for raising funds for the activities of its representatives. Individual representatives could supplement this with whatever they raised by their own efforts. Some were more successful than others, and so they attracted 'followers' with whom they shared out surplus income. Consequently the factions which had already appeared within the LDP from its initial formation because of rivalries between individual leaders acquired a financial basis. Initially numbering eight, by the 1960s there were five factions, with the largest, the Tanaka faction, being by far the most successful. Clearly the existence of the factions had a major impact upon policy-making and the apportionment of government posts within the LDP. Not surprisingly the larger factions also tended to be handed most of the ministerial posts. And ultimately the largest factions determined who was to become the president of the party, and thus normally the Prime Minister. No faction leader was prepared to give up his own faction for the sake of the party. The differences between the factions were based chiefly upon personalities and fund raising ability rather than policies. Nevertheless Tanaka was most successful in raising funds for his faction because he exploited links with the construction industry, and the LDP governments at that time were strongly encouraging infrastructural construction. So government policies could be – and were – skewed in certain directions owing to the funding needs of individual politicians and their factions.

The lavishness of political funding was further exacerbated by the multi-member constituency system. Most constituencies had several representatives who ran against each other, while the electors each only had one vote. This pitted members of the same party against each other. Some constituencies returned as many as five members, so only small variations in voting might separate the candidates. This encouraged candidates from the same party to fight as hard against each other as against other parties. The chief way of fighting was through money. Thus individual members found that they needed to gain access to local funds too, and they set up their own local political support groups (koenkai).[7] These too could raise large amounts of cash, sometimes from dubious sources.

Yet the actual amounts raised were always difficult to know. Although the state had laws on the reporting of political funds, parties and especially individual members were less than punctilious in doing so. Already by the early 1950s it was estimated that candidates needed to spend between five and six times more than what was allowed by law.[8] Factions, if they had a definite identity, were required to report what they had raised, but sometimes they opted to do so by dividing the money out between individual fund raisers within the faction. They would choose to report large or small amounts, according to whichever the public mood expected, or according to whether a particular faction wanted to impress others or to keep a low profile. Donations to political organizations were tax-deductible, and so the largest corporations, which made the largest donations, had an interest in being straightforward about this. But smaller organizations were less punctilious. And in any case those companies which made donations in the hope of an official interpretation of government regulations in their favour might expect better treatment if they kept silent about donations

**Table 9.1** Japan: political parties' reported income, 1953 (millions yen)

| | |
|---|---|
| Liberal (including Democrats) | 229.26 |
| Progressive | 108.71 |
| Socialist (right wing) | 29.27 |
| Socialist (left wing) | 25.50 |
| Farmer-Labour | 1.07 |
| Green Breeze | 5.05 |
| Communist | 11.05 |

*Source*: Nobutake Ike, *Japanese Politics* (New York, Knopf, 1957), p. 201.

**Table 9.2** Japan: political parties' reported income at the national level in selected years (millions yen)

| | 1976 | 1980 | 1985 | 1990 | 1993 |
|---|---|---|---|---|---|
| Communist Party | 15,918 | 19,582 | 21,679 | 32,058 | 32,319 |
| LDP | 7,806 | 18,655 | 18,966 | 30,844 | 26,854 |
| Komeito | 7,130 | 8,388 | 9,807 | 13,490 | 14,462 |
| Japan Socialist Party | 3,874 | 5,110 | 6,649 | 6,794 | 7,199 |
| Democratic Socialists | 1,350 | 2,463 | 1,830 | 2,412 | 2,556 |
| Japan New Party | | | | | 1,165 |
| Shinseito | | | | | 807 |
| New Party Sakigake | | | | | 478 |

*Source*: Home Affairs Ministry figures.

rather than publicizing them, in case the publicity caused embarrassment to the 'patron'.

As mentioned before, the state was not able to demand compliance, because 'everyone knew' that it was impossible. Nor were the parties very effective in policing each other's campaigning. An indication of the strange consequences to which this could lead was, as can be seen from Table 9.1, that in 1953, when the Cold War was at its height, the Liberal and Democratic Parties reported an income that was twenty times that of the Japanese Communist Party (JCP) (the party which most prided itself on honesty). In contrast, in the 1990s, when communism was clearly waning, the JCP was the party which made the declaration of the largest income, 20 per cent higher even than that of the pro-business LDP – as can be seen from Table 9.2.

It was true that this financial largesse on the part of parties caused some spectacular scandals, most notably (until the 1990s) the Tanaka Lockheed scandal in the 1970s. These caused public outcries and some tightening of the laws. But at least at that time the LDP showed skill in public relations when its leaders agreed to allow the leader of the smallest and therefore least prosperous faction, Miki, to become Prime Minister, so as to symbolize an apparent change of heart. And Miki did toughen the regulations on campaign funding, although he was soon forced from office by disgruntled leaders of the larger factions for failing to prevent the prosecution of former Prime Minister Tanaka.

One last consequence of the system should be noted: it was biased in favour of incumbents. While the laws were strict on how long an election campaign could last and what kinds of expenditure and activities candidates could engage in, these served primarily to restrain outsiders. Incumbents were and are able to maintain their profile with electors in between elections by sending them postcards or newsletters at their own expense.

Yet for all the irregularities and the less than frank disclosure of funds, the Japanese system did at least aspire to establish a 'level playing field' between the parties. The rules themselves were not aimed at giving preference to one party. Indeed in the first few postwar years the Allied administration in Japan tried to favour the JSP because they were regarded as a potentially important bulwark defending the new 'peace' constitution which banned Japan from having its own armed forces, provided the JSP could be kept apart from the JCP.[9] As we turn to the other two systems, those of Taiwan and South Korea, we shall find that this evenhandedness has still not been achieved.

## Taiwan and South Korea

Until they began seriously to develop democratization from 1987, both of these states practised authoritarianism (for Korea there was the exception of the brief popular Chang Myon government of 1960–61). Yet it was an authoritarianism which appealed for support to the Free World, and so both states also attempted to create a democratic cover for their actions. They allowed elections at some levels of administration, but they restricted the opportunities for other parties to make a serious electoral challenge, in both cases citing the threat of communism.

*Taiwan*

For Taiwan this meant the banning of other parties under the Emergency Laws. Moreover, no elections could be allowed to the Legislative Yuan for most of the seats because the incumbents had been elected to represent the whole of China in 1947. But elections could be allowed for the seats representing Taiwan, as well as to the provincial legislature for the island of Taiwan and for posts at the county level. However, the opponents of the Kuomintang (KMT) had to stand as independents. They could not organize as parties. An attempt to found a China Democratic Party in 1960 was broken by the arrest of its organizer, Lei Chen, on the dubious accusation of consorting with communist agents. Between 1951 and 1985 KMT candidates won between 80 and 100 per cent of local government posts. In local legislative elections, the KMT won 70 to 85 per cent of the seats in the provincial assembly between 1957 and 1985, and between 75 and 92 per cent of the seats in the Taipei city council from 1969 to 1985.[10]

For Taiwan, the KMT's legally protected superiority was reinforced by its opportunities for patronage. Even more importantly, it also built up its own financial empire. It had always been part of the KMT's ideology that it was aiming at a new society somewhere between capitalism and socialism. Given the difficulties of raising funds for its activities through voluntary contributions in an impoverished China during the civil war on the mainland, it had set up its own business operations in areas which it controlled, just as it also encouraged state-owned enterprises. There was a definite blurring of the distinction between private and public enterprise. Particularly at the end of the Second World War, the Nationalists had seemed to be in league with 'carpet-baggers', who came into areas newly liberated from the Japanese and took over businesses from former 'collaborators', though this did then lose them support to the communists. Then, when the Nationalists lost the mainland and were forced to retreat to Taiwan, they found that they had largely to start from the beginning again, having abandoned most of their assets. They also found themselves confronted by a fairly hostile local population, following massacres on

and immediately after 28 February 1947, when several thousands of protesters were killed. They overcame their lack of
funds by setting up their own business operations, which they
ran in association with the state. Though the KMT has never
published public accounts of its businesses, they prospered as
Taiwan prospered. By the early 1990s rumour suggested that
all of these operations were worth perhaps US$1.5 billion, with
income for 1995 estimated at US$450 million.[11] Whether or
not these figures are accurate, the KMT itself reportedly had
a permanent staff in the early 1990s of 5,000 employees. On
the assumption that they were earning around NT$3,000 per
month, this would put the total wage bill at around NT$1.5
billion per month, that is, US$58 million, or almost US$700
million per year.[12]

When the democratization process began from 1987 onwards,
the KMT was reluctant to give up its organizational wealth, or
the political advantage this wealth could bring. So although as
in Japan campaign laws were drawn up which attempted to
regulate the activities that could be carried on in that period,
nothing was done about party finances for the rest of the time.
This obviously put candidates from other parties at a significant disadvantage, especially as the KMT candidates tended to be
incumbents already and so could continue to use their position
as members of the Legislative Yuan to keep up their profile
in advance of the election. Yet the organization of rival parties
also significantly raised the cost of electioneering. It has been
argued that in earlier times politics was much cleaner, albeit
partly because of popular apathy, than in the more recent era
of democratization.[13] Reportedly already by 1989 a candidate
for the Legislative Yuan might have to spend as much as US$1.2
to $3.2 million on a single campaign, that is more than in elec-
tions for the US Congress.[14] Indeed as the pressures mounted
upon the KMT in the new era of competitive politics, and
as the costs of politics mounted, the party businesses became
if anything more aggressive in their pursuit of new investment opportunities, so as to ensure a regular supply of funds
for the KMT.

As in Japan, the multi-member constituency system has
had some of the same impact upon the internal cohesion of
the KMT. Although it has forced individual candidates to set up
equivalents of *koenkai* to raise funds locally, relatively speaking
the party headquarters controls a larger proportion of the funds

at the disposal of all its candidates. Yet individual candidates from the same party are still pitted against each other in the same constituencies. Attempts by the party headquarters to give assistance to 'weaker' candidates so as to increase the chances of overall party success then cause resentment among the 'stronger' ones, who fear that intervention may cause them to lose their seats.

There are maximum figures set for the amounts which individual candidates can spend on election campaigns at the various levels of government, but enforcement is extremely difficult. For example, as in Japan, it is difficult to distinguish between spending by the candidates themselves, which is restricted, and spending by their supporters, which is not. The government's Election Commission does require reports of campaign spending to be filed by individual candidates, but these are not published. There are in any case no restrictions on the amounts that the party headquarters can spend. This obviously continues to favour the KMT.

Unlike the other two systems considered in this chapter, Taiwan still has extremely limited public support for party activities. A limited amount of time is made available for free television campaign broadcasts, but no public funds are available for other election expenses during the campaign. Once elected, candidates are able to claim NT$2 for each vote which they gained, but this only contributes a small amount towards their overall expenses, and is in any case paid directly to the representative rather than to the party. The chief opposition party to emerge, the Democratic Progressive Party (DPP), requires all its successful candidates to turn over a part of this payment to the party, but even this practice is not always observed.

On the other hand, the DPP also targeted the native Taiwanese business community for possible funds. The consequence has been that political debate has not been polarized into pro- and anti-business discourse. Nevertheless the DPP has experienced considerable and repeated financial difficulties – at one point it was only saved from bankruptcy by a personal donation from the party president.

Still, 'factions' are not as important in Taiwanese politics as they have been in Japan. The residual legacy of Leninism as the basic organizational doctrine of the KMT has restrained the party's representatives from forming several rival factions at the national level. There are 'factions' within the party, but many are local groupings of notables with whom the central leadership of the KMT has worked since the 1960s, and who have preserved a kind of separate identity. In many cases they reflect the divide between mainlanders in the centre and 'native Taiwanese' outside. More recently, however, 'factions' have formed within the KMT over fundamental issues of principle such as policy towards the mainland. They do not, however, have the same organizational significance as factions inside the LDP, and certainly not the same financial role in determining posts in the national leadership.[15]

More recently, however, the increasing salience of money politics has begun to cause a public backlash. Individual KMT representatives have calculated that they would stand a better chance of being elected if they ran against corruption, even if the corruption is associated with their own party headquarters. This has meant that they have actually refused offers of support from the headquarters. Subsequently a few of them broke away to form their own New Party, which they claim is also more firmly committed to the long-term goal of reunification with the mainland than the KMT under Lee Teng-hui.

So there is now a groundswell of popular support for tougher action against corruption in Taiwan, and there are proposals for greater state support for parties, so as both to strengthen the party system overall and also so as to try to ensure greater accountability for party finances.[16] Not surprisingly the opposition parties are in favour of this, but whether the KMT can be brought to accept it remains to be seen.

### South Korea

Compared to Taiwan, South Korea has had a more varied political history since the end of the civil war in 1953. Like Japan, immediately after the Second World War a large number of new parties emerged – proportionately as many for the size of the population. In the 1948 Constituent Assembly elections approximately 48 parties took part. There have been military coups, but also more attempts at guided democracy. But this was unwelcome to first president, Syngman Rhee, as well as to President Park Chung-hee in the 1960s. What is noticeable about Korean democratization is that even when the military were in power, they usually attempted to shore up their legitimacy by allowing restricted elections to the national assembly. In the 1960s President Park formed the Democratic Republican

Party (DRP), which was carefully organized by Kim Jong Pil, for much of the time also head of the Korean intelligence service or KCIA.[17] By the late 1970s it allegedly had several million members. And like the LDP in Japan and the KMT in Taiwan, the 'official' parties sought to enlist the support of rural elites in elections.[18] These were a kind of faction. Yet no sooner was President Park assassinated in 1979 than the DRP was abolished. In the 1980s an analogous attempt was made by President Chun Doo Hwan with the Democratic Justice Party. Despite all the official bias, however, some seats were elected on the basis of proportional representation. This ensured that some opponents of the regime were elected, and opposition leaders such as Kim Dae Jung and Kim Young Sam were surprisingly successful in mobilizing support.

So the regime looked to business for support, and in particular money, to 'win over' as many people as possible. Thus patterns of relationships between party leaders and supporters/ funders developed; in particular there were the very close relationships between the state and the large business corporations (chaebol). As a whole the chaebols owed a lot of their success to privileges granted by the state. It was and still is illegal, for example, for trade unions to engage in any organized party political activity. In return the chaebol were expected to contribute handsomely to the ruling party. This, however, could be shielded from the public not only because of controls on the press, but also because of a highly unusual feature of the Korean economy. Until 1993 it was quite legal to hold bank accounts in fictitious names. So contributions to individual parties could be further disguised under meaningless names, or indeed hidden entirely.

In addition, however, the first Political Funds Law of 1965 introduced the principle of some state funding for political parties, but at that time this was intended to ensure that the money went to regime supporters.

All of this contributed to an escalation in the costs of running election campaigns. As early as 1967 it was estimated that in the National Assembly elections, ruling DRP candidates spent an average of 30 million won, that is, US$100,000, each. At that time the main opposition party was the New Democratic Party, and it could only compete with this amount of cash by tapping contributions from those of its candidates who were successful in the proportional representation seats, allegedly to the tune of 20 million won each, in other words, US$20,000.[19]

Expenditure on elections escalated rapidly. Where the DRP officially reported spending 259,000 won on elections in 1963, by 1967 the figure had risen to 614,000 and by 1971 to 2.5 million. But these figures seriously underestimated real spending. One commentator remarked in 1977 that campaign expenditures in Korea were twenty-five times as large as those of the UK, even though Korea's Gross National Product was only one-seventh of the UK's.[20] According to a former director of the KCIA, in 1971 the ruling DRP spent 60 billion won, a sum equivalent to more than 10 per cent of the overall government budget for that year, on the re-election campaign of President Park.[21]

Thus when the newly-installed president and former general, Roh Tae Wu, decided in 1987 to tolerate the development of democracy, he cast around for ways of keeping the official Democratic Justice Party in power. In the end this was achieved by merging it with the largest opposition party led by then oppositionist Kim Young Sam so as to form the Democratic Liberal Party (DLP). The intention was to create a new party that would stay in power as long as the LDP had done in Japan.

This cosy relationship between top business and political leaders did have the benefit of limiting the factions endemic in the LDP, especially as there were no local elections until 1995, so that the pressure to raise funds to fight local elections was non-existent. It reinforced the tendency for leaders to dominate their parties in fund raising as in everything else. They remained the rather simple patron–client networks dominated by an individual leader such as may be found in many other countries, rather than the complex ones found in the Japanese LDP.[22] On the other hand, elections to the national legislature tended to be characterized in many cases by races between local notables rather than between parties. This still required large injections of cash.

An indication of the money officially declared by parties can be seen in Table 9.3. These figures show the extent to which the ruling party's income far exceeded that of its rivals. In 1994 the ruling DLP reported income equivalent to US$256 million, twelve times greater than that of its nearest rival, the Democratic Party. Yet as in Taiwan and Japan, they only tell part of the story. It has recently been revealed that during his

**Table 9.3** Korea: party revenues 1988–90 (millions won)

| Party | 1988 | 1989 | 1990 |
|---|---|---|---|
| Democratic Justice Party | 32,370 | 23,606 | – |
| Reunification Democratic Party | 14,240 | 5,737 | – |
| New Democratic Republican Party | 12,583 | 6,209 | – |
| Party for Peace and Democracy | 15,481 | 6,243 | 8,775 |
| Democratic Liberal Party | – | – | 39,895 |
| Democratic Party | – | – | 2,199 |

*Source*: Chan Wook Park, 'Financing political parties in South Korea: 1988–91', in H. E. Alexander and R. Shiratori (eds.), *Comparative Political Finance Among the Democracies* (Boulder, CO, Westview, 1994), p. 178.
*Notes*: 1988 was a National Assembly election year, hence the much higher expenses.
Approx. 700 won = US$1.

presidency, Roh Tae Woo collected about US$640 million in secret political contributions from over thirty business tycoons, of which about $274 million went on his party and campaign expenses. In addition something like $2.5 million was given to his opponent, Kim Dae Jung.[23]

In 1993, however, the apparently cosy relationship between big business and the ruling party was thrown into disarray. The president of the Hyundai Corporation, Chung Ju Yung, decided to run for President by setting up his own party, the United National Party. For this he relied largely upon the resources of his own corporation. In the end he was defeated, and the winner, Kim Young Sam, then arranged for a major tax audit of the corporation which found, not surprisingly, that offences had been committed. So Chung was sentenced to a jail term. In fact this was commuted when he agreed to resign from the corporation, since this also marked the end of his political ambitions.

This attempt to buy electoral success worried not only the established politicians, but also the general public. It led President Kim to crack down upon corruption in public office, and also to try to impose restrictions upon the campaign funds of candidates for political office. He increased subsidies to political parties and introduced severe penalties for candidates who broke the law. Most surprisingly of all, he allowed the prosecution and imprisonment of his two predecessors, Chun Doo Hwan and Roh Tae Woo. Yet political scandals have continued to surface, with even the President's own son being implicated in 1997. As a result Kim Young Sam has come under increasing pressure to make the political playing field more even. The practical effects will be seen in the forthcoming presidential and legislative elections in 1997. However, whether the dominance of business interests in politics will be curtailed remains to be seen.

## Japanese reform proposals and the 1996 general election

In all three systems, then, the problem of money politics has been perceived to become more serious. At least in Japan and South Korea attempts have begun to remedy it, more or less simultaneously.

In Japan the spate of financial scandals in the early 1990s finally drove the LDP to try to address the issue, although ultimately it took their loss of power in 1993 for the alternative reform coalition led by the newly-formed opposition party Shinshinto actually to introduce measures. Basically these relied upon a more pronounced role for the state in regulating party activities. Partly this meant increasing the controls on individual contributions. Companies are no longer allowed to give money to individual candidates, but only to parties and recognized political organizations. And now donations of over 50,000 yen – roughly US$500 – have to be reported, where previously the minimum was 1 million yen. Partly too it meant increasing the penalties for infringements of regulations. Previously candidates could only have had their victory quashed if they or their campaign manager could be proved to have been involved. Now if *any* campaign worker is found to have broken the rules, this could lead to the result being overturned. And partly too it involved the re-drawing of parliamentary boundaries, so that all the multi-member constituencies were done away with. This was intended to reduce the competition between different factions of the same party which, it was thought, had contributed to escalating electioneering expenses.

At the same time, the government introduced subsidies for parties that had candidates successful in elections. The overall sum available was set at 30 billion yen, which represented the official size of the population multiplied by 250 yen each. This is roughly equivalent to US$250 million, and was agreed partly because it seemed to be in line with the subsidies available in west European countries, and partly because it represented

**Table 9.4** Japan: political spending reported to the central and prefectural authorities in various years since 1976 (billion yen)

|             | 1976  | 1980  | 1985  | 1990  | 1995  |
|-------------|-------|-------|-------|-------|-------|
| Central     | 69.3  | 112.8 | 145.6 | 184.5 | 170.7 |
| Prefectural | 40.4  | 78.9  | 106.3 | 153.8 | 185.9 |
| **Total**   | **109.7** | **191.7** | **251.9** | **338.3** | **356.6** |

*Source*: Ministry of Home Affairs figures.

roughly half of the figure which politicians had calculated they spent every year on political activities.

Most of these new regulations are aimed at strengthening the political parties at the expense of factions and individuals. The hope is that this will lead to more substantive policy-orientated debate, and to the parties' evolution into more impersonal institutions. It should lead to more funds being made available to the party leaderships, so that they can exercise greater real leadership over their supporters.

The paradox about these arrangements, however, is that the state is intervening not because of a shortage of funds available for political parties, but because of parties' own weaknesses. The state may only be better able to regulate party activity by contributing its own funds and requiring proper accountability. Thus where the original concern was with the need for viable parties to give substance to democracy, now things have changed so that the state needs to intervene to help parties perform a more useful and effective role as part of a democratic system.

Whether this will work obviously remains to be seen. At the time of writing, the most recent official accounts on party funding date back to 1995, and therefore do not yet cover the first general election under the new rules in 1996. But as can be seen from Table 9.4, spending reported by local parties and candidates to prefectural organizations since 1994 has exceeded for the first time that reported by the central parties to the central government. If this trend continues, then it would suggest that the central party apparatuses will still not find it so easy to centralize control over their party branches.

Another curious by-product of the rules has been actually to encourage the splitting of the Shinshinto party rather than to encourage its consolidation. Since the minimum number of

Diet members needed for a party to receive subsidies is five, and the funds are assigned on an annual basis at the beginning of the new financial year, this has no doubt contributed to the decision of former Prime Minister Hata to form his own new party in March. In future the first three months of the new year may see repeated squabbling within parties as disaffected groups decide whether to jump ship in time for the next year's subsidy.

Obviously a real assessment will only become possible when the accounts for election spending in 1996 are published in the autumn of 1997. Anecdotal evidence suggests that less money was spent in the last campaign than in previous ones, and parties have collectively reported 5 per cent less income than in 1993. Some candidates in the election, however, complained that they have had to work much harder when competing in the new single-member constituencies. Nevertheless one sign of a possible improvement can be seen in the fact that in this election only about 700 campaign workers have been accused of breaking campaigning regulations, whereas the previous figure was around 2,500.

## Conclusion

This chapter has shown that there is no simple east Asian model for funding political parties. It is true that the social context of politics in each of these states has imposed particular features upon the activities of parties and representatives which are not so obvious in other parts of the world. It is certainly true that in all three countries money is vital for electoral success. And it is certainly true that business interests have dominated those of labour and other groups in the determination of public policy.

On the other hand, both Taiwan and South Korea are still at a transitional stage as far as the funding of parties in their evolving democracies is concerned. The pre-democratization ruling parties are either still in power (Taiwan) or are substantially so (South Korea) and they give up their inherited advantages only slowly. This is different from Japan where the system itself is now more evenly balanced.

Nevertheless there has been one characteristic of democratizing polities in east Asia which sets them apart from those in, for example, western Europe. Langdon has made the point for Japan but it applies equally well to South Korea and Taiwan. This is that although business groups have made substantial contributions to the funding of political parties and thereby to politics itself, they have been less assertive than in, say, West Germany in using this to raise the profile of business generally. And they have also been less exacting as to the use of the funds. Politicians, both individually and collectively, have been freer to make use of the funds as they chose. Langdon explained this in part by the traditional deference which the people in traditional Confucian societies have shown towards officialdom.[24] Even though political leaders may now be democratically elected rather than appointed, they have still inherited some of the aura of the bureaucrat. And to some extent the officials have reciprocated by being less demanding than their counterparts in the West over accounting for money within companies. Thus each side has been 'generous' towards the other.

There is no doubt about the success of all of these systems in raising funds for political life. None of them has suffered from the equivalent weaknesses of African states. If anything they have been lavish in their political spending. But there are also two conclusions to be drawn. The first concerns the implication from this study for the policies of international economic organizations and governments in the developed world towards Third World development. Since the 1980s, and especially since the end of the Cold War, it has been axiomatic that the 'West' should encourage 'good governance'. This is usually taken to include economic liberalization and political democratization. These two vectors of development are assumed to go together and to reinforce each other.

This account has shown, however, that in none of these states did political democratization and economic liberalization proceed in parallel. In all of them, at early stages of development once peace came after the Second World War and the civil wars, political parties generated funds for their organizations by linking with state officials, who directed national economic development, and with business people who took advantage of special relations with government either to make extra profits or to exploit black-market opportunities. Whatever have been the problems of democracy in these three states, shortage of resources for the political world has not been one of them. Yet the practice of elections, even if, as in Taiwan, no opposition party was permitted to contest them until 1987, sustained the rudiments of a democratic political culture which could then develop when more favourable circumstances permitted.

However, public opinion in all three states is swinging away from the toleration of past practices, since they have now been shown to have led to some individuals accumulating unheard-of wealth. Many Japanese had their breath taken away when one of the godfathers of the LDP, Shin Kanemaru, was arrested in 1993 and 6 billion yen, that is roughly US$60 million, in bank debentures, gold bullion and cash were discovered in his home.[25] Some KMT candidates have now calculated that they stand a better chance of being elected if they openly disassociate themselves from the party's central apparatus and refuse any funds. In that way they think that they will avoid being tarred with the brush of corruption.

So the chances of candidates with less resources winning elections are increasing. Once enough of them do, it is likely that there will be a further tightening of the legislation on the funding of elections, as well as on disclosure of party income.

The second conclusion, however, concerns the possible role of the state in funding political parties. Both Japan and South Korea now allow this, and Taiwan may follow suit in the near future. But the reason for this is not shortage of resources. Rather it is because it allows the state greater access to control over party funding so as to ensure that it is increasingly transparent and legal. In this respect all three states are confronting many of the same problems which the United States and countries in Europe have been addressing in recent years. There too the issue of what should be the relationship between the state and the funding of political parties is contentious.[26]

In that respect, therefore, it is Japan which is more likely to become a 'model', especially in Asia, for it has so far made the most progress in curtailing the spending by parties, and nor is its influence likely to be limited to north-east Asia. Already there have been reports that politicians in Thailand have been watching Japan's efforts with considerable interest, given the extremely venal nature of the last general election there in 1996.[27] Indeed this kind of corruption has become endemic throughout east and south-east Asia. So a great deal of attention will be devoted to this problem, and that will extend to studies of practices in western Europe and the United States in the hope that they will provide useful lessons.[28] As noted above, this could involve a greater role for the state in regulating the behaviour of individual parties, as happens elsewhere in the world.[29]

In fact the experience of western democracies has shown the continuing difficulty of eliminating political corruption. However, in east Asia there is an additional problem. Will the public there accept changes in their relations with elected representatives, for instance ceasing to expect 'gifts' on major family events, as part of the price of change? Unless that happens, the extreme pressures on political funding, often deteriorating into corruption, will continue. Without significant changes in public expectations, the problem of political corruption in Asia cannot be fundamentally addressed.

## Notes

1 P. J. Herzog, *Japan's Pseudo-Democracy* (Folkestone, Japan Library, 1993), p. 135.

2 C. Yanaga, *Japanese People and Politics* (New York, Wiley, 1956), p. 238. According to Kataoka, the figure was 363 (T. Kataoka, *The Price of a Constitution: The Origin of Japan's Post-war Politics* (New York, Crane Russack, 1991), p. 49.

3 Yanaga, *Japanese People and Politics*, pp. 111–12.

4 For a summary account from 1948 until the 1980s, see G. L. Curtis, *The Japanese Way of Politics* (New York, Columbia University Press, 1988), pp. 160–4.

5 Joji Watanuki, *Politics in Post-war Japanese Society* (Tokyo, University of Tokyo Press, 1977), pp. 22–3.

6 Horie Tan, *Seiji Kaikaku to Senkyo Taikei* (Tokyo, Ashi Sho Bo, 1993), p. 115.

7 For a detailed account of how a candidate for the Diet used his *koenkai* in the 1960s, see G. Curtis, *Election Campaigning Japanese Style* (New York, Columbia University Press, 1971), chapters 5, 6.

8 Nobutaka Ike, *Japanese Politics* (New York, Alfred Knopf, 1957), p. 200.

9 Kataoka Tetsuya (ed.), *Creating Single-Party Democracy: Japan's Post-war Political System* (Stanford, CA, Hoover Institution Press, 1992), pp. 48–9.

10 M. L. Lasater, *A Step Toward Democracy: The December 1989 Elections in Taiwan, Republic of China* (Washington, DC, AEI Press, 1990), p. 10.

11 *Far Eastern Economic Review*, 11 August 1994, 62–5. For more details, see Chingsi Chang *et al.*, *Chiekou tangkuo tzupen chuyi* (Taipei, Taipei Society, 1992).

12 Liu Shuhui, 'Chengtang chingfeide yanchiu', in Lin Chiats'ang *et al.* (eds.), *Minchu chihtu shechi* (Taipei, Chang Yungfa Foundation for National Research, 1992), pp. 38–9.

13 Ma Ch'i-hua (ed.), *Tangch'ien Chengchih Went'i Yenchiu* (Taipei, Li Ming Wen Hua, 1991), p. 161.

14 Chyuan-Jeng Shiau, 'Elections and the Changing State-Business Relationship', in Hung-Mao Tien (ed.), *Taiwan's Electoral Politics and Democratic Transition* (New York, M. E. Sharpe, 1996), p. 221.

15 S. J. Hood, 'Political change in Taiwan: the rise of the Kuomintang factions', *Asian Survey*, 36:5 (1996), 468–82; Lai Hsiu-chen, 'Taichungshih tifang p'aihsi t'echih', in *Lilun yu chengts'e* (Taipei, 1994), pp. 97–108.

16 Liu Shuhui, 'Chengtang', in Lin Chiats'ang *et al.*, *Minchu chihtu shechi*, pp. 45–7.

17 For details of this attempt, see C. I. Eugene Kim, 'The Third Republic and the DRP', in C.I. Eugene Kim and Young Whan Kihl (eds.), *Party Politics and Elections in Korea* (Silver Spring, MD, The Research Institute on Korean Affairs, 1976), pp. 25–34.
18 Young Whan Kihl, 'Political roles and participation of community notables: a study of Yuji in Korea', in Chong Lim Kim (ed.), *Political Participation in Korea: Democracy, Mobilisation and Stability* (Santa Barbara, CA, 1980), pp. 85–117.
19 Y. C. Han, 'Political parties and elections in South Korea', in Se-Jin Kim and Chang-Hyun Cho (eds.), *Government and Politics of Korea* (Silver Spring, MD, Research Institute on Korean Affairs, 1972), p. 134.
20 Cited in Sung M. Pae, *Testing Democratic Theories in Korea* (Lanham, MD, University Press of America, 1986), pp. 188–9.
21 Chan Wook Park, 'Financing political parties in South Korea, 1988–91', in H. E. Alexander and R. Shiratori (eds.), *Comparative Political Finance Among the Democracies* (Boulder, CO, Westview, 1994), p. 183.
22 Seongyi Yun, 'A comparative study of party faction in Japan and Korea', *Korea Observer*, 25:4 (1994), 539–65.
23 Yong-ho Kim, 'South Korean party politics' (unpublished paper, 1996).
24 A. J. Heidenheimer and F. C. Langdon, *Business Associations and the Financing of Political Parties* (The Hague, Martinus Nijhoff, 1968), pp. 193, 200–1.
25 C. Wood, *The End of Japan Inc.* (New York, Simon & Schuster, 1994), p. 43.
26 For an attempt to outline a theoretical justification for the state financing in part the activities of political parties because they perform important social functions, see G. van der Beek, *Parteifinanzen: Ein Okonomisch-Finanztheoretischer Beitrag zur Reform* (Hamburg, Steuer und Wirtschaftsverlag, 1994).
27 *Japan Times*, 18 October 1996.
28 See for instance the extended analysis of western practices on campaign funding in Horie, *Seiji Kaikaku to Senkyoh Taikei*.
29 See for example C. Landfried, *Parteifinanzen und Politische Macht* 2nd edn (Baden-Baden, Nomos, 1994).

# 10

# Political party funding in southern Africa

ROGER SOUTHALL AND GEOFFREY WOOD

There has been no systematic treatment of the funding of political parties in Africa. During decolonization, the interest of observers lay elsewhere, notably on the origins, rise and types of parties. Subsequently, during the post-colonial phase, attention shifted first to the consolidation of nationalist parties in government and latterly to the actual decline of political parties, whether because they were displaced by the military or because they were either effectively absorbed or (if in opposition) circumscribed by the state. Then again, even with the renewed interest in African parties which has accompanied the post-Cold War attempted re-democratization of politics, the major focus has been on the reasons and prospects for democratic revival. Absorbed by much grander themes, the literature has concerned itself with the financial base of political parties in Africa only in passing.

This chapter will seek to address this lacuna by examining political party funding in South Africa's new democracy, with some comparative reference to funding practices in some of the countries elsewhere in the southern African region. However, to place this review in some sort of perspective, it is suggested (upon a basis of comments scattered throughout the literature on post-colonial Africa) that party funding in Africa has, broadly speaking, proceeded through three phases.

First, during the early postwar nationalist phase, mass-based political parties were funded in considerable part by party memberships. This practice was imitated less effectively by elite parties, which were more heavily dependent upon the largesse of local notables and patrons.[1] None the less, in some cases a large body of financial support for nationalist movements was provided by external agencies and/or governments interested in influencing the outcome of decolonization.

Second, the effective merging of ruling party with state structures which took place during the post-colonial phase was accompanied by ruling parties moving away from reliance upon membership subscriptions to utilization of state resources. Even so, this was often accompanied by the self-financing of their campaigns by candidates who competed for party office or constituency nominations in contests like the one-party elections which took place in Kenya between 1969 and 1992. Thus Zolberg cites Frantz Fanon's lament that leaders of one-party states rapidly became 'chairmen of the board of a society of impatient profiteers'.[2]

Third, when confronted by the need to embrace a return to multi-partyism in the early 1990s, those ruling parties which had escaped removal by the military continued to rely principally upon their control of state resources. In contrast, pro-democracy challengers to authoritarian or military regimes returned in part to grass-root financing, while also drawing material provision directly or via local non-governmental organizations (NGOs) from foreign donors, both government and unofficial. This trend was to be most pronounced in southern Africa, where external funding of parties has become an integral party of any exercise to broker peace and democracy in countries emerging from vicious civil war.

## Decolonization, independence and the funding of political parties in southern Africa

The evidence concerning party finance in southern Africa is speculative and fragmentary, except for some greater detail available regarding the funding of the attempted democratic transition in South Africa. None the less, it would appear that one may identify party funding as having progressed through the three phases identified in the introduction in this chapter.

In both Botswana and Lesotho, the emergent mass-based nationalist movements, the Botswana Democratic Party (BDP) and the Basutoland Congress Party (BCP), were funded largely by their supporters. In the latter case, the bulk of such support came from migrants on the Rand. This was needed to counter substantial sums provided to the rival, chiefly-based Basotho National Party (BNP), for the pre-independence election of 1965 by, *inter alia*, the South African government and

the conservative West German Konrad Adenaur Stiftung.[3] In
Malawi the Malawi Congress Party (MCP) appears to have
been provided for by a massive expansion of membership which
took place in the months which followed its creation in 1959.[4]
However, the more highly pressured politics involved in the
breakdown of the settler-dominated Federation of the Rhodesias
and Nyasaland saw Kenneth Kaunda's United National Independence Party (UNIP) in Zambia funded overwhelmingly from
outside, notably by Kwame Nkrumah's Ghana, Julius Nyerere's
Tanganyikan African National Union and various African governments including Liberia, Egypt, Ethiopia and Tunisia, as
well as contributions from individuals and groups in the United
States, Britain and Sweden.[5] Nevertheless, an impression which
is confirmed by the performance of the Zimbabwe African
National Union-Patriotic Front (ZANU-PF) in the Zimbabwean
liberation election of 1980 is that nationalist parties were carried
to victory by the massive extent of their support to a far greater
degree than they were by their capacity to deploy resources.
Indeed, only in Lesotho, where workers absent in South Africa
on election day were denied the vote and where, as a result,
the BNP secured a narrow victory, can external funding be said
to have significantly affected an outcome.

The second phase of funding, when ruling party finances become increasingly entangled with those of the state, is exempli-
fied by the case of the BDP. While eschewing the single-party
model, and continuing to draw membership dues and 'especially
voluntary contributions' from the business community and its
more wealthy supporters, the party has benefited substantially
by renting out the bulk of the office space in its headquarters
to government departments and small businesses.[6] More particularly, the government's direction of a prosperous economy
has meant that the BDP has attracted effective sponsorship
from a host of foreign corporations. If donations for 'educa-
tional seminars' from groups like the Friedrich Ebert Foundation are counted, then the BDP may receive as much as half of
its income from foreign sources.[7] The result has been that
when the BDP goes to the polls, it becomes a 'a well-oiled and
financed machine'[8] which has yet to be seriously challenged
by its rivals. Elsewhere, notably in Zambia and Malawi where
the one-party model came to prevail, party resources became
increasingly indistiguishable from those of the government or
parastatals, even if the MCP can be distinguished by the extent

to which party youth were utilized to bully ordinary peasants and workers into buying membership cards. Moyo similarly records how ZANU-PF shamelessly manipulated state institutions to assure its victories in the elections of 1985 and 1990.[9]

### Funding democracy in southern Africa from 1989

The combination of the end of the Cold War, and a diversity of popularly-based and economic pressures upon authoritarian regimes, meant that, as a region, southern Africa was at the confluence of two streams of democratization. On the one hand, countries like Zambia, Lesotho and Malawi were subject to demands, internal and external, for a move away from authoritarianism and a return to competitive multi-partyism. On the other, the rising tide of liberation in southern Africa combined with the more fluid international situation wrought the demise of apartheid, and brought about democratic settlements in Namibia in 1990, and in South Africa and Mozambique in 1994. The evidence suggests that while international financial and diplomatic pressures were vital in bringing about newly democratizing elections in the former countries, there was far less direct foreign involvement in the funding of political parties than in the latter countries, where such activity was seen by diverse interests as intrumental in forging democratic settlements and influencing political outcomes.

### The funding of redemocratization in Zambia, Lesotho and Malawi

Multi-party elections in 1991 in Zambia and in 1994 in Malawi saw the defeat by opposition challengers of the incumbent ruling parties which had entrenched themselves in government since independence. In Lesotho, in contrast, a military government which had seized power from the BNP in 1986 staged a reluctant withdrawal from office following a transition process which culminated in a democratic election in 1993.

In all three countries, coalitions of NGOs – composed of trade unions, churches and student and development organizations – played the crucial role in struggling for the return to democracy in a context where authoritarian governments had become acutely exposed to the economic crisis and decline characterizing the whole sub-continent. Without their backing, neither the Movement for Multi-Party Democracy (MMD) which displaced UNIP in Zambia, nor the United Democratic Front (UDF)-led coalition which defeated the MCP in Malawi, nor the BCP which thrashed the BNP in Lesotho, could have propelled themselves to power. However, while many of the NGOs engaged in struggle would themselves have been in receipt of external funding, there is little evidence that the parties which challenged for power in these elections were in substantial receipt of support from outside. In this sense, they were truly indigenous movements, apparently funded in the former cases at least by the politically alienated and economically disgruntled middle classes (business people, professionals and teachers) which formed their organizational backbone, and in Lesotho – where the majority of BCP candidates' election deposits were paid by local supporters – by a return to the grass-roots.

The popular enthusiasm upon whose back they rode to power was in each case more than a match for their opponents, whose access to use of official resources (vehicles, control of the media, patronage and budgetary bribery) was in any case effectively nullified by the 'negative financing' of international donors. In Zambia, for instance, structural adjustment conditionalities imposed during 1991 required a freeze on many capital projects and an increase in consumer prices on maize of up to 275 per cent: Kaunda's appeal for a freeze on these increases until after the election was turned down.[10] Donors similarly suspended aid to Malawi in 1992 to force the pace of transition, while in Lesotho they associated themselves explicitly with popular demands for 'clean government' and public inquiry into allegations about widespread appropriation of public resources by both the military and the BNP.[11] In contrast, a diversity of international bodies proved happy to bear the expense of the extensive monitoring exercise which accompanied all three elections, and in the case of Lesotho, the actual administration of the election was conducted under the supervision of officials seconded and paid for by the Commonwealth and the United Nations (UN).

*Funding democratic transition in Namibia and Mozambique*

Super-power rivalry had provided the context for South Africa's engagement during the 1970s and 1980s in bitter wars against the Soviet-backed governments in Angola and Mozambique, and against the South West African People's Organization (SWAPO), which was challenging South Africa's continued administration of the UN Trust Territory of Namibia. However, the collapse of the Soviet Union, combined with the rising military cost of defending apartheid beyond the country's borders, led the government in Pretoria to calculate its regional objectives. This was not least because the United States shifted its own strategy in favour of South Africa's withdrawal from Namibia and the forging of formally democratic settlements in Angola and Mozambique, both countries whose economy and infrastructure had been almost totally destroyed by years of civil war and whose governments had been driven into acute dependence upon western financial support. Elections followed in Namibia in late 1989, in Angola in 1992 and in Mozambique in 1994.

Sadly, Angola reverted to civil war, when the União Nacional por Independência Total de Angola (UNITA) declined to accept its electoral defeat. The reasons are complex. Not the least of them, according to US Assistant Secretary of State for African Affairs, George Moose, was that the international community tried to get a settlement on the cheap, and the cost of an adequately supervised election and peace-keeping operation was outweighed by a whole range of other considerations. Indeed, the UN Angolan Verification Mission, the body charged with observing the election, operated on only a quarter of the budget allocated by the UN to bring Namibia to independence.[12]

The circumstances of the latter process were, however, unique. For instead of decolonization being negotiated with a departing colonial power, the settlement featured an election whose principal purpose would be to elect a constituent assembly that would draw up an independence constitution under the supervision of the UN. The implementation of this plan, and the direction of the election, were carried out jointly by the South African authorities as the *de facto* rulers of the territory and the UN Transitional Advisory Group (UNTAG) (composed *inter alia* of 4,500 foreign troops and around 2,500 foreign police and observers) as the representative of the international community. In a situation of remarkable complexity, this resulted in a somewhat flawed electoral process but a result that was regarded as reasonably fair.

Conducted under party-list proportional representation, the election was contested by SWAPO, the Democratic Turnhalle

Alliance (DTA) (a group of multiracial but ethnic-based parties which had emerged under the auspices of Pretoria), and a host of smaller parties which, ranging from white rightists through SWAPO dissidents and ethnic separatists to a leftist Workers' Revolutionary Party, grouped themselves into some eight coalitions. Apart from the human rights orientated United Democratic Front (which obtained nearly 6 per cent of the vote) and the white nationalist Action Christian National Alliance (which obtained 4 per cent), none of these coalitions made a significant impact as SWAPO gained 57 per cent and the DTA 29 per cent of the vote. SWAPO duly took power and oversaw a process that resulted in a thoroughly democratic constitution.

That the outcome was felicitous was fortunate, for the election had proved one of the most expensive in history. Potgieter[13] calculates that if the cost of the UNTAG operation ($500 million) is added to the estimated expenses of the political parties ($42.5 million) and the $3.6 million spent by the South African administration on electoral organization, and if the total of $544 million is divided by the number of voters (701,000), then the cost per capita works out to $77,000! Yet the most expensive votes were those cast for the DTA, whose estimated expenditure of $20 million was backed by the South African state and allied quarters as well as by conservative sources in western Europe, especially Germany. In contrast, SWAPO's outlay of some $18.5 million was drawn from foreign anti-apartheid and solidarity sources. Not surprisingly, by the time of the second election in 1995, when SWAPO swept to a substantially greater victory (73 per cent), foreign interest had declined, and all parties had to operate with considerably more limited funds.[14]

Although expenditure never reached Namibian levels, the Angolan débâcle led to foreign donors and the UN making a considerable investment to secure a settlement in Mozambique after over a decade of South African destabilization and civil war. In particular, to avoid a scenario similar to UNITA's rejection of defeat at the polls, Italy, the United States, newly-democratic South Africa and Namibia agreed to contribute $11 million to fund the electoral campaign of the rebel Resistencia Nacional Mocambicana (Renamo).[15] The latter constituted the major opposition to the Frente de Libertacao de Mocambique (Frelimo), which had formed the government since independence.

In the event, Frelimo won both the presidential and the parliamentary votes with just over 50 per cent of the vote, in an election which attracted over 90 per cent participation and which, in the ultimate analysis, was regarded by the international community as well organized, and both free and fair. However, it had also been remarkably tense, for it had been severely tested by Renamo leader Oscar Dhlakama's various attempts to pull out in protest at alleged fraud. Intense pressure from both Renamo's own supporters, who defied calls to boycott, and the UN, the western powers, and not least, South Africa and Zimbabwe, compelled Dhlakama to accept the result as the basis for a peaceful settlement. But this acceptance came at a price (which foreign funders were prepared to accept). Renamo had used very little of its external funding on actual election campaigning. Even so, by late July 1994, its funds were largely depleted, and it soon demanded an additional $5 million, threatening to withdraw from the electoral process.[16] Once again, to avoid a repetition of the Angolan débâcle, foreign donors coughed up, even though it was recognized that Renamo leaders had begun to live in an extravagant style. However, importantly, these handouts gave Renamo a concrete stake in the electoral process.[17] Currently, Renamo receives some $50,000 a month from the state. In addition, it has gained some further revenue by granting concessions for the extraction of timber and other natural resources from areas in the centre of the country which remain under its direct control.[18]

Frelimo has similarly moved beyond the normal activities of a political party, for since the 1970s and 1980s it has acted also as a commercial enterprise, with considerable interests in both agriculture and industry. Increasingly, however, many of these enterprises are being sold off for nominal amounts to members of the Frelimo elite. Consequently, any profit from these sources will now be reduced. Furthermore, while in the past Frelimo enjoyed a direct state subsidy, it will now only receive greatly reduced amounts, along with all the other parliamentary parties. However, as with Renamo, some of its officals impose unofficial levies in areas under their direction, the large proportion of which never find their way into party coffers.

In terms of the settlement, all (three) parties (Frelimo, Renamo and the tiny Uniao Democratica) which had won representation in the Assembly were now entitled to an official subsidy drawn from a $17 million UN trust fund to promote Mozambican democracy. In contrast, observers reckoned that those which had failed to gain seats would be likely to cease to exist for the simple reason that most of them had been founded with the express purposes of securing access to a share of a trust fund that the UN had established for new political parties.[19]

*Party funding in the new South Africa*

South Africa's negotiated settlement led to the establishment of an Independent Electoral Commission (IEC), charged with supervising and managing the country's first democratic elections, conducted under the party-list system, held in April 1994. Political parties had to adhere to a strict code of conduct, which forbade defamatory advertising materials but stressed the rights of parties to freely engage in political activity in all areas of the country.[20] Although the IEC's principal task was to supervise and monitor the electoral process, it was also charged with distributing a sum of some R22 million (increased to R69 million in February 1994) to finance the campaigns of registered parties.

To qualify for state funding, parties had to gather at least 10,000 signatures from five of South Africa's nine provinces, or register at least 2 per cent support nationwide in an independently conducted poll. In the case of parties only contesting provincial elections, 3,000 signatures were necessary. Meanwhile, minimal financial aid was given to various eccentric splinter parties, a number of which IEC officials felt to have been launched simply to qualify for state funding. In sum, the R69 million was distributed as per Table 10.1.

As can be seen, those parties with the largest demonstrated support gained the lion's share of the allocations, while those parties who could not meet the initial qualifications received no allocations whatsoever. Meanwhile, in addition to this state funding, a Dutch foundation, the Stiftung Voor Het Nieuwe Zuid Afrika, supplied *bona fide* political parties with a flat sum donation, and a proportional allocation based on indicated support. Subsequently, after the elections, all political parties were allocated a constituency allowance of R30,000 per month per MP,[21] plus an allowance for parliamentary support staff, again allocated according to representation. The latter ranges from R2 million per month for the African National Congress (ANC), which secured 62.5 per cent of the national vote, to R238,000 for the liberal Democratic Party (DP), which obtained 1.7 per cent, with somewhat less being allocated to the even smaller

**Table 10.1** South Africa: state allocation to political parties, the April 1994 elections (million rand)

| Allocation | Amount |
| --- | --- |
| Equally shared between all qualifying national level parties prior to elections. However, provincial-only parties to get a quarter of national party allocations | 34.50 |
| Proportionately shared after elections according to votes | 17.25 |
| After election, divided amongst all parties that won at least one provincial or national parliamentary seat | 17.35 |
| **Total*** | **69** |

*Source*: Independent Electoral Commission.
*Note*: * To nearest whole number.

Pan Africanist Congress (PAC), and the African Christian Democratic Party (ACDP).

Given an estimated 60 per cent illiteracy among the electorate, the major parties conducted highly visual campaigns, the ANC and the National Party (NP) both staging highly publicized roadshows centred around their leaders, Nelson Mandela and F. W. De Klerk respectively. These cost an approximate R20,000 per day, with roughly 40 to 50 million pamphlets being released. In total, it seems that the ANC spent some R300–400 million on campaigning in the 1994 elections, and the NP some R100–150 million. The sources and consequences of such spending deserve examination in closer detail.

*The ANC*

During its long years of exile the ANC was overwhelmingly dependent upon external material support. By the mid-80s, it was reportedly receiving some US$24 million per annum in kind from the Soviet Union, and some US$20 million per annum in cash from Scandanavia.[22] Other sources included funding by church and solidarity groups in the West.

The relative importance of Scandanavian, principally Swedish, funding increased when Eastern-bloc aid ceased with the collapse of the Soviet Union. In the last seven months of

1993 alone, Swedish assistance totalled some R40 million.[23] However, this support came to an abrupt halt in late January 1994, when the Swedes ruled that the ANC had transformed itself from a liberation movement into a conventional political party. In order to plug a massive funding gap, Mandela therefore mounted a vigorous fund-raising campaign overseas, just as a statutory ban on such fund raising by political parties was lifted.[24]

In addition to personal campaigning, the ANC distributed a book and video to potential overseas fund raisers. The latter included Mandela 'making the most important appeal of my life'. In response, Dutch official sources gave some R5.5 million to the ANC for voter education (sic). A donation of R20 million was also received from the Indonesian government, while other monies were channelled through the Malaysian government. However, one of the ANC's biggest backers proved to be the Taiwanese government, which not only donated R10 million but granted tax concessions to Taiwanese firms who suitably 'invested' their money in South Africa.

After the elections, the Taiwanese, the Malaysians and the Indonesians all attempted to benefit from their financial support for the ANC. Most particularly, Taiwan managed to roll over the diplomatic relations which it had established with the apartheid regime into a continued formal link with the new government, and South Africa remained the most significant country which did not officially recognize the People's Republic of China (PRC). In this regard President Mandela repeatedly stated that South Africa would never abandon its friends and that it would pursue a controversial 'two Chinas' policy. However, this constituted a major affront to the PRC which, although it had favoured the rival PAC during the years of exile, was now looming ever larger as a potential market for South African exports. Consequently, after much agonizing the new government reversed its stance and, in November 1996, announced that it would sever diplomatic ties with Taiwan and establish them with the PRC in 1997.

While Malaysia has rapidly emerged as one of South Africa's major sources of investment, the Mandela government has come under significant pressure from both internal quarters and its Lusophone neighbours on the East Timor issue. Indeed, following protests by the Indonesians at a visit by an official East Timorese delegation to South Africa in late 1996, Mandela felt compelled to issue a public statement that donations by the Indonesian government 'would not make a hostage of South African foreign policy'. Although this elicited a statement from Jakarta that 'Indonesia's donation to the ANC was made as a gesture of friendship and as a token of solidarity ... with no intention of any political influence', the suspicion remains that Indonesia is expecting a very clear return on its money.[25]

Less controversial foreign funders of the ANC included many European social democratic parties (including the British Labour Party), and their related foundations, including the (Swedish) Olaf Palme Foundation and the (German) Friedrich Ebert Stiftung.[26] Both these bodies gave donations specifically for the training of ANC campaign workers. Similarly, both the New Zealand and Australian Labour Parties not only donated money, but also despatched voluntary workers, while the former also gave the ANC free use of its intellectual property. In addition, having formed the Matla Trust as a conduit for donations from the United States, the ANC received financial assistance from the Democrats, as well as separate donations from their black caucus which allowed for the establishment of the Voter Education and Elections Training Unit (VEETU). Although primarily giving assistance to the ANC, VEETU also offered training to the civic organizations and the PAC.[27]

For the 1994 election the ANC was overwhelmingly dependent upon its overseas backers. In contrast, its local fund-raising initiatives yielded mixed results. On the one hand, its formal membership fee of R12 proved too costly for perhaps the majority of its supporters, who doubtless deemed themselves members of the movement by identification anyway. Similarly, although it managed to obtain some backing from smaller local businesses during the staggered local government elections of 1995 and 1996, it operated on remarkably modest budgets during these campaigns. On the other hand, responding to appeals by Mandela that they support the transition, a number of leading South African firms gave donations to both the ANC and the NP in 1994, while a 'President's 1000 Club', which charged a R10,000 admission fee, proved highly successful among African business people. In addition, the party received the backing of the Congress of South African Trade Unions, itself the recipient of substantial overseas aid.[28]

None of this information on funding was made freely available to the public. When later pressed on this matter, the ANC responded that it had never revealed the sources of its finances, which were regularly audited and subject to checks required under its constitution. However, for a party whose rhetoric espoused accountability and transparency in public institutions, these assurances rang particularly hollow, especially when it was subsequently admitted by Mandela that, prior to the election, he had received a substantial donation from casino magnate Sol Kerzner without informing his party colleagues. What was particularly damaging to the ANC, and to the president's own lofty moral image, was that Kerzner was widely known to have been under investigation for bribing politicians to win commercial favours.

Kerzner had amassed a considerable fortune under apartheid through his securing a monopoly on casino concessions in the former 'independent' homelands when gambling was banned in 'white' South Africa. Courtroom evidence indicates that Kerzner bribed former Transkei leader George Matanzima in return for casino licences in that territory. Shortly thereafter, Matanzima was toppled in a 1987 military coup led by General Holomisa, who briefly handed over power to Stella Sigcau (the daughter of Transkei's founding president, Botha Sigcau), before seizing power for himself, claiming that both leaders had been personally corrupt. Subsequent judicial proceedings led to the conviction and imprisonment of Matanzima for receiving the Kerzner bribe. A warrant was issued for Kerzner's arrest, but South African authorities refused to extradite him to Transkei.

Holomisa and Sigcau's membership of the influential establishment of traditional leaders in the Transkei helped ensure that, despite their mutual aversion, both received senior positions in the ANC, with Sigcau obtaining a cabinet seat, and Holomisa a deputy ministership. However, matters came to a head when, in July 1996, Holomisa gave a statement to the Truth and Reconciliation Commission (the body charged with investigating human rights abuses in the apartheid era) accusing Sigcau of receiving a R50,000 cut of Matanzima's bribe. No effort was made to refute this claim, but Holomisa was subsequently to be ejected from the ANC for endangering party unity.

This indignity followed his allegations that Kerzner had given R2 million to the ANC's 1994 election campaign, in addition to giving free hotel accommodation to Minister of Sport, Steve Tshwete, and footing the bill for Vice-President Thabo Mbeki's lavish fiftieth birthday party, all in turn for the sidelining of the charges laid against him. Holomisa further alleged he had been summoned by Mandela to Johannesburg's Carlton Hotel in 1994 to tell him about Kerzner's donation, and to discuss the possibility that the bribery charges against Kerzner could be quashed. It was only after initial denials by ANC officials that Mandela then conceded that the ANC had indeed received the R2 million, but not for any services rendered. For his part, Kerzner claimed to have only donated R50,000. Meanwhile, his trial has yet to take place, ostensibly because of personnel shortages in the office of the Transkei Attorney-General.[29]

The ANC has a long-standing alliance with the South African Communist Party (SACP). The latter remains a somewhat secretive organization, assuming the role of a self-styled elite within the ANC alliance. The SACP retains a highly restrictive membership policy – potential members must serve a six-month probation period. However, despite a Stalinist tradition, the SACP has conditionally endorsed not only a multi-party system, but also much of the neo-liberal economic policy adopted by the ANC.[30] In the past, the SACP's main funder was the former Soviet Union, although it also received considerable assistance from the East German *stasi* (this support reportedly included supplies of forged South African rands for expenditure by its underground operatives within the Republic). Currently, the SACP claims that its main sources of funds are membership subscriptions and 'modest investments', but it also may be receiving limited assistance from the PRC.[31] There is little doubt, however, that the SACP has very limited financial resources. Again, it has very limited operating expenses – SACP candidates contest elections on ANC tickets, and produce little of their own publicity to back up their candidatures. In addition, the SACP can rely on a small core of highly-dedicated and disciplined volunteers.

*The NP*

One of the NP's major funding sources remains its several trust funds, whose dates of establishment range from 1912 to 1979. Historically, the NP has managed to cover a large part of its running expenses out of the interest received from these accounts, although it is believed that it was forced to dip into its capital when confronted with the first democratic election in 1994.

Since its early years, the NP has had a close and mutually beneficial relationship with the Afrikaans business community, and much of its financial backing still comes from this source. However, it has now lost the backing of a number of key Afrikaans firms, including insurance giant Sanlam, and the Kolosus meat conglomerate. In addition, Nasionale Pers (the main Afrikaans newspaper grouping, previously one of the NP's most fervent backers) now gives equal sums of money to the NP and the DP. The NP leaders claim that such losses have, in turn, been offset by their gaining financial support from firms which had previously backed the DP, but which now viewed the NP as the most effective opposition.[32]

The NP fought a highly capital-intensive campaign in 1994 centred around their principal asset, F. W. De Klerk, who built up a strong personal following, especially in the Western Cape. In order to gain maximum exposure, De Klerk toured the country, with a videotape being widely distributed in those areas he could not visit. The latter was compiled by the local affiliate of the British advertising firm, Saatchi and Saatchi, which has been responsible for much of the NP's media since the mid-1980s. None the less, NP campaigners battled to gain access to many African areas, and were denied permission by Holomisa to campaign in Transkei.[33]

As with the ANC, the NP's major expense during the 1994 elections was media advertisements. Full-page colour coverage in the major national Sunday newspaper, the *Sunday Times*, cost roughly R250,000. However, given that only 15 per cent of the nation read newspapers, and that many areas of the country were off limits to the NP, the effect of such campaigning was somewhat limited. As an alternative means of spreading its message, the NP made widespread use of pamphlets. Yet these proved costly in another way, notably when the IEC seized over 11,000 copies of an allegedly racist NP flyer ('Will You Survive the Storm?') which was distributed in the ethnic coloured areas in Cape Town. Such pamphlets were delivered by voluntary workers recruited from the coloured community.[34]

Coloured volunteers similarly provided the backbone of a very high profile and expensive campaign,[35] apparently extensively financed by Sol Kerzner, which the NP mounted in the greater Cape Town area during the subsequent local government elections. Significantly, two major casino licences were due to be issued by the Western Cape NP-controlled government, and a consortium headed by Kerzner was bidding to win one (there have been further allegations that another consortium, linked to senior NP members, would like to obtain the other licence in order to open a casino in the rural centre of Caledon).

There seems little doubt that, in addition to providing donations to the ANC, Kerzner also contributed to the NP. During the second half of 1995, there were persistent allegations in the South African press that financial handouts he had made to the NP in the late 1980s and early 1990s were linked to the then government's opposition to his extradition to Transkei. To be sure, the NP issued a statement denying that it had received any money from Kerzner during 1990–94.[36] But shortly thereafter, it was forced to concede that it had indeed received some R50,000 from Kerzner immediately after the 1994 elections.

Meanwhile, like the ANC, the NP has a number of overseas backers, most notably European conservative parties. There is, again, considerable sharing of intellectual property, in addition to the fact that, as noted above, Britain's Conservatives and the NP have, for many years, employed the same advertising agency, Saatchi and Saatchi. Given that it has now lost control over the output of South African Broadcasting Corporation, which it was shameless in using to promote its message in earlier whites-only elections, the costs of its political marketing seem destined to rise. Not surprisingly, perhaps, the NP now routinely accuses the Corporation of bias towards the ANC.

## The DP

For many years, approximately 80 per cent of the DP's funds have come from individual donatiohs, above all in the form of standing orders on bank accounts. This has always been backed up by large numbers of dedicated voluntary workers, who have catered principally to the party's overwhelmingly white, middle-class constituency. In addition, since the inception of the precursor Progressive Party in 1959, there have been close relations with sections of the English-speaking business community.

Anglo-American patriarch Harry Oppenheimer was one of the Progressive Party's founding MPs, and was influential in ensuring that business contributions increased substantially in the 1970s. Indeed, coterminous with something of an electoral breakthrough by that party in 1974 (when its representation in the all-white parliament increased from one to seven MPs), a 100 per cent increase in donated funds, and a 200 per cent increase in large donations, was recorded. From 1973 to 1977, the party's national treasurer was Gordon Waddell, an executive director of the Anglo-American Corporation. In 1978, Houghton branch chair, Irene Menell, stated that there were few big Johannesburg companies which had not been approached or which had not given.[37] Indeed, over the years, Anglo-American Corporation has paid for the running expenses of the national office of the 'Progs' and their successor parties, including the DP.

None the less, a major constraint on corporate fund raising in the apartheid era was the compulsory state audit. This led to many companies with sizeable government contracts being extremely reluctant to donate monies, while some donations were heavily concealed, being routed via firms of attorneys.[38] Firms are now somewhat less circumspect in donating money to the DP as a result of the more open political climate, while some corporations have adopted a policy of giving equal or proportionally allocated sums to a number of major political actors. In addition, it seems that some of the DP's traditional financial backers which switched to the NP for the 1994 elections have now returned to the fold.

Following the lifting on the ban on overseas fund raising, the DP embarked on a fund-raising drive abroad. This campaign enjoyed a considerably lower profile than the ANC's, and, not surprisingly, it raised considerably less money – roughly R1 million.[39] However, the DP has received some support from the Friedrich Neumann Stiftung (linked to the German Free Democrats), which, for example, paid for a workshop for all DP public representatives in late 1996.

The DP pioneered large-scale media advertisements in the 1981 elections. In an interview, Senator James Selfe ruefully admitted 'that it probably was not a good idea in that it gave other political parties ideas', fuelling a merry-go-round, whereby electoral expenditure 'has tended to rise exponentially'.[40] In 1994, the DP spent R6 million on media advertisements alone, resulting in somewhat depleted finances by the time of the 1996 Cape Town municipal elections.

### The Inkatha Freedom Party (IFP)

Prior to the 1994 elections, the IFP, the Kwazulu-Natal ethnic-based party led by Chief Mangosuthu Buthelezi, received financial support from conservative American sources, although this has gradually dried up since then. Again, in the past, the IFP received some financial support from elements of the business sector, notably the sugar industry in Natal. However, this has also somewhat diminished as the transition has progressed,[41] and as the party has come to be increasingly identified as a 'spoiler' of South Africa's new democracy. Indeed, currently, the IFP has 'no easy relationship to business',[42] and unlike the ANC, has few linkages to supportive NGOs capable of independent fund raising overseas. However, as with all the other political parties, the IFP has received some donations from the Stiftung Voor Het Nieuwe Zuid Afrika, the Dutch foundation that has been noted above.

Probably the IFP's biggest individual backer is right wing British businessman and zoo-keeper, John Aspinall. However, Aspinall has tended to reserve final say as to how this money is spent. Among other things this led to the employment of British consultants, led by Ian Grier, to manage the IFP's election campaign in the 1996 Natal local government elections. The radical free market message promoted by these consultants seems to have had little appeal to the IFP's traditional rural constituency, and probably greatly contributed to a poor performance by the IFP in these elections. Another prominent European supporter of the IFP has been controversial billionaire Sir James Goldsmith, who died in 1997. However, it seems that Goldsmith donated considerably less to the IFP than Aspinall. He also expressed an interest in obtaining a casino licence in the depressed Point area of Durban.

However, from at least the early 1980s, the IFP – which was viewed as a rival to the ANC by the apartheid state – received covert financial (as well as operational and quasi-military) assistance from both the South African Defence Force's Civil Co-Operation Bureau and the Security Police. In addition, although it officially entered the contest only days before the 1994 elections, it did thereby qualify for IEC financial support, even though its late entry into the fray meant that it was in no position to make effective use of the monies. However, post-election allocations enabled the IFP to defray some of a massive debt accumulated as a result of campaigns aimed at raising its general profile during the final pre-elections negotiations.[43]

Since the general election, the IFP has funded its national office out of its constituency allowances, with no money whatsoever being allocated for constituency level activity. However, as one prominent IFP member (who wished to remain anonymous) remarked, the parliamentary speaker's office 'began smelling a rat'. As a consequence, there are now moves to tighten up these allowances, which will have serious implications for the IFP's future operations. While all IFP MPs are expected to contribute R1,000 of their monthly salaries to the party, this will do little to overcome the shortfall, and it seems likely that in the future the party will not be able to mount the same intensity of campaigns as it has done in the past.[44]

## The Freedom Front

During the closing stages of the negotiations process, the major Afrikaner right wing organizations, most notably the Conservative Party (CP) and the Afrikaner Volksvront, formed an alliance with the IFP and former Bophuthatswana homeland leader, Lucas Mangope. However, dissatisfaction with the alliance led to a breakaway white right wing grouping, the Freedom Front (FF), being formed in March 1994, with the express aim of contesting the elections.

The FF mopped up most of the white right wing support, only a small minority heeding the calls of the rump CP and a plethora of often neo-facist splinter groupings to abstain. Led by a former Defence Force chief, General Konstand Viljoen, the FF mounted a campaign centred around the personality of its leader, under the slogan 'Comes the Hour, Comes the Man'. As with most of the other smaller political actors, it was heavily reliant on state funding, in addition to receiving the normal allocations from the Dutch foundation mentioned above at the time of the 1994 elections. However, the Front has gradually diversified its financial support base, and has now built up a network of standing orders, in addition to limited donations from right wing elements in the business community.[45]

## The PAC

As with its rival, the ANC, the PAC – which went into exile in the 1960s but suffered from intractable divisions – sought overseas backing prior to the 1994 elections, but in its case to little avail. This reflected both the extremist image the PAC cultivated in the run-up to the elections, and its total eclipse by the ANC. Indeed, in a submission made to the Truth and Reconciliation Committee in early May 1997, the PAC admitted responsibility for a series of violent attacks and robberies which took place in the early 1990s, mainly in the Eastern Cape, motivated primarily by the search for funds and equipment. It argued, 'The liberation movement was at war with a very strong regime. The PAC had no superpower backing them and we had to form repossession units.'[46] The PAC also attempted some fund raising in more extreme quarters of the Arab world, but even long-term backers, such as Libya, were not forthcoming. This reluctance followed upon a split with the previously closely aligned Islamic fundamentalist grouping, Qibla, with the latter favouring a boycott of the elections.[47]

In early 1994, PAC leaders made appeals to local businesses to ensure a fair campaign by being even-handed in donations. Not unexpectedly, given periodic threats by PAC leaders to redistribute property without compensation, little such support was forthcoming. Similarly, pledges of financial support collected from members were widely dishonoured. This did not, however, deter the PAC from at one stage giving a 50 per cent pay rise to staff members.[48]

In the end, the main source of PAC funding during the 1994 elections was the IEC's contribution, which led to the party offering a limited campaign. Indeed, PAC finances were in such a parlous state that it had to appeal to VEETU for travel assistance to get its voluntary workers to voter education training workshops.[49] A week after the elections, it faced eviction from its Salt River offices for unpaid rents, while during the campaign itself its offices had their telephones disconnected as a result of accounts arrears.[50]

Worse, it seems that much of the IEC's allocation may have been embezzled. At its 1996 Congress, the conference convenor, Ike Mafole, conceded that there had been widespread misappropriation of party funds, which together with poor leadership directly accounted for the PAC's consistently dismal performances at the polls.[51] The PAC subsequently launched a campaign 'for disciplined financial organization and management', stressing that action would be taken against those found guilty of having misappropriated party funds. As at the time of writing, no culprits had been identified.

As with the IFP, the PAC's major source of income today is probably in the form of parliamentary allowances for its five MPs. Again, little seems to be spent in constituency work, and indeed, although the PAC had a small network of paid organizers during the 1994 election, these have now been retrenched.

With the move to tighten up on constituency allowances, the PAC's national office will be facing a serious financial short-fall. However, one of the few areas in which the PAC has demonstrated an aptitude has been in weathering seemingly terminal financial crises.[52]

### The ACDP

Since its launch in the early 1990s, the ACDP has been closely aligned to conservative Christian fundamentalist groupings, with the latter playing a major role in promoting its image. The party has based its limited publicity material around a narrowly fundamentalist world view, with pamphlets citing *Old Testament* strictures as justification for its policies over a wide range of areas, including homosexuality, abortion and the death penalty.

During the 1994 election, the ACDP received R400,000 from the Dutch foundation that has already been referred to, and R600,000 from the IEC. However, the chair of the Gauteng region could not, after the elections, satisfactorily account for a significant portion of the IEC allocation. This led to his suspension, although he was later reinstated following a court order, and the dispute has yet to be resolved.[53]

The ACDP has had little financial support from the business community or overseas donors, although some professional supporters have given some infrastructural backing to the party on an *ad hoc* basis. According to one of the party's two MPs, 'it is very debatable if a small party is able to reach out to all persons, to get the support it deserves'. However, unlike the IFP, the ACDP has taken great pains to promote linkages with the NGO sector. *Inter alia*, it is involved in developmental work, and promoting literacy in the Pietermaritzburg area, through Project Gateway. While it is not relying on NGOs to promote its message, it hopes that 'through good works' it may be possible to raise its profile, especially in pre-selected areas, where the party believes it has potential room for expansion. However, it is felt that lack of finances are a major barrier to expansion in the townships, where 'people share the vision' but lack financial resources.[54]

The ACDP has tended to rely heavily on volunteers, although for short periods during the run-up to the election a few part-time paid workers were employed. Today, the party has only three full-time secretaries, one based in each of the three provinces where it has MPs or members of the provincial assembly. However, with the Speaker's permission, the ACDP has used its constituency allowances to employ a lawyer to assist in the monitoring of legislation, given the limited experience of its two MPs. None the less, the party favours the tightening-up of constituency allowances, and in future plans to devote the money to constituency level activity.[55] ACDP MPs have to 'tithe' R5,000 per month of their salary, while city councillors also have to give a portion of their allowances to the party.

*Other political actors*

Other political parties contesting the 1994 elections included the African Muslim Party (AMP), the African Democratic Movement, the African Moderates Congress Party, the Dikwankwetla Party, the Luso-South Africa Party (LSAP), the Minority Party, the Federal Party, the Soccer Party, the Kiss (Keep It Straight and Simple) Party, the Women's Rights Peace Party, Workers List Party and the Ximoko Progressive Party (XPP). These groupings reflected homeland/black town council interests (Dikwankwetla, XPP), minority interests (LSAP, the Soccer Party), or simply served as vehicles for the self-promotion of a single personality (the Federal Party, Kiss). None of them had any significant financial backing, and most have since disappeared without trace. However, Lucas Mangope has now been charged with having misappropriated in excess of R10.4 million of public funds in favour of his United Christian Democratic Party, which he formed after his removal from office in Bophuthatswana (Eastern Provincial Herald, 6 September 1996). In the end, Mangope's party did not contest the national elections in 1994.

## Conclusion

As elsewhere in the world, political parties in southern Africa require funding, either by their members and supporters, or by other external agencies. It has been argued that, in the case of the tropical southern African states, while funding by members was often critical during the early nationalist phase, external funding was equally or more often provided by foreign governments or agencies who were interested in shaping the post-colonial situation. Second, during the one-party/dominant party phase, ruling parties were financed by the state. Third, during the most recent wave of democracy, it has been suggested that external resourcing of political parties was again fundamental, albeit during this round located within a wider context of the external funding of a broader process of democratization, where provision for civil society (notably NGOs) and electoral administration and monitoring was viewed as being as important as the direct funding of political parties by the international community.

As a result of political isolation and restrictions on overseas funding, political parties in apartheid South Africa derived their revenue in a somewhat more complex manner. There is little doubt, however, that following democratization, South Africa, like many other southern African states, followed the third pattern of funding outlined above. This development was clearly related to the decline of Cold War contestation in southern Africa, and the associated re-legitimization of multi-partyism and competitive elections within Africa. Most important of all, there has been a determination by western powers to back drives for political settlements in the previously strife-torn countries of Namibia, Mozambique and South Africa. As has been noted, where this determination has been lacking, in Angola, the search for peace remains elusive.

There are clear dangers in all this. The first is, quite simply, that if external resourcing of democracy in southern Africa is important to the continuance of that democracy, then the inter-national community will need to go on paying. It is, then, most certainly *not* being argued that 'democracy' has arrived or returned to Africa simply because of western beneficence. None the less, it is argued that democracy in southern Africa is fragile – heavily dependent upon the health of civil society, and yes, of political parties as well. To be sure, the vitality of civil society and of parties rests primarily upon the energy, imagination, effort and – too often – the bravery of key segments of society. Yet countless NGOs in Africa remain dependent upon external financial support. This may be undesirable, and self-reliance may be the preferred goal, but the reality is that in poverty-stricken, ravaged economies continuing external dependence is probably unavoidable for the foreseeable future. Yet the contradiction is that, just as the western powers preach 'conditionality' and 'democracy' in southern Africa, the obsession with IMF/World Bank structural adjustment means financial cutbacks which are cutting swathes through NGOs. Thus a survey of some 128 NGOs in South Africa in June 1995 indicated that, compared with the previous year, they were facing a two-thirds shortfall in their operating budgets, and many were contemplating closure.[56] At the time of writing (in early 1997), plans are in hand for the creation of a National Development Agency, which in addition to being a forum where 'civil society' will be able to debate with government, will serve as an official agency for directing foreign and state funds to selected NGOs. Yet for the moment NGO financing remains precariously balanced and many are said to have gone under.[57] While it is unlikely that NGOs and political parties are in direct competition for the same funds, the broader point is that with apartheid now dead, external western enthusiasm to fund democracy – whether support for 'civil society', or in the form of direct funding of parties or international monitoring exercises – is now likely to decline. What remains to be seen is the likely impact which state funding of NGOs (unlikely to exceed 50 per cent of any one body) will have upon the quality of democracy.

The second problem with external funding of political parties is, of course, that so often it implies an attempt to purchase influence. Where foreign funding is involved, this is traditionally regarded as being peculiarly nefarious, especially where it is seen as attempting to purchase foreign policy outcomes (even though as Taiwan has learnt to its cost, foreign policy is not always for outright sale). For the moment, one is inclined to suggest that the foreign funding of ruling parties, especially of ZANU-PF and the ANC, may accompany a wave of new investment in these countries taking place under specifically Malaysian sources.[58]

None the less, as external agency funding of parties seems both necessary and inevitable, and if funding and attempts to purchase influence seem inextricably bound, then the case for transparency and accountability will need to be continuously restated. Political parties – witness the ANC – are notoriously reluctant to reveal their sources of funding, yet the public has an undoubted right to know. For this reason, current attempts by the DP in South Africa to secure agreement around codes of conduct, disclosure and limits on elections spending are greatly to be welcomed,[59] not least in an era when competing parties will be tempted to import increasingly capital-intensive (and thus, often, rather inappropriate) means of electioneering from overseas. Against this, it seems inherently unlikely that the ANC – or any other ruling parties in southern Africa – will concede total transparency. Perhaps the best that can be hoped for in the circumstances is that DP-style legislation be implemented to require strict accounting of all public electoral expenditure (which might set limits on the extent of manipulation of budgets by ruling parties). Also, public demands for transparency may set at least some ground rules and imply there will be political costs if wholly inappropriate external funding (such as by foreign investors awaiting government contracts) came out into the open.

The final difficulty with external funding is that often it becomes impossible to separate personal from party financing. Infusions of cash too often translate into personal wealth for a few. Again, there are no obvious remedies, except to argue the case for accountability, linked to a pragmatic commonsense which recognizes that, in peculiarly fragile situations like Mozambique, it may well be better to pay warlords to live in peace than to go back to war.

None the less, for all the inevitable dilemmas that it poses, the continued external funding of political parties, and especially of oppositions, seems an important requirement if democracy in southern Africa is going to survive. In a final postscript it can be recorded that in early May 1997 the South African government gave notice that it would be tabling a Promotion of Multi-party Democracy Bill in Parliament. This proposes the establishment of a fund for financing parties that will be credited with money appropriated by Parliament, together with contributions from local private and foreign sources, and administered by a permanent electoral commission. Smaller parties in particular would benefit from the funding, according to Mr Valli Moosa, the Minister of Provincial Affairs and Constitutional Development.[60]

## Notes

1 T. Hodgkin, *African Political Parties* (Gloucester, MA, Peter Smith 1971), pp. 68–9.
2 A. Zolberg, *Creating Political Order: The Party-States of West Africa* (Chicago, Rand McNally, 1966), p. 141.
3 B. Leeman, *Lesotho and the Struggle for Azania*, vols. 1 and 2 (London, University of Azania), pp. 122–3.

4 P. Short, *Banda* (London, Routledge & Kegan Paul, 1974), p. 126.

5 J. Pettman, *Zambia: Security and Conflict* (London, Julian Friedmann Publishers, 1974), pp. 21–3.

6 J. Parson, *Botswana: Liberal Democracy and the Labour Reserve in Southern Africa* (Boulder, CO, Westview, 1984), p. 49.

7 J. Holm, 'Elections and democracy in Botswana', in J. Holm and P. Molutsi (eds.), *Democracy in Botswana* (Gaberone, Macmillan Botswana, 1989), p. 197.

8 Parson, *Botswana*, p. 49.

9 J. Moyo, *Voting for Democracy: Electoral Politics in Zimbabwe* (Harare, University of Zimbabwe Publications, 1992). On Malawi see D. Cammack, 'The democratic transition in Malawi: from single-party rule to unity in a multi-party state', in M. Szeftel, R. Southall and J. Daniel (eds.), *Voting for Demcoracy: Elections and Politics in Contemporary Africa* (Aldershot, Dartmouth, forthcoming 1997).

10 C. Baylies and M. Szeftel, 'The fall and rise of multi-party politiics in Zambia', *Review of African Political Economy*, 54 (1992), 81.

11 On Malawi, see Cammack, 'The democratic transition'; on Lesotho see R. Southall, 'Lesotho's transition and the 1993 election', in R. Southall and T. Petlane (eds.), *Democratisation and Demilitarisation in Lesotho: the general election of 1993 and its aftermath* (Pretoria, Africa Institute, 1995), p. 32.

12 C. Pycroft, 'Angola – the forgotten tragedy', *Journal of Southern African Studies*, 20:2 (1994), 250 and 262.

13 P. J. J. S. Potgieter, 'The resolution 435 election in Namibia', *Politikon*, 18:2 (1991), 26.

14 D. Simon, 'Namibia: SWAPO wins two-thirds majority', *Review of African Political Economy*, 63 (1995), 108–9.

15 *The Economist*,13 August 1994.

16 *Mozambiquefile* (Maputo) 1/1994.

17 R. Haines and G. Wood, 'The 1994 election and Mozambique's democratic transition', *Democratization*, 2:3 (1995), 362–76.

18 *Africa Confidential* (London) 36:2 (1996), 4.

19 *Ibid.*; *Mozambiquefile* 10/1994.

20 IEC, *Election 1994: Path to Democracy* (Pretoria, 1994), 11/3/1994.

21 Although the election system was conducted by list-system proportional representation, MPs were subsequently made responsible for individual 'constituencies'.

22 *Africa Confidential*, 27 May 1986.

23 *Weekend Argus* (Cape Town), 19–20 February 1994.

24 Section 3 of the Political Interference Act. The ruling obliging political parties to have their accounts audited was retained.

25 *Mail and Guardian* (Johannesburg), 20 September 1996 and 4 October 1996.

26 Interview, Bill Sewell, Cape Town, September 1996.

27 *Ibid.*

28 R. Southall, *Imperialism or Solidarity? International Labour and South African Trade Unions* (Cape Town, University of Cape Town Press, 1995), pp. 170–83.

29 *Mail and Guardian* 8–15 August 1996; *Sunday Independent* (Johannesburg), 4 August 1996; *Daily Despatch* (East London), 11 October 1996.

30 H. Adam and K. Moodley, *The Opening of the Apartheid Mind* (Berkeley, CA, University of California Press, 1993), pp. 81 and 100.

31 *Mail and Guardian*, 22–28 November 1996.

32 Interview, Roelf Meyer, then NP Secretary-General, Cape Town, September 1996.

33 *Argus* (Cape Town), 17 March 1994.

34 *Argus*, 9 April 1994; *Argus*, 18 March 1994.

35 Meyer, interview. However, this has been disputed. In one interview, a senior DP member remarked, 'we always see the same familiar (white) faces doing much of the NP's day-to-day campaigning'.

36 *Daily Dispatch*, 10 October 1995.

37 B. Hackland, 'Incorporationist ideology as a response to political struggle: the Progressive Party of South Africa, 1960–1980', in S. Marks and S. Trapido (eds.), *The Politics of Race, Class and Nationalism in Twentieth Century South Africa* (London, Longman, 1987), p. 381.

38 Interview, DP Senator James Selfe, Cape Town, 1996.

39 *Ibid.*

40 *Ibid.*

41 Interview, K. O'Malley, IFP Research, Cape Town, September 1996.

42 Interview, senior adviser to Chief M. Buthelezi, Cape Town, September 1996.

43 *Ibid.*

44 Interview, Cape Town, September 1996.

45 K. Viljoen, Cape Town, September 1996.

46 *Eastern Province Herald* (Port Elizabeth), 7 May 1997.

47 *Cape Times* (Cape Town), 19 April 1994. Libya was involved in training members of the PAC's armed wing and provided some financial support from the early 1970s (see for instance Leeman, *Lesotho*, pp. 58–9). The PAC received its last donation from Libya in early 1990, acccording to the *Sunday Times* (Johannesburg), 10 April 1994.

48 *Argus*, 18 March 1994; *Cape Times*, 7 May 1993.

49 Interview, Bill Sewell, Cape Town, September 1996.

50 *Argus*, 30 October 1994.

51 *Daily Dispatch*, 23 September 1996.

52 Press reports predicted the PAC's collapse as a result of financial difficulties 'within eight weeks' in May 1993. See *Cape Times*, 7 May 1993.

53 Interview, Lous Green (ACDP MP), Cape Town, September 1996.

54 *Ibid.*

55 *Ibid.*

56 R. Amner and L. Vergnani, 'Findings of survey on financial situation of 128 Non-governmental organisations (NGOs) and community-based organisations (CBOs)', *Leading Edge*, 4 (1995).

57 This assessment is based on informal discussion with various activists and by reference to items on the Internet.

58 This is very definitely speculation on the writers' part, but it is seen as a possibility because of the growing love-match between South Africa and Malaysia. See R. Southall, 'Party dominance and development: South Africa's prospects in the light of Malaysia's experience', *The Journal of Commonwealth and Comparative Politics*, vol. 35, 2, 1997, pp. 1–27.

59 *Eastern Province Herald*, 23 October 1996.

60 *Sunday Times*, 4 May 1997.

# 11

# Conclusion

ALAN WARE

It is a relatively easy exercise to specify the standards that party funding would have to meet in an ideal democracy. Unfortunately, these standards are not met even in long-established liberal democracies, and, arguably, it may be that much more difficult for regimes that are in the process of democratizing. Most especially, regimes that started to democratize in the late twentieth century (or to re-democratize in these years) may find it difficult to establish methods of funding parties that come anywhere close to realizing these desiderata. To understand why this should be so, and what if anything, democratizing regimes might do about it, we must begin by outlining what these desiderata are.

1 *The level of funding to parties should be such that, between them, they are capable of establishing links with nearly all voters.* Parties need money for a variety of specific purposes – building up permanent organizations, electioneering, and so on. The sum total of these activities should result in the development of links with mass electorates. When a significant number of parties fail to develop stable relationships with large sections of the electorate, the stability of the regime itself may be weakened. The classic example of this is the Weimar Republic, where the centre and right-of-centre parties achieved very little penetration of German society; one of the factors contributing to the success of the National Socialists was that their potential electoral rivals on the right had established so few permanent links with voters. Anti-system movements and parties are much less likely to succeed if they must try to detach their likely supporters from loyalties to pro-democracy parties. Despite some evident resistance in contemporary eastern Europe to the idea that

parties need to be built up in order to preserve democracy, the history of liberal democracy indicates that weak party–voter links can be a major source of regime instability. For this reason, those regimes, such as Brazil and Russia, in which electoral competition has come to involve more individual candidates than it has parties, might face a more difficult task in preserving democracy should, say, economic conditions become intolerable. To those who might argue that the United States provides an example of the successful practice of candidate-centred competition, it should be pointed out that there are important institutional differences between the United States and most other 'presidential' regimes. In particular, legislatures constrain American chief executives (the President and state governors) to a much greater degree than they do in most other presidential regimes, and this provides a counterbalance for the weakness of parties.

2 *The pressure to acquire funds must not be so great that it either becomes the prime activity of most parties or makes it likely that they will act merely as the agents of those who do fund them.* It is not just the lack of funds that can weaken linkages between parties and mass electorates; the distortion of party effort in the direction of fund raising, because of the need to remain competitive electorally, can also lead to a weakening of various kinds of party–voter links. However, the other danger if there is a general frenzy towards the acquisition of money by parties is that particular parties may have an incentive to make specific deals with funders. In an ideal democracy parties have a high degree of automony, in that powerful individuals or organized interests can be dealt with as equals; in turn, that makes it more likely that most parties will seek to aggregate interests rather than act simply as vehicles for particular interests. This autonomy may be undermined should the demand for funds be so intense that a party may be tempted to cut an explicit deal in exchanging the promotion of specific policies for funds. (Another temptation, which could also help to undermine democratization, is that, having gained power, a party then tries to raid the public purse to reimburse itself for the expenses it incurred in winning office.)

3 *Between them, the parties acquire funds from a wide sector of society; overall, the pattern in the giving of money to political parties should reflect the structure of interests in*

*the society.* There are really two aspects to this condition. On the one hand, there is a need to avoid too many parties becoming the mere instruments of just a few interests. This is a more general point about party autonomy than the one made above in relation to the pressure on parties to acquire funds; even when that pressure is not especially high, if most parties are heavily dependent on only a few financial backers, their willingness to try to aggregate interests may be limited. On the other hand, even if a party is more than a front for a single interest, how much attention it pays to a given sector of the electorate may well depend on the contribution that sector makes to party success. Financial contributions are only one such source – time or effort put in by party activists or members is another; but to the extent that different types of contribution are not substitutable, it matters when funding is not widespread, for those who cannot, or do not, contribute may find their interests less well protected.

In the long-established liberal democracies the first desideratum is met. The total amount of funding has been sufficient for parties to develop reasonably strong links with mass electorates. However, the third desideratum has never really been met and, increasingly, the second one is not being met either. One of the problems in meeting the second condition is that the very act of competing with other parties is likely to drive up the demand for money. Particularly, in election campaigning the desire to do well at the next election may well lead party elites to the conclusion that a necessary condition for doing so is spending more and thereby increasing the 'presence' of the party among voters. The overall rise in campaign expenditures in the United States in the late nineteenth century is an example of such pressures. Nevertheless, it is not true that the history of liberal democracy is one of ever-spiralling expenditures by parties, so what factors have held them in check in the past?

The central factor for most of the first half of the twentieth century was the use of free labour donated by party activists or members – labour that could be used for a variety of purposes – in organization building, in electoral campaigning, and so on – and which reduced the need for money. Furthermore, through building up support within communities, this labour could result in party building of a kind that money could not.

Competition between parties was about building up and maintaining an organization – it was about recruiting members and getting them to perform various tasks efficiently. As late as the 1970s the German Christian Democrats were trying to develop a larger mass membership organization because they believed that their small membership meant that their 'voice' was not being heard in the community; spending money, on advertising, for example, was not a substitute for this form of activity. However, the advent of television from the 1960s onwards, together with such techniques as opinion polling, focus groups, direct mail solicitations and many others, has tended to reduce the relative importance of volunteer labour, even though most parties would struggle without some volunteer corps. Money is now relatively more important as a resource for parties and the forces of party competition are tending to result in much greater effort being directed to the acquisition of funds.

The other factor favouring the building up of party organizations was that parties could make activism attractive to potential participants. Many parties provided social and recreational facilities that acted as complementary incentives to their ideological ones. In the case of some parties, such as those in North America, opportunities to acquire patronage further made participation attractive to a wide range of people. The various mixes of incentives provided by different parties ensured that most parties usually had sufficient labour to perform tasks linking them to mass electorates. However, changes in lifestyle in the mid-twentieth century started to make party work much less attractive than it had been – parties were no longer valued as centres of recreational activities, for example. The result was a decline in party membership; most European parties – the notable exceptions being Belgium and Germany – experienced such a decline between the 1960s and the 1980s.[1] This had two effects on parties. First, it increased the pressure to move away from reliance on volunteer labour and more towards methods of linkage with voters that could be purchased. Second, to the extent that members and activists had been a source of party funding, it tended to depress levels of party income.

Nevertheless, it would be misleading to assume that those parties that had been able to attract a large number of activists or members had been able to rely on them for funding party work. They had not. In the case of the United States a broadly-based system of funding, drawing on the loyalty of party identifiers, gave way in the later part of the nineteenth century to a much more instrumental relationship between interest groups and parties. In the mass-membership European socialist parties membership dues might pay for everyday activities, but in election campaigns financial contributions from labour unions were often vital. Rising campaign costs and declining memberships would only make organized interests more attractive as sources of money to parties, and, in turn, this would take parties even further away from the democratic ideal of their being funded by a wide spectrum of interests within the society.

The fact is that the funding of political parties is one of the more problematic aspects of democracy in the older liberal democracies. However, there are good reasons for thinking that the issues may be more complex still in many of the emerging democracies in the late twentieth century. First, it might be questioned whether in all of these regimes there would be sufficient funding currently available to enable parties to build stable links with mass electorates. Especially, in those countries experiencing major economic changes it might be questioned where adequate funding would come from to enable voters to be connected with the political system. A high level of party fractionalization makes this problem worse. In time those parties that survive, and could demonstrate an ability to win consistently, say, 5 per cent of the vote, might well be able to attract funds. But during economic transformation, and while there are still many parties, money for parties may be tight.

Second, the perceived need for money – that it helps make a party competitive electorally – is being manifested in an environment in which there are greater limitations on the use of alternative resources. Volunteer labour is poor, for example, at designing television broadcasts or constructing opinion polls. In that way party building may be more difficult than it was earlier in the twentieth century when activists living in stable communities offered alternatives to paid labour in the performance of various party tasks. The Spanish case provides good evidence of this. Parties competed in trying to obtain funds for electoral purposes, and they became overstretched in their efforts to obtain them. With the initial exception of the Communists, parties did not try to make use of or build up mass organizations because that was not useful to modern forms of campaigning.

Third, by comparison with even one hundred years ago, the much greater scale of business organizations means that funding from interest groups in democratizing regimes is likely to produce a much more skewed distribution of funding. The democratic ideal of broadly-based funding was not fully realizable in the early years of the older democracies, and it is that much more difficult to attain in a world of large corporations, many of them transnational corporations. Building parties that have a relatively high degree of autonomy from the economic organizations operating in their society is that much more difficult.

Fourth, one of the earlier routes towards creating autonomous parties is not open to parties today. The use of patronage as a means of party building was widely accepted in nineteenth-century North America but commands much less support now. For one thing, the scope of government activity has changed, and the technical skills needed for many positions in government would make patronage a wholly inefficient system of appointment. Moreover, changed norms about political spoils means that patronage rarely commands the widespread support that it used to.

Fifth, at least some of the democratizing regimes – especially those in southern Africa – have large sectors of their populations whose income is so low that it is doubtful that they could make any financial contributions at all to political parties. Broad-based funding is not possible in such regimes, even if, in theory, it was possible in the industrial democracies of the early-to-mid-twentieth century.

If the ideally democratic system of party funding is a receding dream in the established democracies, and is even less likely to develop in regimes that are in the process of democratizing now, what are the more limited objectives to which a democrat might aspire in relation to the funding of parties? If a broadly based system of funding is unattainable might it be possible to devise ways of funding that:

a  provided sufficient funds so that parties could develop links with voters;

b  did not make the raising of money the main party activity, to the detriment of others; and

c  gave parties at least some degree of autonomy in their relations with particular interest groups?

In attempting to answer this question about (the more limited) objectives to which a democrat should aspire it is useful to consider the range of legal mechanisms that various established democracies have utilized in attempting to regulate political financing. The most common mechanisms are:

1 the public reporting of financial contributions to political parties and candidates, and/or the reporting of particular kinds of expenditures made by parties and candidates.

When successful, this may contribute to the realization of objective (c), though it is not likely to have any direct effect on the other two objectives.

2 a prohibition on financial contributions from some sources.

The aim of this is largely to promote party autonomy (objective c), though it might also be a means of restricting the 'chase' for money (objective b).

3 restrictions on certain kinds of expenditures that may be made by parties, or by those who are their 'agents'.

If successful this would have the effect of reducing the demand for money through restricting the purposes for which it can be used. This aims at meeting objective (b), and possibly objective (c) as well.

4 a prohibition on parties purchasing particular services and/ or a requirement that these services be provided free of charge to parties.

The justification for this might be made with respect to either objectives (a), (b) or (c) – depending on the circumstances and on the scale that the service might be provided.

5 the provision of funds to the parties by the state.

The aim of this is usually to promote all three objectives.

Each of these mechanisms will be considered in turn, and their potential for the problems facing party politics in emerging democracies will be indicated.

## Reporting party income or expenditures

Requiring parties to report either their income or certain components of their expenditure – for example, what they spend in election campaigns – allows, at least in theory, a party's opponents to expose to the public just who is backing it or just how much a party is 'trying to buy' an election. If reporting works as a control mechanism, it works because other political actors

– parties and journalists included – can use information to embarrass a given party. For that reason, it is argued, accurate reporting is essential to making competitive electoral politics function. Indeed, there are some political scientists who argue that under some conditions tight reporting requirements are the only effective possible form of control – including those in the contemporary United States.

The recent experience of Russia indicates the incentives facing both parties and organized interests to arrange contributions that take place unobserved. However, it would be a mistake to believe that the problems posed by such funding can necessarily be eliminated by comprehensive legal regulation even in fully functioning democracies. To the contrary, evidence from the long-established democracies indicates that devising an effective legal framework that makes most financial contributions visible is a matter that cannot be resolved once and for all. Rather the legal framework is likely be in need of continuing revision.

One consideration is that, even when a given form of reporting is successful, changes in the long term in how parties operate may reduce the significance of such legislation over time. For example, the British Corrupt Practices Act of 1883 ensured that virtually all expenditures made by individual candidates are reported, and conform with the spending limits laid down in the legislation. The cost of elections per voter did decline significantly over the next few decades. However, the 1883 legislation did not cover general expenditures by national parties, and these increased greatly from the mid-twentieth century with the rise of television-centred national campaigning. Moreover, the 1883 legislation did not cover the income of political parties, and to this day British political parties can conceal from public scrutiny who donates money to them and how much is donated.

Moreover, there is a strong incentive for parties to try to find legal means of evading public reporting procedures. The demand for money makes even highly questionable sources attractive to parties, and it is important to find ways of keeping such funds hidden from public view. In 1974 the United States passed some of the most stringent legislation ever enacted on the reporting of donations to candidates. Whereas previous legislation had led to widespread evasion, the 1974 law prevented concealment. At least it prevented concealment in the form of direct gifts to candidates, but over the next twenty years loopholes were exploited including those permitting the giving of 'soft money' through the political parties themselves. The 1996 national elections generated a whole series of scandals connected with this: 'Some watchdog groups suggest that the party committees have become nothing more than "black bag" operations, conduits for interested parties to pour unregulated money into campaigns.'[2]

Finally, there is the serious issue of what kind of effective sanctions could be used against parties that broke reporting requirements. Without threatening the fundamental basis of democratic politics, parties cannot be banned, say, from participating in given elections in the way that sporting teams that cheat might be banned from competition or commercial monopolists broken up and prohibited from colluding. The main sanction is that of the party's reputation being seriously tarnished. But the impact of this is much less if all the parties are breaking the rules – and most of them are likely to have an incentive to do so. The scandals in Germany in the 1980s and Italy in the 1990s embraced a number of parties and not just one. There is safety in numbers for parties, and the expectation is likely to be that the party will survive scandal even if a few senior leaders or officials have to be sacrificed in the event of discovery. The three major parties involved in the Flick scandal in Germany in the 1980s are still the three main parties in the country.

Now a case can be made that once a party system has been consolidated in a new democracy – that is, once the dozens of parties that are likely to have formed in the early stages of democratization have been reduced to less than, say, seven or eight – there is an incentive for the parties to behave less recklessly. Some of the financial practices in Russian parties that border on gangsterism are much more threatening to parties that clearly have a stake in the persistence of the party system. But the incentive to evade rules on reporting remains, and that is why this most basic of legal controls remains problematic even in mature democracies.

## Prohibitions on particular sources of funds

Attempts to preserve the autonomy of parties have led to legal prohibitions on parties receiving funds from particular kinds

238 FUNDING DEMOCRATIZATION

of potential contributors. Obvious candidates for exclusion are foreign governments and, possibly, foreign-owned corporations. The point here is clear – the autonomy of the state might well be compromised were parties in government beholden to such actors. Thus, for example, both Taiwan and Indonesia anticipated policy favours for their regimes from the South African government as a result of their donations to the ANC; publicity for this kind of influence often leads to demands for prohibitions on certain kinds of foreign donors. But there may be bans on some internal political actors as well; for example, German trade unions may not fund political parties, while Brazil prohibits contributions from professional associations as well as trade unions. However, even leaving aside obvious questions about enforceability that have been raised already in connection with compulsory reporting of funding, donations from domestic economic interests raise issues that are difficult to resolve.

There are two main arguments for permitting economic institutions to be able to make financial contributions to parties. First, if parties are to be well enough funded so that they can develop long-term links with voters, it is these institutions that are the most promising private suppliers of such funds. For reasons identified earlier, it cannot be expected that broadly-based contributions from party activists could finance more than a rather small proportion of party work. By contrast, firms, industrial associations, professional associations and trade unions may well have the amount of money at their disposal that would be required for these tasks. There are also principles of free speech involved. Few would doubt the right of an individual to spend his or her own money in an election campaign opposing the policies of parties that threatened his or her interests; the same principle arguably applies to corporate entities as well. Thus, it would be argued, the Tate & Lyle company's advertising in the early 1950s opposing the British Labour Party's plans to nationalize the sugar industry were quite properly lawful. But, if that is granted, why should a corporate body not be able to do what an individual can do – namely defend its interests through contributing to particular parties, rather than simply through its own campaign?

The argument against unrestricted rights for corporate economic interests to make financial donations to parties, of course, is the need to prevent parties being 'bought' – that is the need to preserve party autonomy. The problem arises not when there are relatively large numbers of such economic actors, all of a similar size, but when there are economic giants whose scale of funding others cannot match, or whose dominant position in their sector of the economy provides them with a special incentive to influence government, or whose economic sector depends particularly on state action. The railroads in the United States in the second half of the nineteenth century fell into all three of these categories – they were economic giants, whose actions influenced many other sectors of the economy, and their activities were directly affected by state and federal government policies. The case against such entities being permitted to fund parties is the same as the case against, say, trade unions and professional associations being allowed to do so: their interests as monopolists or near-monopolists make it especially important for them that they have influence.

The argument of those who favour reporting as the main instrument for preventing the 'purchasing of favours' is that public knowledge of very large donations would be likely to discredit those parties that received them while smaller donations could not really buy influence. Leaving aside the general difficulties about reporting noted above, there is a further limitation to the role reporting can play. This is that where parties are not highly centralized, it may be possible to 'buy' key individuals rather than the party itself. In nineteenth-century America it was not the parties themselves but individual members of Congress who were in the pockets of the railroads. The potential for this form of influence in, for example, contemporary Brazil derives from the fact that candidates are largely self-financing. In such de-centralized parties the opportunities for economic interest groups to make their money count is that much greater, if only because keeping track of a trail of money is far more difficult than analysing even the detailed accounts of a centralized party.

This is one of the reasons why the possibility of restricting the financial contributions to parties of certain corporate economic entities remains within the arena of political debate. If policing is difficult then more drastic solutions may come into the debate; yet, arguably, they can come into that debate only if there is an alternative to major private donors – and that would really mean bringing in the state as a source of funding.

### Restrictions on certain expenditures that parties can make

During democratization one restriction that has nearly always been placed on parties at a relatively early stage has been that of spending money on buying votes directly, though it is a practice that still occurs in some countries, including Thailand.[3] However, there are other ways in which restrictions might be placed on expenditures. One means of attempting to stop a 'feeding frenzy' among parties in their search for funds is to restrict how much they spend on a very costly activity – namely election campaigning. At least, in theory, this is a way of preventing a push for fund raising that can both distort what a party is doing and also lead to it coming unduly under the influence of particular major donors. The problem with elections is that they are expensive to contest and the costs are not spread evenly over the years. As it did in Spain, the desire to be competitive in elections can drive parties into major financial debt.

*Ceteris paribus*, if parties were starting from rather similar positions of organizational strength, there is something to be said for attempting to limit campaign expenditures. After all, it is this activity that largely prompts the 'frenzy' for funds. But at least in some regimes there is not comparable organizational strength. Ex-communist parties in former communist regimes may well have organizational resources far superior to those of other parties, simply because they have inherited the remains of the communist structures. To impose uniform campaign spending limits in these conditions may well aid the ex-communists in making their other advantages count.

But this is not the only possible difficulty with the spending limits approach. The rights of affected interests to spend money on their own behalf, to defend those interests, may provide loopholes through which parties or candidates can evade spending limits. Distinguishing between the genuinely independent campaign on an issue and a front for a particular party or candidate may not be easy, and may prompt complex legal actions. Then again, the problem of evasion mentioned above in connection with the reporting of funds applies also to spending limits. This is not to say that spending limits legislation is always ineffective. The 1883 British legislation limiting expenditures by candidates was highly successful, but this blueprint would not necessarily work in other contexts.

## A ban on purchasing particular services and/or a requirement that they be provided free of charge

This approach has been applied particularly with respect to television. Many democracies, though notably not the United States, have prohibited parties or candidates from buying advertising time on television. Usually, this restriction of access to certain media advertising goes hand-in-hand with the provision of free television time during election periods, and sometimes, on a more limited basis, in other periods as well. The idea of this approach is to prevent the frenzied drive for money that the possibility of saturating the airwaves with advertising might generate; it is also intended to provide a certain equality of access to viewers – at least equality among similarly sized parties. A small party might not have the same number of minutes of air time made available to it as a large party has, but all large parties would have the same time.

Given the relative cost of commercial television advertising, restrictions of this kind are likely to have some effect in damping down the demand for money by parties. It also ensures a certain level of public exposure for small-to-medium-sized parties, though it is likely to do little for the very small party that is seeking to make an electoral breakthrough.

Generally this approach has not been extended beyond television and radio. It has been used there because in all countries the state plays some role in regulating the licensing of television and radio stations, and in some countries there are also state-owned stations whose operating policies can be controlled directly. It would be far more difficult to use such an approach in other areas of campaign technology or advertising. Presumably opinion polling firms could not be required to run polls for all parties. Or consider the case of billboards. They are privately owned, and requiring private firms to devote a certain proportion of their total space to electoral advertising, and then to ensure that the space available was divided fairly between different parties, would be extremely difficult to police. It would be much easier for the state just to pay a subsidy to parties with which they could buy whatever services they required. This leads directly to the case for public funding.

### Public funding of parties

Financing parties and elections from public coffers has been one of the main themes addressed by political scientists in recent years, especially in connection with the more established democracies. Because of the considerable attention it has received, this is not the place to rehearse all the arguments again, but there are a number of key points that must be noted here. An obvious point is that public funding of parties and elections can take a variety of forms – including reimbursement of election expenses (up to a certain amount), grants for maintaining party organizations and research institutes, and a system of 'matching' public funds with those that a party can raise from private sources. Public funding was unknown in the first half of the twentieth century but has become common in the second half. Many of the established liberal democracies have some form of public funding, and some of the newer democracies, notably those in eastern Europe, have embraced this approach. Well-financed parties can provide linkage with mass electorates; a wholly publicly-funded system would prevent the distortion of party priorities in the direction of fund raising; and even partly publicly funded systems might reduce the inequalities in resources between parties and candidates. (Although a system of 'matching' funds could well have the opposite effect, in rewarding those parties that are successful in attracting private money.) Viewed in this way it looks like a panacea for all the problems of party financing. However, in practice it is not.

Public funding is expensive. In a country, such as South Africa, where the initial elections in the democratizing regime have been costly, replacing private funding with a wholly public funded system would lead to the displacement of other public policy priorities and may be difficult to sell to many sectors of the electorate. On the other hand, if public funding operates alongside private funding, scandals involving links between parties and organized interests may well occur anyway, just as they do in wholly privately funded regimes. Public funding does not always drive out the adverse effects of private funding. Germany, the first European state to introduce public funding, is a case in point, and among the more recently democratized regimes Spain provides another example. Spain reveals other possible problems as well. First, depending on the kind of public funding used, intermediate institutions (in this case, banks) can be influential in determining the actual allocation of money originating in the public sector. Second, the distribution of money can be used as a way of removing smaller parties and bringing about party consolidation – for example, by making proportionately larger grants to parties that win more seats in the legislature. Consequently, equality of access to resources may pertain among larger parties but not among all parties, and may be a device for squeezing small parties. More generally the point can be made that public funding can give a false appearance of fairness and legitimacy in the funding of political parties when, in reality, there is unequal access to private funds for which public funding does not compensate. A final consideration is that public funding can contribute to parties becoming more remote from their members, because (as in Israel) they put much less effort into building up a membership base.[4] Such an outcome works against the objective that parties establish stable links with mass electorates.

What may be concluded from all this? An obvious point to make is that there is not a single model of party financing – either being used in the mature democracies or being developed in emerging democracies – that offers a uniquely best way of meeting the objectives we would expect to be met in a democracy. There are a number of possible devices for generating sufficient funds to establish links with voters, preventing an excessive frenzy in fund raising, and providing for party autonomy; however, there are difficulties with, and disadvantages, to all of them. What may work in one set of circumstances will not necessarily work in another. For this reason party financing is likely to remain a contentious issue for the foreseeable future.

## Notes

1 R. S. Katz, P. Mair et al., 'The membership of political parties in European democracies', European Journal of Political Research, 22 (1992), 334.

2 'As soft money grows so does controversy', Congressional Quarterly Weekly Reports, 16 November 1996, p. 3272.

3 See S. Bunbongkarn, 'Thailand's November 1996 election and its impact on democratic consolidation', Democratization, 4:3 (1997), 158–61.

4 J. Mendilow, 'Public party funding and the schemes of mice and men: the 1992 elections in Israel', Party Politics, 2 (1996), 329–54.

# Index

Note: 'n.' after a page reference indicates the number of a note on that page.